Practical Azure SQL Database for Modern Developers

Building Applications in the Microsoft Cloud

Davide Mauri
Silvano Coriani
Anna Hoffman
Sanjay Mishra
Jovan Popovic

Apress®

Practical Azure SQL Database for Modern Developers: Building Applications in the Microsoft Cloud

Davide Mauri
Redmond, WA, USA

Silvano Coriani
Legnano, Milano, Italy

Anna Hoffman
Sherman Oaks, CA, USA

Sanjay Mishra
Redmond, WA, USA

Jovan Popovic
Belgrade, Serbia

ISBN-13 (pbk): 978-1-4842-6369-3
https://doi.org/10.1007/978-1-4842-6370-9

ISBN-13 (electronic): 978-1-4842-6370-9

Managing Director, Apress Media LLC: Welmoed Spahr
Acquisitions Editor: Jonathan Gennick
Development Editor: Laura Berendson
Coordinating Editor: Jill Balzano

Cover image designed by Freepik (www.freepik.com)

Distributed to the book trade worldwide by Springer Science+Business Media LLC, 1 New York Plaza, Suite 4600, New York, NY 10004. Phone 1-800-SPRINGER, fax (201) 348-4505, e-mail orders-ny@springer-sbm. com, or visit www.springeronline.com. Apress Media, LLC is a California LLC and the sole member (owner) is Springer Science + Business Media Finance Inc (SSBM Finance Inc). SSBM Finance Inc is a **Delaware** corporation.

For information on translations, please e-mail booktranslations@springernature.com; for reprint, paperback, or audio rights, please e-mail bookpermissions@springernature.com.

Apress titles may be purchased in bulk for academic, corporate, or promotional use. eBook versions and licenses are also available for most titles. For more information, reference our Print and eBook Bulk Sales web page at http://www.apress.com/bulk-sales.

Any source code or other supplementary material referenced by the author in this book is available to readers on GitHub via the book's product page, located at www.apress.com/9781484263693. For more detailed information, please visit http://www.apress.com/source-code.

Printed on acid-free paper

This book was written during one of the most difficult times faced by our generation – the COVID-19 epidemic that took lives of thousands of people across the world and impacted many other lives in several different ways; and the events leading to the #Whatmatters2020 movement.

What we need more is kindness and compassion toward different ideas, different points of view, and different experiences as in those lies the road to progress.

This book is dedicated to the spirit of kindness and compassion in every living being, which we need in abundance to get through these difficult times.

Table of Contents

About the Authors

Davide Mauri is Program Manager in the Azure SQL Database product group. He has been working in the IT field since 1997 and was awarded Data Platform MVP status for 12 consecutive years. He started his career as a full-stack and back-end developer and then focused on databases and data science for 15 years while still keeping alive his passion for development (mainly in C# and Python). He then moved to the Internet of Things (IoT) and big data space where ingesting, processing, and analyzing millions of data points in near real time was his everyday challenge. Building from that experience, he joined Microsoft to help companies worldwide to leverage stream processing at scale. He now works for Azure SQL Database as the developer's voice inside the product group, working to make sure that Azure SQL Database is, and will be, the best database option for developers.

Silvano Coriani has worked on SQL and other data technologies for more than 25 years. He started as an embedded systems developer in industrial automation and moved to data acquisition, processing, and analysis in distributed solutions. He has worked on several RDBMS engines (SQL Server 6.0 and later releases, Oracle, IBM DB2, and more recently PostgreSQL) and on NoSQL and other analytical engines such as Spark and Hadoop. He also has experience in C/C++, Visual Basic, Java, and .NET. He has worked in several industries, including manufacturing, retail, and financial services. Since joining Microsoft in 2003, he has been busy helping ISVs and enterprise customers to learn and adopt Microsoft technologies. His experience includes being a Developer Evangelist and Software Engineer in the SQL Customer Advisory Team and most recently working in SQL Customer Success Engineering for the Azure Data team. He is also an active speaker at industry conferences such as PASS Summit and Microsoft Ignite.

Anna Hoffman is Data and Applied Scientist on the Azure Data team at Microsoft. She has worked in Microsoft Research, AI Engineering, and Microsoft Services in her time at Microsoft. She spent several years working on .NET, Python, R, and Java to democratize AI via tools and services such as Azure Cognitive Services, Azure Machine Learning, and SQL Server (Machine Learning Services and Big Data Clusters). She now spends most of her time working on the Azure SQL Database product team and participating in the community. She has an undergraduate engineering degree and a Master of Science in Analytics from Georgia Institute of Technology. You can follow her on Twitter at @AnalyticAnna.

Sanjay Mishra is a product leader in the Microsoft Azure Data organization. He leads product management for the Azure SQL Database. Prior to this role, he served as Technical Advisor to the VP of Azure Data PM and led the eminent SQL Customer Advisory Team (SQLCAT).

Jovan Popovic is Senior Program Manager working on Microsoft SQL Server, Azure SQL Database, and Azure Synapse Analytics. He is working in Microsoft Development Center Serbia as Program Manager on several developer-facing SQL Server/Azure SQL features such as T-SQL language enhancements, JSON/temporal support, columnstore/in-memory technologies, and built-in intelligence. He has more than 15 years of experience in various Microsoft technologies with a focus on SQL Server, Azure, ASP.NET, C#, and JavaScript. He has been working in various Microsoft Data Platform teams since 2012. He is a former Microsoft MVP for ASP.NET and has a PhD in software engineering from the University of Belgrade. He is a public speaker at top Microsoft conferences and is an author of several books and open source projects. He enjoys exploring technologies (especially SQL Server capabilities) and finding the best ways to implement the most efficient solutions using them.

About the Technical Reviewer

Drew Skwiers-Koballa is a Program Manager at Microsoft for the Azure Data SQL Tools and Experiences team, which focuses on graphical and command-line tools for Azure SQL and SQL Server. Prior to joining Microsoft, he had a decade of experience as a database administrator and developer, including publishing several open source extensions for Azure Data Studio.

Acknowledgments

Davide Mauri

As this is my first book as main author, I'll go for the most common and obvious path of saying a big, huge "thank you" to my wife Olga, my amazing kids Riccardo and Anna, and my whole family Maurizio, Ornella e Claudio for…well everything. From little things to big, life-changing events, you have always been supportive and encouraged me to be my best self, either with words or, even more important, showing the way. And while these thanks are common and obvious, they are nonetheless heartfelt and true. So thanks, thanks, thanks. I love you all.

I also want to say thanks to Lara, Chuck, and Sanjay: without you, my experience in Microsoft wouldn't have been the dream experience I've had – and I'm still having – so I really want to say thanks to you for everything you have done to help and support me in my journey. Thanks, thanks a lot. I also want to say a big "thank you" to Itzik, Lilach and Lubor, for being so welcoming from the first day we moved into the United States. You made us feeling at home right away, thanks!

Silvano Coriani

When I wrote my first "solo" book on ADO.NET and SQL Server, around 17 years ago, I promised myself that it was also going to be the last ☺ but when my friend and colleague Davide proposed me this team effort together with a group of great professionals like Anna, Sanjay, and Jovan, I couldn't say "no." My first big "thank you" is clearly for them, for their help and support during this adventure. During my 25+-years-long career, I've been blessed to be surrounded by a lot of great folks and learn from all of them, but the years I've spent in SQLCAT with Mark, Sanjay, and team have been a great gift and helped me to grow as a human being and a professional. I'd like to thank each and every one of them! And the story continues now within the Azure SQL team, where I have the privilege of keep working with wonderful individuals, colleagues, and bosses: thank you all!

On a personal level, first and foremost I'd like to thank my family: my lovely wife Serena and my kids Caterina and Lorenzo. Their patience, love, and support, especially during those long lockdown days when I was writing this book, were invaluable. Last but not least, a big thank to my broader family, my parents and parents-in-law, for their support and encouragement.

Anna Hoffman

Being relatively new to Azure SQL and the world of developers, I am so grateful to Davide, Silvano, Jovan, and Sanjay for the amazing opportunity to work on both topics with some of the world's greatest SQL veterans. Through this experience, I have learned and grown from all of them in big ways. I also want to thank the SQL community, inside and outside of Microsoft, for being unlike any other community I've been a part of. Every day, I learn from you all, so thank you. I am thankful to every PM and engineer on our team, but specifically, I'd also like to thank Alain Dormehl, Bob Ward, and Buck Woody for providing much time and patience as I learn about Azure SQL and SQL Server. I also want to thank Asad Khan, our fearless SQL leader, for taking a chance on me two years ago in joining this team and for his continued support. Personally, I want to acknowledge my husband, Phil, who is my biggest cheerleader and helps me with our puppy (Moose, the best quarantine decision we ever made) when I spend long hours obsessing over Azure SQL. Finally, I want to thank my parents, Shaji and Leigh Ann Thomas, who inspire me every day to be better (and who started the Computer Science trend in our family) and my brother, Zachary, who is continuing that tradition in his final year at Duke University (I am so proud of you and can't wait to see what you accomplish!).

Sanjay Mishra

I recently completed 15 years at Microsoft. In my early years in Microsoft, two people went out of their way to help me get settled and grow in my role, and I would like to acknowledge their contribution and influence – Mike Ruthruff and Prem Mehra. Mike spent countless hours with me in my early days helping me understand the new database product I was dealing with, which was so similar, yet so different from the database product I knew so well coming into Microsoft. Mike was my go-to person for everything from installing Windows (yes, installing and configuring Windows wasn't easy on those Itanium boxes) to attaching a debugger and debugging an early build in our SQLCAT lab, with a complex customer workload. Mike's kindness and generosity with his time helped me cut my teeth in SQL Server; else, this book would have been a distant dream.

Prem took me under his wings and coached me on dealing with customers at all levels – from a database developer to a CTO. Every time Prem was in a meeting with a customer, I would just sit there and observe him deal with them – irrespective of whether the customer was angry or happy, frustrated or confused, Prem's mood would always be constant; I never saw him get unsettled. Customers respected him a lot. If I had to meet a customer alone, and I knew that Prem had worked with them earlier, I would introduce myself saying that "I work with Prem," and it would immediately earn me a camaraderie with the customer that would have taken days and months to build. In later years, I earned a lot of kudos from various people for my customer empathy, but all of it has been Prem's coaching.

Prem is enjoying his retired life, and Mike is having fun at his startup, but I miss them every single day at work. My 15 years at Microsoft and this book would not have happened if not for Mike and Prem's influence in my early days. Thank you, Mike! Thank you, Prem!

Jovan Popovic

I would like to thank my daughters and wife for their patience and support during this adventure.

Foreword by Rohan Kumar

Today's business environments are evolving rapidly. Keeping up with the speed of change requires companies to undergo a digital transformation that includes a plan to update their applications. Some organizations choose to update their legacy software and business processes as cloud solutions. Others choose hybrid approaches that combine the benefits of on-premise and cloud capabilities. All the while, cloud-native solutions proliferate. IDC predicts the creation of over 500 million new applications in the next five years.[1]

This trend creates enormous opportunity – and some significant challenges – for today's development community. Developers want to bring their solutions to market as quickly as possible and differentiate themselves from other software vendors. To accommodate customers' growing needs, developers need a proven back-end database solution that eases the coding process.

We like to describe the Azure SQL Database as an "all-inclusive" database. By saying that, we mean that the platform offers the components and capabilities needed to streamline and accelerate application development. Application vendors need essential features like an excellent database engine, highly responsive performance, exceptional scalability, and high security. They also need a solution that embraces modern application constructs like Geospatial, Graph, and JSON, expressed in their familiar T-SQL language. The platform must support multiple deployment options too. Developers need the freedom to design their applications to run in an elastic pool, a hyperscale scenario, as managed instances, or in a serverless environment. Benefits like these have encouraged thousands of developers to choose the Azure SQL Database as their preferred solution.

We want to extend our heartfelt thanks to so many people in the SQL community who shared their feedback over the years and helped us make Azure SQL all it is today. Here at Microsoft, our team remains focused on advancing the Azure SQL Database to offer even more value for developers. Thank you for giving us an opportunity to support your efforts and innovations!

—**Rohan Kumar**
Corporate Vice President, Azure Data at Microsoft

---

[1]Source: IDC, `www.businesswire.com/news/home/20191029005144/en/IDC-FutureScape-Outlines-Impact-Digital-Supremacy-Enterprise`

Foreword by Mark Souza

Today, embracing digital transformation and cloud computing is key to customer success. There is a critical need for organizations and technologies to evolve to meet new business requirements (and shifting priorities in response to the current COVID crisis) and new data ecosystems. Azure SQL Database has been a central technology in this evolution, and modern developers need to keep suit. If you're an experienced database software engineer or a modern developer looking to upskill your knowledge and technical intensity in this space, this book is for you.

With over 30 years' experience in the tech industry focused on customers and digital transformation, I'm thrilled to see this work come to fruition. With the benefit of hindsight, it's not surprising that there has been tremendous evolution and growth in the database space over the last 25–30 years.

I joined Microsoft in July 1993 to help build a Microsoft database business. Microsoft SQL Server on Windows Server (then called Windows NT 3.1) had just released. At that time, we had only 17 Microsoft SQL Server software engineers. Today there are more than 2300. In 2000, I moved into the product group to establish one of the first highly technical, customer-facing teams within engineering at Microsoft, called SQLCAT – SQL Customer Advisory Team. The team was super technical and interacted directly with our top customers around the world. Our engineers listened and learned from these customers. They then took these learnings and drove customer feedback, feature suggestions, and bug reports into important product improvements and created best-practice guidance and made it available to all customers, large and small. In 2011, the SQLCAT team became AzureCAT and focused on helping our customers accelerate their journey to the cloud.

Microsoft SQL Server evolved significantly over the past 25+ years. We saw the creation of new enhancements and capabilities to the SQL platform such as Graph, Geospatial, JSON, columnstore compression, memory-optimized tables, temporal tables, and more. Its most significant evolution came as Microsoft evolved on-premise computing and storage services to the cloud, when SQL Server became the foundation for the cloud-based Azure SQL offerings like Azure SQL DB, SQL MI, and much, much more. The developer experience for SQL Server has really evolved and today supports all of the popular languages: Python, Node.js, Go, Ruby, PHP, Java, Native C/C++, and of course .NET languages C#, F#, and so on.

This book also caters heavily to the new generation of data analytics developers, especially if you are focused on your own digital transformation journey.

The best part is the authors are most of my old SQLCAT/AzureCAT friends who are still part of the Microsoft Data Group in engineering, so it promises to be technical, practical, and very valuable to jumpstart your cloud journey. I was honored to be asked to write this foreword. While I recently moved out of engineering to run the Microsoft Customer Success organization (part of the worldwide commercial business), Microsoft data services remains close to my heart. Thank you, team, for writing this timely book for our customers and data developers across the world. I know it will be a big hit.

—**Mark Souza**
Corporate Vice President – Microsoft Customer Success

Introduction

This book encapsulates our combined experience on what developers need to build resilient, scalable, and secured database applications. Azure SQL Database provides a solid foundation for database applications, and we believe this book will provide a solid foundation for the developers to build the applications for future.

Chapter 1 starts off with the motivation for the book and sets the stage for developer mindset.

Chapter 2 gets you kick-started with Azure SQL, how to provision and build your first database, and how to use the samples.

Once you have your database, you would like to connect to it and start querying it. **Chapter 3** gets you there. It also takes you through on configuring the right connection attributes and building the connection retry logic for resiliency.

Chapter 4 takes you through the foundations of building the constructs and writing a database application.

Chapter 5 builds on Chapter 4 and discusses more advanced concepts.

Chapter 6 discusses practical use cases and best practices for using tables and indexes.

Chapter 7 discusses more advanced concepts, such as consistency, scalability, and performance.

Chapter 8 discusses the multi-model capabilities in Azure SQL that help you build modern applications.

Chapter 9 discusses advanced data storage capabilities, such as columnstore indexes, memory-optimized tables, temporal tables, and so on.

Having written your application, you would like to monitor its performance and debug it.

Chapter 10 takes you through that.

The journey of a developer isn't complete without the discussion on DevOps.

Chapter 11 discusses DevOps technologies, tools, and processes for database applications involving Azure SQL database.

CHAPTER 1

A Database for the Modern Developer

The advent of cloud computing has brought a lot of innovation in all fields, and relational databases have been taking advantage of that innovation too. They evolved up to the point that many of them, Azure SQL included, now incorporate features that have traditionally been found in non-relational databases, distributed systems, and analytical platforms. Such evolution provides a great number of options in terms of flexibility and scalability, and yet still offers all the consistency and the guarantees provided by the solid mathematical foundations of relational algebra, so that a developer can have the best of both worlds: well-established technologies along with new and disruptive ideas in just one place.

Why did we write this book?

As you will learn throughout this book, there are a lot of features that you probably won't expect to see in Azure SQL databases. As you may have guessed already by now, that's why we felt that a book like the one you are reading is needed. As a developer, you need to know what are the tools and the features that you have at your hand to your job at best, and this book is here to help. Starting from a new, fresh approach to development and data management, the book will go through a shift in mindset, which is needed to deal with an always-evolving environment like the one offered by the cloud, up to the discussion of which role a modern database like Azure SQL can play in today's modern software architectures, all while explaining, using a very practical approach, all the features that Azure SQL makes available to you and where and how they can be used in modern solutions.

In fact, sooner or later you will have to deal with data, and it doesn't really matter if it will be a huge amount or just a little of it. The earlier you learn how to do it properly and use it at your advantage, the better. With a good knowledge of Azure SQL, you can

1

© Davide Mauri, Silvano Coriani, Anna Hoffman, Sanjay Mishra, Jovan Popovic 2021
D. Mauri et al., *Practical Azure SQL Database for Modern Developers*,
https://doi.org/10.1007/978-1-4842-6370-9_1

simplify your architecture and keep code clean and with a clear separation of concerns (`https://aka.ms/seofco`), all while improving performance by orders of magnitude just by using the available features, scaling up to almost any possible need you may have now or in the future. Yes, this sounds too good to be true, but it is real. And it's not magic. Those features are the result of almost 30 years of research and development, mixed with today's cloud elasticity and scalability.

A relational database, in fact, being completely based on mathematical concepts, is still amazingly good at handling today's challenges, despite being introduced in the market 50 years ago. Just like the sum operation in math, probably the most ancient operation we know of, it really doesn't grow old. If the idea behind is solid and mathematically proven, it will always work. What may become old, instead, is how it is used and implemented in available hardware and software. Here's where evolution and constant improvement come into play: we know that the relational model works and works well. What needs to be pushed far away are the limits imposed by the existing hardware and software constraints.

Azure SQL is a relational database that, especially in its new Hyperscale version, has been renewed and refactored completely to provide the elasticity expected from a cloud service, even though it shows the usual, well-known, programming model and data management features that have been used with so much success since the 1970s.

This dual soul, with roots both in a well-established and mature field on one side – keep in mind that Azure SQL is SQL Server in the Azure cloud – and in new exciting frontiers of scalability and data management on the other, makes Azure SQL a pretty unique, one-of-a-kind database, capable of handling today's most demanding and scalable workloads.

As a result, it comes loaded with so many features that every developer will find something to love; this also implies that there is a lot to learn for those who have never used it before. This book is here to help.

The growth mindset

In 2006, the psychologist Carol Dweck published a book titled *Mindset: The New Psychology of Success* where she introduced the idea of the *growth mindset*. She describes that people who understand that talent and abilities can be developed, acquired, and improved through continuous effort, learning, and persistence, despite failure and setbacks, are more likely to succeed than those who instead have a *fixed mindset*. People with a fixed mindset work to defend the reached status quo, trying to show no weakness and always showing off like there are no challenges or failures, as they already know a lot, if not everything.

A fixed mindset cannot work in today's ever-changing world.

On the opposite, the growth mindset idea goes perfectly hand in hand with the Agile methodology and the more general idea that key to success is the ability to *embrace changes*. The ability to keep learning and to be able to adapt to new situations is at the foundation of the ability of embracing changes. Of course, this doesn't happen overnight, and failures, and what comes as a learning from them, are part of such a process as much as success is.

This approach also brings another important behavior to the table: the ability to constantly check if what we have learned so far, or even our beliefs, are still true and applicable.

As you can now imagine, everything just described, which at first glance may seem completely out of place in a technical book like this, is instead much more profound and interconnected with a developer's everyday life, as in the cloud changes are constantly happening. The ability to deal with such a high rate of change becomes one of the primary traits of a good developer.

Is not by chance, in fact, that within Microsoft the idea of a "growth mindset" is pervasive: it is needed to evolve, grow, and stay competitive.

It wasn't until one of the authors joined Microsoft, where he learned about the growth mindset, that he realized while some developers always have this mindset, others don't. And this is especially true for everything that's related to data and databases. Developers usually don't like databases that much and simply try to deal with it in the simplest and quickest possible way, if they deal with it at all.

But in the information age, it should be quite clear that data, and then information and then in turn knowledge, are the center of gravity of everything we build and do for a living. The ability to efficiently manipulate data will immediately turn a developer into a *better developer*.

A growth mindset is a way to start to look at this challenge. But how is that applicable to development? How can anyone be a *better developer*? Why is this important and, above all, what this has to do with Azure SQL?

Let's try to give some answers.

Reviewing old beliefs

"The relational model is old and doesn't scale." "You need to use some new paradigm to be able to scale at cloud level." Or even, "You can't deal with more than a few millions of rows of data in a relational database." No matter if you're a new developer born in the cloud or a veteran that has assembled his or her first computer on its own and still know what a *nibble* is, chances that you have heard the aforementioned sentences are pretty high.

Now, since someone said them, or even wrote books and blogs about it, they must be true. Well, they may have been true at some point in time, something like 40 years ago. Time has passed since then, and so it is time to check if such beliefs and myth are still true.

Well: no. Azure SQL evolved from SQL Server that through the years had so many improvements and upgrades that if you weren't really focused on the data space, you may have missed them. From a developer point of view, you still deal with tables and columns – and this is already not entirely true to be honest, as you'll learn in the next chapters – but behind the scenes the database engine has been updated so much that, as the well-known SQL Server guru Bob Ward said, "SQL Server 2019 is not your Grandpa SQL Server" (`https://aka.ms/ssnygss`).

Just to mention a few of the amazing features that are now available in SQL Server and thus Azure SQL, you can find columnstore tables where data is saved in a highly compressed, column-structured format that enables fast vector computations using AVX and SIMD instructions (yes, the same used by videogames); lock-free structures are also available where locking is not used to keep data consistent, but something much more advanced like Multi-Value Concurrency Control (MVCC) where the same data can exist at the same moment in different versions, depending on how the observer is interacting with it; tables can automatically keep track of all changes that happen on the data they hold, even allowing for "as-of" queries, literally allowing a query to travel back in time; JSON documents and graph models are available and deeply integrated with the query optimizer, a marvel of human engineering, that is able to optimize the execution of any query for you, taking into account how much data there is in a table, what are the resources available, and what are the possible alternatives to reach the best performance goal.

All these features - and more - also come with the ability to run at scale. Cloud scale. Several of the most used websites, online and mobile games and applications, if fact, use Azure SQL every day, scaling to serve millions of users worldwide.

Azure SQL offers a lot of features that you should check out to make sure you are not reinventing the wheel every time.

But this is only half of the picture.

Continuous learning

In another great blog post, this time by Grant Fritchey (Figure 1-1), that you can find here: "Why don't people use columnstore indexes" (`https://aka.ms/wdpuci`), the issue – among others – is described extremely well. We were used to learning something once and using what we had learned for many years to come. It was already true long ago that in information technology you were expected to continuously learn and stay updated, but the pace at which innovation was happening was much slower that the pace you see today.

You're not spending your time learning. You're learning once. You're evaluating a technology once. You're picking up the common knowledge one time, then never assessing it, ever again.

I get it. You have work to do. Learning isn't a part of your work. Oh, but there you're wrong. It is. Technology moves. You are a technologist. You must learn in order to move with the technology. You must get in the habit of reassessing assumptions and reevaluating that the common knowledge that you have, might be wrong, old, not applicable.

Figure 1-1. *Words of wisdom*

The need to learn new concepts, technologies, and ideas was something you could easily do every couple of years and sometimes even more. Today the speed at which technology is moving is completely different. In the cloud, new updates are released every month. Azure SQL is constantly updated not only to correct bugs or improve existing features, but entire new features are released so that developers from all around the world can take advantage of them, to create simpler, yet more scalable and powerful solutions.

It's clear that the key to becoming a successful developer today is not only the ability to master one language or another. One of the key factors is the ability to learn and keep learning, so that your solution can take advantage of the latest and greatest innovations, leveraging the work done by other hundreds or even thousands of people, allowing you to create solutions that would be impossible otherwise.

You can't just learn a thing once and hope that's enough. It is clearly not enough. Not anymore. Challenge yourself, keep learning, keep an eye on what's new, and do this as part of your job routine. It's just like creating unit or integration tests for the code you wrote. Years ago, almost no one was doing it. Now it is natural as breathing, and you won't move forward in your project without some tests in place to give you the guarantee that you're not introducing bugs or breaking existing code. Continuous learning is the same: no one should ignore the power of what the cloud offers just because you're too busy writing code. You may be wasting hours and days on something that is already there.

A better developer

Developers that know how to properly take advantage of data and databases are, without any doubt, better developers – better not only because they can use the right tool to process data, but also because, on the cloud, every inefficiency means higher costs. For example, a very chatty application that continuously moves data from the database to a processing service to crunch and elaborate data may need to execute thousands of queries per second. That will require a close placement of the processing service to the database to reduce the network latency at minimum, as some network delay will incur for *every* query, as data needs to be moved in and out of the database; in addition to that, code will be more complex and will require more CPU resources; at the same time, the database will be used as a dumb storage wasting CPU cycles only to deal with the huge amount of queries sent by just one user, with the result that scalability will be more costly as compute power will be needed more and more as new users will use the service. This chain of issues can be avoided by making a better use of batching techniques via Table-Valued Parameters or Bulk Load. Better developers will know when it makes sense to write code and when they should leverage the database to operate with efficiency on data. It's just one simple choice but can have an impact with many zeros in a lot of places: from the cloud bill your company will need to pay at the of the month, to the amount of time needed to maintain and evolve the system, through the ability to isolate different parts of the solution to work on them in parallel.

Be a better developer by knowing your tools, being pragmatic, and keeping in mind that "You are not Google" (`https://aka.ms/yang`); don't just embrace new and exotic technologies just because the big companies do so. Use the one that better serves your overall needs, considering costs, performances, features, supportability and availability.

Not just a passive container of data

A relational database is much more than a container of data. It doesn't just offer a way to persist data, as some architects and developers – with very extreme views – may instead think. If you need just a persistence layer, even a text file may be fine, especially today where you can put a text file in an Azure Blob Storage and be pretty much sure it will be high available, secure and globally distributed. But is that enough?

The challenge starts when more than one entity, be it human or a software, needs to access that data. Who is going to make sure that all those who need to access don't step on each other's feet? And what about making sure that access to parts of stored data is secured so that different entities may only access the data that they are allowed to see? Who is in charge of guaranteeing that such data is handled in the correct way, so that if an application crashes while modifying that data, the modifications done are not left halfway finished?

For sure you can put all this logic somewhere in your solution, if that will be the only one accessing the database. While this sounds amazingly elegant from an architectural point of view, it is also costly to implement and maintain. Again, it's about deciding if reinventing the wheel makes sense or not. If you are creating a new vehicle to explore Mars, then reinventing the wheel surely makes sense. But in most of the cases, you're not going to Mars. So it would be much better to focus your development efforts on something that is unique to your business challenge instead of using something that is already available and has been battle-tested for almost half a century. All evolutions are built on the shoulder of who was there before us: it makes sense to follow the same approach in software development too.

Gatekeeper of data

Databases are gatekeepers of data. It would be a beautiful world if all developers were good developers, if no bugs would be created, and if human error or hardware failure were not something we have to deal with. But that's not the world we live in and, likely, it will never be. Reality is that not all developers are good developers, hardware has failures, and therefore data needs to be protected from any voluntary or involuntary corruption.

Data is the ultimate asset, the one that carries the value as it can be transformed to information and knowledge, and it must be protected at all costs. A database like Azure SQL, among other duties, finds its main purpose in protecting the data from anything – bugs, errors, inconsistencies, and malicious users.

A database is the last chance to make sure data is correctly modified and served, at scale, and with the expected performance. Moving all these features outside the database would mean creating a new database management system. But then you'll be exactly at the starting point. Following the same analogy used before, it would be like if the wheel you created to explore Mars can now be used on the Earth too, and on every type of terrain: it is surely more flexible, but has exactly the same pros and cons of existing wheels, with the added complexity that only few know how to correctly use it.

So, better learn how to make good use of existing one.

Where should business rules go?

Business rules: They should go into the application, not in the database. The answer is simple and straightforward. The problem is that the definition of business rules is not that straightforward.

While a deep dive into such discussion is well outside the scope of this book, we need to draw, at least, a line to make clear what should be pushed to the database and whatnot.

Business rules usually act on data. Among other duties, they also process, read, change, and create data. It's fair to say that all *data manipulation* should be pushed to the database where data lives. If the creation of a new user, for example, requires the creation of a row in the User table, that statement should be executed within the database itself, not by creating some spaghetti code where data manipulation logic and business logic are intertwined together in a very inelegant and not-so-maintainable code.

An even better example is when aggregation of data is needed, maybe to calculate some complex end-of-month report for monitoring business KPIs. Due to what is known as *data gravity*, it is much, much easier to move this complex computation to where data already is, instead of moving data into the business layer. Data has a size and thus a weight: moving it can be very challenging a definitely requires a lot of effort.

This is especially true in distributed systems, where each different system may want to access and modify the same data. By having data manipulation logic in each and every one of those systems, some complex – really complex – distributed coordination would be needed. By allowing the database to do its job – orchestrate data access – such complexity can be avoided entirely.

With this line drawn, it is much easier to obtain a clear separation of concerns, bringing clarity and simplicity to the solution that, in turn, will be easier to create and less expensive to maintain and evolve. It will be more Agile.

Tell me about Polyglot persistence

Polyglot persistence came to be known to the world in the last years, where microservice architectures showed all their power and became mainstream. The idea is that every service should use the best database technology (Relational, Key-Value, Graph, Document, etc.) for the task it is doing.

While in theory this seems absolutely correct, there is one big, huge challenge that lies within this approach: how data, living in different systems, can be integrated and kept consistent so it can be trusted to be free of errors and used to make decisions?

Not only that, if using different databases to store data, all of those different technologies need to be known enough so that they can be used appropriately; otherwise, security, consistency and performance issues will quickly arise and become a day-to-day nightmare.

But there is something more. What if, at some point, some data needs to be gathered and then re-distributed to all systems? Integration is a really, really hard problem. In fact, not only will you need a process to just keep data integration going on, but at some point, you'll also need something where the "golden master" of your data will be stored – somewhere where Business Analytics systems can get data from to allow meaningful forecasts and, nowadays, reliable data to feed machine learning algorithms. You'll need a system to manage your *master data*.

As you can see complexity increases at every step, and *caching* hasn't been put in the picture yet! Now, if complexity is needed, that's fine. As long as you're in control of the architectural decisions, and such complexity is needed (as your business is complex like managing an online word processor for millions of concurrent users), and you are ready to handle it, everything is good. But unfortunately it is very easy to be caught in the unexpected landslide of issues that a complex architecture brings with it, if not well planned and managed, easily becoming more and more complex every day, eating every dollar possible from the IT budget.

Polyglot persistence and high specialization are great choices, but not always and not for every project: sometimes, an integrated solution, which provides all the options but just in one place, is much better. Azure SQL can be that integrated solution.

Batteries included

Keep it simple, as simple as possible. But not simpler! That's why Azure SQL can help a lot. Just like Python, that is said to be "batteries included" (`https://aka.ms/pep0206`), we like to use the same definition for Azure SQL. It offers almost everything a developer needs for any project. From relational support to Graph models, from JSON documents to Columnstore indexes, it is possible to take advantage of the same pros that you would find adopting the Polyglot Persistence ideas, with way less complexity and cons.

This book will help you to learn all the features you can use to create modern solutions, using Azure SQL to offload all data manipulation and management to the cloud so that you can just focus on something that no one else can do for you: implementing the business logic and the correct architecture that will be unique for the solution you're working on.

Is Azure SQL a developer tool?

Many developers would argue that managing a database, and more in general data, is not part of their job. This was probably true 20 or more years ago, but things have changed a lot since then.

In today's world, where agility and ability to adapt and change is a key factor for success, figures like full-stack developers or back-end developers are more and more common every day. While those figures do not need to have the deep knowledge around data that is expected by a database administrator or a data engineer or a data scientist, their job will ultimately result in manipulating some data too.

Now, this doesn't mean that you should stop learning C#, Java, Python, or any language you want or need and just go head down learning SQL. What is needed is just to understand that Azure SQL is a tool in your toolset just like any other tool you may have, from Design Patterns to the `WeakReference` class, just to mention two things that are on the complete opposite side of the knowledge spectrum.

As any other tool, the more you know it, the better you'll use it.

Keep it super simple

As a developer, you have to know that doesn't make sense, for example, to create an amazingly sophisticated caching mechanism to improve performance of your solution, if you haven't correctly designed your database so that it can take advantage of indexes. Let me tell you it loud and clear: there is nothing you can do to gain the same performance improvement that a good indexing strategy can give you. If you try to do something different and cleverer, sooner or later you'll be ending up by replicating the same solution already available in a database, right inside your application (most likely, some form of b-tree) – just with much higher costs and complexity. It just doesn't make sense from a professional standpoint. Stories of overengineering like this one aren't just hypothetical, and told just to scare new junior developers: it happened for real to one of the authors. He was asked to optimize a complex near real-time data processing solution that was using complex multiple caching layers, state-of-the-art microservice architecture, and the greatest and latest hardware, but still was performing badly and with unsustainable costs. After a deep analysis, the proposal was to dismantle a big chunk of the existing architecture and replace it with a couple of indexes on the database – more precisely, Columnstore Indexes. The developers who created the solution didn't know that they existed as they were still stuck with ideas of features available in SQL Server 2005. After some debate, some struggles, and discussion around growth mindset, the code was refactored and rearchitected, and the reviewed working solution went from using seven virtual machines to host a complex distributed caching solution to one Azure SQL database at one tenth of the cost and much, much better performances.

By using the correct tool, solutions that are complex by nature can be shredded down to smaller pieces, each one simpler to manage with the correct tools. Azure SQL is one of them that usually fits well when it comes to data manipulation. Give it a try even if you think it is not up to the challenge and be prepared to change your mind. That's how you become a better developer.

Be a generalized specialist

Development is much more about making decisions than writing code. Sure, code is how you bring to the world what you have decided to do in order to solve some business problem or to implement a feature, but the development process started long before in your mind, the moment you started to evaluate what options you have at your hands to realize what you're asked to work on.

As a developer, one of the most important steps toward the goals one has in mind is the ability to be in control and to decide what is the best architecture and implementation strategy to reach them. By knowing more than one language and more than one data management solution, one can pick, or suggest, the best one for the specific solution being worked on. Sometimes it can be something as complex and flexible as Apache Spark, some other time something simple and easy as Redis. Many times, a modern database like Azure SQL can give, in just one place, an amazing number of features that provide a good balance of options, costs, and performances.

To make the best choice, one needs to know at least a few tools that are on the border of the development space as they will help to deal with everything outside that space. In many cases, "everything" means "data". The more one knows about it, the better the solution will be. To use the same definition used in the Agile methodology, one needs to become a *generalizing specialist* (`https://aka.ms/swkogs`).

Be the master of some skills, but actively seek to learn others.

If you want to know more

This book aims to give you a very practical view of Azure SQL and how it can be helpful in your daily life as developer or architect. Of course, to understand why something described is important or better than some other alternative, a bit of theoretical background is needed. We want you to learn by understanding concepts, not just learning them by memory. This is a foundational mindset as you will be the one asked to make some development or design choices. While we cannot be there to help you, this book can, but only if you understand the details of the explained concepts. We put in this book what we think is enough to get you started and to give you an idea of what you can achieve. It's more than enough to be in control of your development and design decisions. However, you may want to know more and to go deep into some concepts; after all, the more you know, the more you want to know. So, in every chapter, you'll find a section with this very same name, where you can find a list of books, articles, or posts as a reference for going deeper into database knowledge. Here's the list for this chapter:

- Database in Depth: Relational Theory for Practitioners – `www.amazon.com/Database-Depth-Relational-Theory-Practitioners/dp/0596100124`

- Practical Issues in Database Management: A Reference for the Thinking Practitioner – `www.amazon.com/Practical-Issues-Database-Management-Practitioner/dp/0201485559`

- SQL and Relational Theory: How to Write Accurate SQL Code – www.amazon.com/SQL-Relational-Theory-Write-Accurate/ dp/1449316409

- Data Modeling Essentials, Third Edition – www.amazon.com/ Modeling-Essentials-Third-Graeme-Simsion/dp/0126445516

- Database Design and Relational Theory: Normal Forms and All That Jazz – www.amazon.com/Database-Design-Relational-Theory-Normal/dp/1484255399

- Hot Patching SQL Server Engine in Azure SQL Database – https:// techcommunity.microsoft.com/t5/azure-sql-database/hot-patching-sql-server-engine-in-azure-sql-database/ba-p/849700

CHAPTER 2

Azure SQL Kickstart

The first mention of Azure SQL, referred to as "Microsoft SQL Services" at the time, was when Microsoft announced "Project Red Dog" (Microsoft Azure) at Microsoft's Professional Developer Conference (PDC) in 2008. This cloud-hosted version of SQL Server was one of the first services available on Azure. From the beginning, it was meant to provide a Platform as a Service (PaaS) offering of SQL Server, where you don't have to provision hardware or patch software and you can enjoy benefits that come with running in the cloud – availability, performance, security, and scale – without deploying complex and expensive systems on premises. Since then, Azure SQL has continued to grow and evolve with the Azure platform. As you read this book, it's important to remember that things are always changing. While some of the "little rocks" or details throughout the book may change slightly as the platform evolves, the "big rocks" you will learn in this book will provide a solid foundation for you to grow in the space of developing with databases.

For readers who are new to Azure or new to Azure SQL, this chapter will serve as a kickstart to get you ramped up and ready to start building applications with Azure SQL. You'll learn about the flexibility in deployment that exists today in Azure SQL, as well as some common scenarios that can help you decide what deployment option, service tier, and other options you should choose. You'll also learn about some of the tools and samples that are available for working with and managing Azure SQL.

While (or after) you read this chapter (and the chapters that follow), we recommend you leverage the code samples that are provided with the book, so you can get some hands-on experience with the topics.

Today, when you hear the words "Azure SQL," this refers to a suite of products, not only Azure SQL Database. Within Azure SQL, there are different deployment options, which basically amount to different products within the Azure SQL brand. It's easy to break the deployment options, as shown in Figure 2-1, into three categories, based on abstraction and access level: OS level, server level, and database level.

© Davide Mauri, Silvano Coriani, Anna Hoffman, Sanjay Mishra, Jovan Popovic 2021
D. Mauri et al., *Practical Azure SQL Database for Modern Developers*,
https://doi.org/10.1007/978-1-4842-6370-9_2

Azure SQL
The family of SQL cloud databases

Figure 2-1. *The Azure SQL family of offers*

OS-level access means that Azure handles everything until you get to the OS level. The data center, hardware, virtualization, and so on are managed by Microsoft, but the OS, SQL Server, and database(s) are managed by you. You essentially get an Azure Virtual Machine with SQL Server installed. This is often referred to as an *Infrastructure as a Service* (IaaS) type of offering. With IaaS, while you are responsible for managing and patching the OS, SQL Server, and database(s), you also get access to all the features contained in those levels. For example, if you want to run a third-party application on the same machine as SQL Server, you can do that with IaaS. Additionally, there are a few features from SQL Server 2019 (latest release at time of this book) that are not yet available in the other deployment options, like PolyBase. If you want 100% parity with SQL Server, an Azure SQL virtual machine may be your best option. For more information, see `https://aka.ms/azuresqlvm`.

As you move away from scenarios that require OS-level access, and you begin looking for more managed offerings, there are a few Azure SQL options that fall within the *Platform as a Service* (PaaS) type of offering, and these options will be the focus of this book. With a PaaS service, you get things like automated backups, patching of both the database engine and OS, a service-level agreement (SLA) for availability, advanced security, monitoring, and scalability out of the box. For developers, this means you can get a connection string, stop worrying about maintenance, and spend less time troubleshooting.

For example, let's imagine you don't want to have to worry about OS patches and SQL Server upgrades. You just want an instance of SQL Server. You might opt for *Azure SQL managed instance*, which abstracts the OS away from you, leaving you with an evergreen managed instance of SQL Server. Here, you can get almost all of the instance-level features; for example, SQL Server Agent, Service Broker, Linked Servers, and Common Language Runtime are supported. This deployment option is ideal for companies that want to move to a PaaS offering, but still need to control and access many of the server-level pieces. Azure SQL managed instance also offers native virtual network support, which allows you to integrate the service into your on-premises network if desired.

Now, consider a scenario where your company is in the process of transforming into a cloud-native entity or one where you are working in a cloud-born company. Perhaps you are not interested in managing SQL Server at an instance level and do not need the server-level features. Even more, you may not even know what SQL Server is, as you may never had the chance or the need to use it on premises. What you are looking for, then, is the next layer of abstraction that Azure SQL can offer, which is *Azure SQL Database*. In this offering, you get all the PaaS benefits that Azure SQL managed instances give you, but you just get a database and the database-level capabilities. For this deployment option, you'll have a logical server for organizational and administrative purposes, but no access to instance-level features or views.

When choosing between Azure SQL managed instance and Azure SQL Database, there are a few additional trade-offs you can consider determining what is best for an application's requirements. One way to think about Azure SQL managed instance vs. Azure SQL Database is like the way you think about virtual machine vs. a container. If you use a virtual machine (VM) to deploy an application, you have more power, disks, and security services, but you can only have 2–10 VMs per host. On the other hand, if you use containers, you get lighter and faster with greater elasticity and hundreds of containers per host. If you apply that train of thought to Azure SQL, with Azure SQL managed instance, you get more features and control, but with Azure SQL Database, you get faster, smaller, and with potentially lower costs. Let's consider the trade-offs.

First, you may consider costs. While Azure SQL Database and Azure SQL managed instance are priced the same for storage and compute, if you are going to have just a few databases that consume less than the minimum configuration for Azure SQL managed instance, then Azure SQL Database may be cheaper, as it allows a smaller minimum configuration (lower cost). Azure SQL Database is also able to guarantee resources for a specific database because no sharing is occurring with other databases as in Azure SQL managed instances. You might also consider speed and elasticity. Since Azure SQL Database is deployed in the secure public cloud, Microsoft can provide provisioning and scaling in a matter of minutes or less. An Azure SQL managed instance is deployed in complete isolation (which has security benefits), but the result is that provisioning and scaling can take a matter of hours. From a feature perspective, Azure SQL managed instance allows access to instance-level features, which, if you are not using today, you may want the option to use later, and allows customizations for time zone and collations (covered later in this chapter) that you don't get with Azure SQL Database.

Moving forward, let's look at a scenario where you have many databases or many instances of SQL Server. Perhaps you are a *Software as a Service* (SaaS) provider where your software serves multiple customers, meaning you need multi-tenancy. Or perhaps you have many different SQL Servers that you want to move into the PaaS offering. So far, we've looked at scenarios for single databases or single instances, but for these scenarios, you may consider the "pools" options, which allow you to have multiple databases or servers that are collocated and share resources. This can allow for cost optimization and reduced overhead. For multiple databases, you may consider *Elastic Pools*, and for multiple instances, you may consider *Instance Pools*.

While there are a lot of choices, the Azure SQL platform has the flexibility to meet the requirements that you have. Throughout the book, the capabilities and nuances that exist between different PaaS deployment options will be explored at a deeper level, and it will be done so from the perspective of developers for developers.

If you're completely new to Azure SQL, all these options could scare you, but don't fear. If you want to start easy with something that in 90% of the cases will give you exactly what you need, you can start with Azure SQL Database. But rest assured that all the other options are there for you to make sure that even the most exotic and demanding edge cases you will encounter as a developer will be covered.

Creating Azure SQL Database

In order to create a single database (or managed instance, Elastic Pool, or Instance Pool), you first need a few basics with respect to Azure. First, you'll need an Azure account and a way to pay for services. If you haven't created a free account before with Azure, you can go to `https://azure.com/free` and get a one-time credit. This should be enough for you to complete most, if not all, the hands-on exercises in the book. If you have already used your free account, you may have an Azure credit with a set monetary value each month if you have a Visual Studio subscription that supports that. If neither of those are options, you'll need to use or obtain an Azure account where you have access to create and manage resources.

Once you're set up to use Azure, you'll create a *Resource Group*, which is basically a logical container for a set of Azure resources tied to a certain subscription. You can use any operating system you prefer, the Azure portal, PowerShell, or the Azure CLI (command-line interface) to perform tasks related to deploying and managing resources. After you've installed the Azure CLI (`https://aka.ms/install-azure-cli`), for example, you can get connected and create a resource group with the following code.

Listing 2-1. Set up Azure CLI and create a resource group

```
# log in to your Azure account
az login

# view your available subscriptions
az account show

# copy the "id" of the subscription you want to use and set it as default
az account set --subscription <SubscriptionId>
# view regions available to your account, note the "name" of the region you
want to use (for example, "westus")
az account list-locations

# create a resource group (specifying region and name)
az group create -l <DeploymentRegion> -n <ResourceGroupName>
```

Notice that you must provide a *region* where the resource group is to be created. All resources are tied to a region (e.g., West US, South India, East China). Since a resource group itself is essentially a metadata entity, the location you select during creation represents where the metadata is stored. Each resource in a resource group could, in theory, be created in a different region. Once you have a resource group, you can start deploying other resources (applications, networking, databases, etc.) into it. To view all the regions available to your account and find the region name which is used in the preceding script, you can run the following command:

Listing 2-2..

```
az account list-locations -o table
```

In order to deploy Azure SQL Database, you'll first need a *logical server*, which, like a resource group, is used to group Azure SQL databases in a logical container. You can have elastic pools and single databases all in the same logical server. To do this using the Azure CLI, you can use the following code.

Listing 2-3. Create an Azure SQL Database server

```
# create a logical server
az sql server create --admin-password <AdminPassword>
--admin-user <AdminUsername> --name <LogicalServerName>
--resource-group <ResourceGroupName> --location <DeploymentRegion>
```

Once you have a logical server configured, you can deploy databases (single databases or databases part of an elastic pool) into that server with the following code.

Listing 2-4. Create an Azure SQL Database

```
# create an Azure SQL Database with the default configuration
az sql db create --name <DatabaseName> --resource-group <ResourceGroupName>
--server <LogicalServerName>
```

We'll discuss the details around the many options, tools, and sample databases in the following sections, but the easiest way to get one of the sample databases (if you want to leverage AdventureWorksLT) is to specify one of those during deployment. Instead of the previous `az sql db create` command, you can add one parameter, as follows.

Listing 2-5. Create a database with a sample

```
# create an Azure SQL Database with the default configuration
# and the AdventureWorksLT sample database
az sql db create --name <DatabaseName> --resource-group <ResourceGroupName>
--server <LogicalServerName> --sample-name AdventureWorksLT
```

This will take a few minutes to deploy, but once it's finished, you'll have an Azure SQL Database with the AdvenureWorksLT sample restored on it.

Once your database has been deployed and you've got some data in it, the next step may be to connect to it and verify everything was deployed correctly. In order to connect from your local machine, you'll need to specify the IP address range that you want to be able to connect to the database. Optionally, you can create a firewall rule with value "0.0.0.0" for the starting and end IP address to allow all Azure-internal IP addresses. This will allow other services (e.g., Azure Functions, Azure virtual machines) to connect to your database. The code is the same for both options mentioned; just substitute the IP address range desired in the following code.

Listing 2-6. Create firewall rules

```
az sql server firewall-rule create \
--name <FirewallRuleName> \
--resource-group <ResourceGroupName> \
--server <LogicalServerName> \
--start-ip-address <StartIpAddress> \
--end-ip-address <EndIpAddress>
```

You should now be able to connect to your Azure SQL Database from an allowed IP address from your tool of choice (more on tools soon).

The process and commands for creating an Azure SQL managed instance vary slightly, because with a managed instance, you create a "managed" SQL Server (not a logical server) and then you create "managed" databases.

Before deploying, you'll need to address new parameters for the *VNetName* and *SubnetName*. This is because Managed Instance is required to be deployed in an Azure virtual network in its own subnet or in a subnet with other managed instances only. The easiest way to set this up is by using the Azure Resource Manager (ARM) deployment template available here: `https://aka.ms/sqmicvs`. An ARM template is a JSON file that uses declarative syntax to define infrastructure and configuration to be deployed. There are many ARM templates available to get started building simple or complex solutions in Azure (`https://aka.ms/armtemplates`). Using the ARM template, you can simply select the "Deploy to Azure" button and fill in your subscription and resource group information, and it will deploy the virtual network and subnet that is required for a managed instance.

You can read more about the different commands here: `https://docs.microsoft.com/en-us/cli/azure/sql/mi`, but a sample script follows.

Listing 2-7. Azure CLI commands to create Azure SQL managed instances

```
# create an azure sql managed instance with default parameters
az sql mi create -g <ResourceGroupName> -n <ManagedInstanceName> -l
<DeploymentLocation> -i -u <AdminUsername> -p <AdminPassword> --subnet
/subscriptions/<SubcriptionId>/resourceGroups/<ResourceGroupName>/
providers/Microsoft.Network/virtualNetworks/<VNetName>/subnets/<SubnetName>

# create a new managed database within an existing azure sql managed instance
az sql midb create -g <ResourceGroupName> --mi <ManagedInstanceName> -n
<ManagedDatabaseName>
```

Tools to use and manage Azure SQL Database

In the previous section, you saw how you can use the Azure CLI to deploy and manage Azure SQL. Depending on what you're trying to accomplish and your preferences, there are other tools available for you to leverage. For example, if you're more familiar with PowerShell, you can get about the same functionality as with the Azure CLI. Since SQL Server and Azure SQL have been around for 25+ and 10+ years respectively, there are also many command-line tools available. And if you're looking for a tool that provides a graphical user interface (GUI), there are several for you to choose from. In this section, you'll get an overview of what's available from GUI to CLI.

There are about five main tools that provide a GUI, the most popular being *SQL Server Management Studio* (SSMS). This tool has been around for 20+ years and can be used to access, manage, and develop components of SQL Server and Azure SQL. It contains graphical tools and script editors.

Azure Data Studio (ADS) is a newer, source-open tool that also provides a GUI and much of the functionality that SSMS has. ADS was built on top on Visual Studio Code, so if you're familiar with that, you'll feel comfortable in ADS. ADS is also cross-platform and supported on Windows, macOS, and Linux. When choosing between SSMS and ADS, it's often a preference or a matter of functionality. For example, if you want to leverage Jupyter to create SQL, PowerShell, Python, and so on notebooks (a notebook is most simply explained as a mixture of code cells that can be run with results saved and formatted text cells), then ADS is the only tool that currently supports that. Similarly, there are things that you'll find in SSMS and not ADS. Microsoft is actively investing in both tools, so expect them to continue to evolve.

There are also two extensions directly linked to Visual Studio, *SQL Server Data Tools* (SSDT) and *mssql*. SSDT is a tool for designing and deploying many things related to SQL, including Azure SQL, and it gives a similar experience to developing applications with Visual Studio. Similarly, the mssql extension for Visual Studio Code allows you to leverage the lightweight editor to connect to databases and instances with a good editing experience.

The fifth tool that provides a GUI for management and development is the Azure portal. From deployment to integration with other applications and services, the Azure portal is an easy, user-friendly way to build applications with little coding required.

Moving to the command-line tools, there are quite a few. Most of the command-line tools are cross-platform (Windows, macOS, and Linux). Some are for very specific tasks; a few common examples follow:

- *mssql-cli* is an open source command-line tool specifically for querying, with interactivity and helpful features like IntelliSense and syntax highlighting (`https://aka.ms/mssqlcli`).

- The *sqlcmd* utility allows you to use the command prompt for T-SQL statements, script files, and system procedures.

- The *bulk copy program* utility (bcp) is used specifically for bulk copying data.

- *mssql-scripter* can be used to help with creating, editing, and storing scripts (`http://aka.ms/mssqlscripter`).

- *sqlpackage* automates tasks related to extracting, publishing, exporting, and importing live databases, database schemas, and user data (`http://aka.ms/sqlpackage`).

Some of the tools are built for more broad usage. For example, the Azure CLI and the SQL Server PowerShell snap-in provide commands for accessing, deploying, and managing Azure SQL. It's almost certain that you will not just use one GUI tool or one CLI tool, but a combination of both (and even multiple within the categories). As you'll see in other chapters, there are things that will be easier to do with varying tools.

Throughout the book, you'll be exposed to the different tools more in depth. If you ever want the reference materials for any of the tools, here's a useful link that will guide you: `https://aka.ms/sqltools`.

Choices, choices, choices

Once you have an idea of which deployment option of Azure SQL is best for your scenario (Azure SQL Database single database or Elastic pool, or Azure SQL Managed Instance single instance or Instance pool), there are many other choices that you can make to tailor the solution to meet your needs. In an earlier section, you saw how to deploy an Azure SQL Database using Azure CLI, but many of the defaults were selected. In this section, you'll learn about all the choices and configurations you can make during deployment and some guidance on how to choose. This section follows the order and flow presented currently in the Azure portal, but the order and specifics may change depending on your deployment tool of choice (Azure portal, Azure PowerShell, Azure CLI).

A quick recap

In the first section of this chapter, "Creating Azure SQL Database," some of the Azure basics were covered, including Azure subscriptions, resource groups, regions, and logical servers for Azure SQL Database. To review, you'll need an Azure subscription to do anything in Azure (even if it's free), resource groups are logical containers or metadata entities for the resources or services you deploy in Azure, the region is where your services will be deployed, and the logical server acts as a central administrative point for multiple single or pooled databases and other settings/configurations associated with that logical server. For Azure SQL managed instance, the server name you select is not a logical server, but the actual service, which you can then deploy databases into (sometimes referred to as "managed databases"). In all deployment options, you'll then have to provide an admin login and password. If you're familiar with SQL Server, this is the equivalent to the system admin in SQL Server. This account will connect using a username and password that you provide, and only one of these accounts can exist. If you're familiar with Azure Active Directory, you can also choose to configure an individual or security group account here or after deployment (optional).

DTU or vCores

After you've set up the admin login, when deploying Azure SQL Database, your next choice is if you want the database being deployed to be part of a new or existing Elastic Pool. If you do, you'll then have to configure the service tier, storage, and compute options for the Elastic Pool. Note that in Elastic Pools, you share resources between all the databases in the pool. You can also resource govern among databases in the pool if you want to limit certain databases. Similarly, if you're deploying an Instance Pool, you'll need to use a different Azure portal flow or set of commands, as you first need to deploy the Instance Pool, before you can deploy Managed Instances inside of it.

Next, you'll select what's referred to as the *purchasing model*, and there are two options: *virtual core (vCore)-based* or *database transaction unit (DTU)-based*. The DTU model is not available in Azure SQL managed instances. The DTU-based model is an early purchasing model within Azure SQL Database. The idea is that you get a bundled measure of compute, store, and I/O resources (that is a DTU), and you pick the DTU level that meets your needs. One of the challenges with this model is you cannot scale independently between the three, and it's hard to determine what you are getting. The vCore-based model was introduced due to customer requirements to independently choose compute and storage resources. This is the recommended model from Microsoft. In addition, using the vCore model allows you to leverage *Azure Hybrid Benefit for SQL Server* to gain significant cost savings. This benefit allows you to apply existing unused licenses you may own already in return for big discounts. In the vCore model, you pay for compute resources (based on the service tier, number of vCores, amount of memory, and the hardware generation), the type and amount of data and log storage, and the backup storage.

In this book, we'll mostly focus on the vCore purchasing model since it's the recommended and modern model from Microsoft, but if you're interested in further comparing vCores and DTUs, you can refer here: `https://aka.ms/sdpm`.

Service tiers

Once you select the purchasing model, you have options underneath that are called *service tiers*. These service tiers represent different tiers of performance and availability. The tiers available include General Purpose, Business Critical, and Hyperscale. It's important to carefully consider your options, but a general recommendation would be to start with the General Purpose tier and adjust as needed.

The *General Purpose* tier offers a budget-oriented, balanced, and scalable set of compute and storage options. Within the General Purpose service tier for an Azure SQL Database (single database), there currently exists two options for selecting compute: *provisioned* and *serverless*. Provisioned compute is meant for more regular usage patterns with higher average compute utilization over time or multiple databases using elastic pools. This is the tier you may want to start with. Serverless compute is meant for intermittent, unpredictable usage with lower average compute utilization over time.

For example, consider an expense-reporting internal business application that typically only gets used during business hours, but occasionally sees spikes in usage after big internal conferences or at the end of the month. This means that every night, between 5PM and 8AM, there is little to no activity happening. However, after big conferences and at the end of the month, significant activity occurs. You then must make the choice of overprovisioning to meet the spikes in demand or underprovisioning to keep costs low for the relatively quiet application. With serverless, you can leverage auto-pause and resume capabilities, with a customizable time delay. This means that when your database is inactive for a certain amount of time, your database will pause. During this time, you only pay for storage, and your compute costs go to zero. Once someone tries to access the application again, SQL will turn back on, and your compute will scale on a per-second basis between the minimum and maximum vCores that you set. In this example, when demands are high, Azure SQL Database can autoscale up to what's required and then use an interesting cache reclamation system to scale back down once the demand decreases. Remember, serverless is currently only available in Azure SQL Database single databases, but check the documentation for most up-to-date information at `https://aka.ms/sdserverless`.

Currently, apart from the Azure SQL Database General Purpose tier, all other tiers and deployment options only have the choice of provisioned compute. Once you choose a service tier, you can scale up and down as needed and even switch between service tiers. The next service tier that's available in all deployment options is *Business Critical*. This is meant specifically for business applications with low-latency response requirements. This tier also offers the highest resiliency to failures by leveraging several isolated replicas (one of which you can also use as a read-only replica). Some industries that tend to leverage this tier include gaming, emergency, and financial. While Azure SQL Database generally has a high service-level agreement that sets the expectation for uptime and performance (SLA), Business Critical can guarantee the highest SLA at 99.995% uptime. For more information about the Azure SQL SLA, refer here: `https://aka.ms/sdsla`.

The Business Critical tier is also the only service tier within Azure SQL that supports in-memory technologies. In-memory technologies will be covered at a much deeper level in Chapter 9. At a high level, in-memory technologies can help improve the performance of various SQL workloads (analytic and transactional), and the Business Critical tier supports in-memory OLTP, clustered columnstore indexes, nonclustered columnstore indexes, and memory-optimized clustered columnstore indexes.

The General Purpose and Business Critical tiers currently support database size of maximum 4–8TB (depending on deployment option and service tier). The final service tier available within Azure SQL Database is *Hyperscale*, which was built to take advantage of cloud elasticity and to allow a database to grow almost without limits, freeing the developer from all encumbrances of managing huge databases. Microsoft rearchitected Azure SQL to be able to run in a Hyperscale fashion by refactoring the original SQL Server engine into different, smaller, independent, distributed services that work together as one entity, but much more elastic and scalable than the original. This service tier is meant for most business workloads that may need in future highly scalable storage, up to 100TB at the moment. Hyperscale also supports deploying multiple read replicas for read-intensive workloads, where data is served by all replicas, leveraging a scale-out strategy to increase concurrency and performances. Because the file snapshots are stored in Azure Blob storage, Hyperscale supports "nearly instantaneous" database backups and restores in minutes, because it's no longer a size of data operation. As you can guess, this feature is topical in the management of very large databases. Hyperscale can provide higher overall performance than the General Purpose tier due to higher log throughput and faster transaction commit times (regardless of the volume of data). If you're interested in how Microsoft architected this and what the architecture changes enabled, you can review additional details here: `https://aka.ms/sdsth`.

To summarize, the recommendation from Microsoft has been to start with General Purpose and adjust as needed. With the elasticity of the cloud, you can then scale up or down the resources as needed, and if the performance is not good enough, you can move to Business Critical or Hyperscale. Remember that performance is higher in Hyperscale but highest in Business Critical, and cost typically follows the same pattern. For a detailed, current comparison between the service tiers, refer here: `https://aka.ms/sdbsth`.

Hardware generations

Once you've selected a service tier, depending on the deployment option, the vCore model provides multiple choices for the *hardware generation*. The hardware generation selection allows you to select which physical hardware you want to be used for compute and memory. The most common hardware generations used today are Gen4 and Gen5. Without getting too much into the specs, Gen4 hardware allows substantially more memory per vCore, but Gen5 hardware allows you to scale compute resources much higher. It's important to note that hardware generations available will constantly change and evolve as the technology improves. Gen4, for example, has been around for a long time and is no longer available for new databases in certain regions. Additionally, Fsv2-series (compute-optimized) and M-series (memory-optimized) hardware options recently became available for public usage. Another example is that Azure SQL Database serverless is currently only available on Gen5 hardware. Your requirements for cost and performance may make a certain generation of hardware a better choice. You can review the most current choices and specs of hardware here: `https://aka.ms/sdstvhg`.

If you're looking for other compute cost-savings opportunities, one option to consider is pre-paying for compute resources at a discount with Azure SQL Database reserved capacity (RI). For more information, see `https://aka.ms/sdri`.

If you are building a new application and starting from an empty database or instance, Azure SQL's elasticity allows you to grow and scale your compute and storage as needed. If you happen to be migrating an existing workload to Azure SQL Database or managed instance, translating that workload to a service tier, compute level, and max data size can be complicated. Fortunately, Microsoft has built a few tools that can help with this. First, you can leverage the *Data Migration Assistant* (DMA) tool to identify any blockers and determine which deployment option is best. Specifically related to the deployment choices, the DMA tool also has a feature called *SKU Recommender*, which analyzes your existing workload and recommends the service tier, compute level, and max data size. This tool provides an estimated cost per month and creates a PowerShell script you can use to bulk provision after analysis.

Networking

After you've selected your starting points for compute and storage, the next step is to configure the network connectivity. Choices for networking for Azure SQL Database (single database and Elastic pool) and Azure SQL managed instance (single instance and Instance pool) are different. When you deploy an Azure SQL Database, currently the default in the portal is that the "Allow Azure services and resources to access this server" blade is set to yes, meaning that other Azure services (e.g., Azure Data Factory or an Azure VM) can access the database if you set up the connection. Additionally, after deployment, you can alter the Azure SQL Database firewall rules to meet the requirements of your application.

With Azure SQL managed instances, you deploy the service inside an Azure *virtual network* (VNet) and a subnet that is dedicated to managed instances. VNets are like networks you'd deploy to your on-premises environments, but specific to Azure. A subnet is simply a way to create segments within a VNet. By deploying Azure SQL Managed Instance into a managed instance-only subnet within a VNet you own, you're enabled to have a completely secure and private IP address. This ability allows you to connect your on-premises network or other on-premises data stores to Azure SQL managed instance (e.g., using linked servers is supported). You can optionally enable a public endpoint so you can connect to a managed instance from the Internet without VPN, but this access is disabled by default.

The principle of private endpoints through VNet isolation in Azure SQL managed instance has made its way to Azure SQL Database in the form of Azure Private Link: `https://aka.ms/aplo`.

Connection methods

During deployment, in Azure SQL managed instance, you're also able to choose the connection type. In Azure SQL Database, you can also choose the connection type, but only after deployment. You can keep the default (combination of Proxy and Redirect) or change to solely Redirect or Proxy. At the highest level, in Proxy mode, all connections are proxied through the Azure SQL gateways, but in Redirect mode, after the connection is established leveraging the gateway, the connection goes directly to the database or managed instance. The direct connection (Redirect) allows for reduced latency and improved throughput, but also requires opening additional ports for services external to Azure, which is why it is not entirely enabled right away; opening additional ports is something that needs to be evaluated with respect to security risks that decision implies, and therefore Azure resorts to the most secure option by default.

As discussed in an earlier section, during deployment of a database (of Azure SQL Database or within an Azure SQL managed instance), you have the option to set up a *data source* using an existing backup from another Azure SQL Database or managed database in Azure SQL managed instance (they must match; you cannot use a managed database to create a new Azure SQL Database). In Azure SQL Database only, you also have the option to choose an existing sample database (AdventureWorksLT).

Collations

Another choice that you should carefully consider when deploying Azure SQL is the
collation. Collations in Azure SQL provide the sorting rules, case, and accent sensitivity
properties for the data in your database(s). The collation set will affect the characteristics
of many operations in instance or database, so should be set carefully. In Azure SQL
managed instance, you can set the server collation upon creation of the instance, but you
cannot change it later. This sets the default collation for all the databases in that instance,
but you can modify the collations on a database and column level later. In Azure SQL
Database, you cannot set the server collation; it's set at "SQL_Latin1_General_CP1_CI_
AS" which is the most common collation. Every collation name is formatted similarly:
"SQL" means it is a SQL Server collation (as opposed to a Windows or Binary collation),
"Latin1_General" specifies the alphabet and language to use when sorting, "CP1"
references the code page used by the collation, "CI" means it should be case insensitive,
"AS" means it should be accent sensitive, and there are other options available related to
widths, UTF-8, and so on (`https://aka.ms/srdc`).

Time zones

Time zone setting, like collation setting, is a seemingly small decision that can have a
big impact on your application. The Microsoft recommendation is to use Coordinated
Universal Time (UTC) for all instances and databases. In Azure SQL Database, you cannot
change the time zone; you just get UTC (but no fear, there are plenty of built-in features
in any Azure SQL database to manipulate time zones if needed and handle conversion
to local time). However, for Azure SQL Managed Instance, choice of time zone during
deployment was introduced to address the needs of many customers whose existing
applications store and call date and time values with a context of a specific time zone.

Advanced data security

The final choice that is available from the Azure portal deployment (but can also be done
with PowerShell) is *Advanced data security* (ADS). In the portal, you're prompted if you
want to start a free trial and enable ADS, which provides functionality related to data
discovery and classification, vulnerability alerts, and threat detection. For Azure SQL
managed instance, ADS can be configured after deployment. You can learn more about
ADS here: `https://aka.ms/sdads`.

As you can see, there are a lot of options available for you to make Azure SQL meet your needs in an efficient and cost-effective manner. Throughout the book, features available in different options will be explored further, giving you additional insights in selecting the best options for any scenario at hand.

Using sample databases

Whether you're getting started with Azure SQL and T-SQL or you're a well-seasoned professional, there are always new things to explore. Exploring some new or nuanced features and scenarios requires a database, and leveraging some of Microsoft's sample databases can help tremendously. Additionally, the Azure SQL and SQL Server community is huge (just search on Twitter for #sqlfamily), and members of the community are constantly contributing new content and samples to explore the latest feature or explain complex topics. Oftentimes, the examples you find online or in books will be tied to one of the sample databases from Microsoft, because they are rich samples that are easy to find and use.

In the first section of this chapter, you learned how to create an Azure SQL Database with a sample database preloaded. In this section, you'll learn more about the sample databases available and how to get started with them on Azure SQL Database and Azure SQL managed instance.

There are two main sample databases used most frequently, AdventureWorks and WideWorldImporters. The AdventureWorks sample is based around a fictional retail company AdventureWorks Cycles, and WideWorldImporters is a fictitious wholesale company with global trade operations. The AdventureWorks sample database was originally published to work with SQL Server 2008 and the WideWorldImporters with SQL Server 2016. As you saw in the first section of this chapter, using the Azure CLI, you can deploy a "light" version of the AdventureWorks database "AdventureWorksLT". There are additional database samples: the WideWorldImporters database for the features in standard edition of SQL Server "WideWorldImportersStd" and the WideWorldImporters database for the features in the enterprise edition of SQL Server "WideWorldImportersFull". Over the years, the samples are generally updated to go with the latest features. Those databases need to be deployed manually, just like for any other existing database that you might already have. Let's see how to do it.

There are different ways of getting the sample databases into Azure SQL Database vs. Azure SQL managed instance. For Azure SQL Database, you can do that by leveraging a bacpac file (a Windows file that has the extension ".bacpac" and contains a database's data and schema). You can download the WideWorldImporters file from here: `https://aka.ms/wwi10`.

If you are not running in the service tier of Business Critical (or Premium in the DTU model), there are some dependencies in the sample that will require you to use the samples ending in "Standard" or "std", since the General Purpose tier doesn't support memory-optimized tables. If you are running in Business Critical (or Premium), then you can use all samples (including those ending in "Full").

You'll need to create a storage account (`https://aka.ms/sdrsac`) and then copy the bacpac file into an Azure Blob container. There are many ways to copy the bacpac file over, but using Azure Storage Explorer (`http://aka.ms/storage-explorer`) and uploading via the Azure portal are two easy ways. Once the bacpac file has been copied into an Azure Blob container, you can leverage the following code to import the database into your Azure SQL database with Azure CLI.

Listing 2-8. Import bacpac file into Azure SQL Database

```
az sql db import \
    -g <ExistingResourceGroup> \
    -s <ExistingLogicalServer> \
    -n <ExistingSqlDatabase> \
    -u <AdminUsername> \
    -p <AdminPassword> \
    --storage-key-type StorageAccessKey \
    --storage-key <StorageKey> \
    --storage-uri https://<StorageAccount>.blob.core.windows.
      net/<BacpacFilename>
```

There is similar functionality available in PowerShell as well as a GUI experience in the Azure portal. This method can work well for migrating databases to Azure SQL Database in cases where the bak file can be exported to a bacpac file.

Your options for getting sample databases in Azure SQL Database are using the Azure portal, using Azure CLI, or using Azure PowerShell. In Azure SQL managed instances, these options are available as well (with slightly different syntax), but you also can natively restore using T-SQL. First, you'll need to have access to the backup ".bak" file. In this case, the backup file could be stored in an Azure Blob container, in the same way as for the Azure SQL Database example earlier. This time, you'll also need to generate a shared access signature (SAS) key (guidance for doing this with the Azure CLI: https://aka.ms/ascsas) so your managed instance can access the backup file. After deploying your instance, you can use your T-SQL querying tool of choice to connect to the instance to create a credential to the backup. If you copy and paste any of the below T-SQL commands, you may need to re-type the single quotes.

Listing 2-9. Create a credential to a backup

```
CREATE CREDENTIAL [https://<BakFilename>]
WITH IDENTITY = 'SHARED ACCESS SIGNATURE'
, SECRET '<Generated SAS Key without any leading "?">'
```

To check if the credential works, you can run the following T-SQL to get a list of the backup files. For "WideWorldImporters-Standard.bak", you should see the mdf, ndf, and ldf files returned.

Listing 2-10. View the files in a backup

```
RESTORE FILELISTONLY FROM URL = 'https://<BakFilename>'
```

Finally, you can restore the database from the URL using the following code.

Listing 2-11. Restore the database from a URL

```
RESTORE DATABASE [Wide World Importers] FROM URL = 'https://<BakFilename>'
```

This restore process is asynchronous and retriable, meaning that Azure SQL managed instance will keep trying to restore the database in the background even if the connection breaks or some timeout occurs. While this example was tied to WideWorldImporters, the process for restoring a database in Azure SQL managed instance with T-SQL will be the same for other backup files. For more information, refer here: https://aka.ms/sdmirsdq.

If you want to know more

Creating an Azure SQL database or managed instance is a simple operation, compared to on premises, but still requires some choices to be made to make sure you don't waste your money on things you don't need. This is more or less the same concept you apply on premises. Big difference is that scaling up is much easier. Keep in mind that in the cloud, resources can be managed just like salt: you can always add more.

Some links to go more in details of several concepts discussed in this chapter are as follows:

- Choose the right deployment option in Azure SQL – `https://docs.microsoft.com/azure/sql-database/sql-database-paas-vs-sql-server-iaas`

- What is PaaS? – `https://azure.microsoft.com/overview/what-is-paas/`

- Azure SQL service tiers – `https://docs.microsoft.com/azure/sql-database/sql-database-service-tiers-general-purpose-business-critical`

- Azure SQL Database servers and their management – `https://docs.microsoft.com/azure/sql-database/sql-database-servers`

- Azure SQL Features – `https://docs.microsoft.com/azure/sql-database/sql-database-features`

- Azure SQL Fundamentals – `https://aka.ms/azuresqlfundamentals`

CHAPTER 3

Connecting and Querying Azure SQL

Once you have created and configured a database instance, your next task will be to connect a newly developed or existing application to it and start executing data manipulation or retrieval commands.

Azure SQL is a cloud-native database service that communicates with external applications and processes through multiple Inter-Process Communication (IPC) mechanisms, like TCP/IP sockets, named pipes, or shared memory. Both commands in T-SQL (SQL Server's own SQL dialect) like SELECT/INSERT/UPDATE/DELETE and resultsets returned from the service are packaged into an application-level protocol called TDS (Tabular Data Stream, `https://aka.ms/mstds`).

As an application developer, of course you don't have to code against these low-level protocols in your own application. They usually are abstracted by a comprehensive series of drivers and libraries covering pretty much every modern programming language and framework available on the market and running on Windows, Linux, and macOS operating systems.

All the examples in this chapter are edited using Visual Studio Code editor (`https://code.visualstudio.com/`) and built and executed through command-line tools and SDKs for respective runtimes like .NET Core 3.1, OpenJDK 11, and Python 3.6.6 and on Windows, macOS, or Linux operating systems.

35

© Davide Mauri, Silvano Coriani, Anna Hoffman, Sanjay Mishra, Jovan Popovic 2021
D. Mauri et al., *Practical Azure SQL Database for Modern Developers*,
https://doi.org/10.1007/978-1-4842-6370-9_3

Driver and libraries

Most drivers are designed around some basic constructs, mainly representing common entities like

- A connection with server/database

- A command to execute over that connection

- An object to iterate and access records on a returned resultset

Some libraries do also offer more advanced data manipulation capabilities, like disconnected caches that can store retrieved rows, track offline modifications, and provide current/previous versions of contained rows to be used in pessimistic concurrency multi-user scenarios (e.g., ADO.NET DataSets/DataTable).

Higher-level frameworks and libraries are also available to cover specific scenarios in areas like performance (e.g., think about connection pooling for libraries that don't provide it natively, like JDBC drivers) or productivity tools like Object-Relational Mappers and MicroORMs to speed up development times. This table recaps all client drivers for Azure SQL on various programming languages and available for all platforms (Windows, Linux, macOS):

Language	Driver library	Version
.NET languages (C#, F#, etc.)	Microsoft ADO.NET for SQL Server	V1.1+
Java	Microsoft JDBC driver for SQL Server	V8.2+
PHP	PHP SQL driver for SQL Server	V 5.8+
Node.js	Node.js Tedious driver for SQL Server	V8.0.1+
Python	Python ODBC bridge (pyodbc)	V4.0.30+
Go	Microsoft SQL Server Driver for Go	
Ruby	Ruby driver for SQL Server	V2.1.0+
Native languages (e.g., C/C++)	Microsoft ODBC driver for SQL Server	V17.5.1.1+

What Azure SQL driver works best for me

For languages like C#, C++, Node.JS, or Python, multiple options are available for drivers, depending on platforms and application needs, so it's important to understand what combinations are available and recommended.

If your application is targeting *full .NET Framework* (on Windows) or the multi-platform *.NET Core* (on Windows, macOS, Linux, or Docker) using a language like *C#*, you have two main options:

- Rely on the classic *ADO.NET Provider for SQL Server* in *System. Data.SqlClient* namespace, which is available as part of the full .NET Framework version installed at the machine level.

- Reference in your project the new *Microsoft.Data.SqlClient* driver, hosted in GitHub (`https://aka.ms/ghmdsc`) and NuGet (`https:// aka.ms/ngmdsc`).

The latter option provides a much more flexible and direct way for Microsoft to introduce improvements in client libraries for .NET, so it's the recommended version to use when developing a brand-new app. Installing and referencing this package for a project is pretty straightforward using `dotnet` CLI:

```
dotnet add package Microsoft.Data.SqlClient
```

Programming languages like Perl, PHP, and Python are providing lightweight wrappers and interfaces around native ODBC drivers (e.g., pyodbc, DBI, etc.). To support all newest features available in latest Azure SQL releases (e.g., Always Encrypted, Data Classification, AAD authentication, etc.), *Microsoft ODBC Driver 17 for SQL Server* (or higher) is recommended. This driver is available for most major Linux distros and releases, in addition to Windows. Packaged with this driver are also traditional SQL Server client utilities like *sqlcmd* and *bcp*. Installation procedures for the ODBC driver largely depend on your target operating system and distribution, and all details can be found at this URL: `https://aka.ms/azuresql-odbc-install`.

Java developers should use *Microsoft JDBC Driver 8.2 for SQL Server*, which is a Type 4 JDBC driver supporting JRE 8, 11, and 12 and works on all main operating systems where Java is supported, including Sun Solaris. When using Maven, JDBC driver can be added to a project by adding it as dependency in the POM.xml file:

```
<dependency>
    <groupId>com.microsoft.sqlserver</groupId>
    <artifactId>mssql-jdbc</artifactId>
    <version>8.2.0.jre11</version>
</dependency>
```

As typical in the Java space, JDBC drivers don't provide native connection pooling capabilities so many external libraries are available on the market. While we're not endorsing any particular one, *HikariCP* (`https://aka.ms/hikaricp`) is one we often encounter when working with customers connecting to Azure SQL instances and has proven to be fast and reliable.

For other programming languages like *Python*, usually multiple options are available although Microsoft places its testing efforts and its confidence in *pyodbc* driver (`https://aka.ms/pyodbc`) that, as discussed previously, relies on the ODBC driver for SQL Server and supports most operating systems. You can easily install *pyodbc* using the following line in command prompt:

```
pip install pyodbc
```

Similarly, for Node.JS, the Tedious driver can be added to a project through canonical package manager typing

```
npm install tedious
```

Getting started

Official Microsoft documentation offers a great "Getting started" section for developers (`https://aka.ms/sdcq`), which is the best place to start familiarizing with application development for Azure SQL family using a step-by-step approach.

While you will have time to evaluate all these samples, we will start from scratch here with some of the most popular programming languages and explain key aspects of how to connect to Azure SQL and run some basic queries.

All samples in this chapter are referring to a database named "WideWorldImportersFull" that can be deployed as Azure SQL Database stand-alone or managed instance. In Chapter 2, you'll find instructions on how to deploy this sample database. Please update connection strings accordingly to make these samples work.

Listing 3-1. Data access method in a .NET *Core application*

```
public async Task<IEnumerable<Order>> GetOrders()
{
    List<Order> orders = new List<Order>();
    using (SqlConnection cnn =  new SqlConnection(
                config.GetConnectionString
                        ("DefaultConnection")))
    // Connection string pattern: "Server=tcp:<servername>.database.
       windows.net,1433;Initial Catalog=<database>;User ID=<username>;
       Password=<password>;Connect Timeout=30;"
    {
        SqlCommand cmd = new SqlCommand
            (@"SELECT TOP 5
                 [o].[OrderID],
                 [o].[OrderDate],
                 [c].[CustomerName]
              FROM [Sales].[Orders] AS [o]
                 INNER JOIN [Sales].[Customers] AS [c]
                 ON [o].[CustomerID] = [c].[CustomerID]", cnn);
        await cnn.OpenAsync();
        SqlDataReader dr = await cmd.ExecuteReaderAsync();
        while (dr.Read())
        {
            orders.Add(new Order()
            {
                OrderID = Convert.ToInt32(dr[0]),
```

```
                OrderDate = Convert.ToDateTime(dr[1]),
                CustomerName = Convert.ToString(dr[2])
            });
        }
    }
    return orders;
}
```

In this basic example, you can find a typical .NET Core data access method that can be reused in multiple application types, from a Console app to a WebAPI or Azure Function. Once you add a reference to Microsoft.Data.SqlClient package from NuGet, you can use *SqlConnection* and *SqlCommand* classes to interact with Azure SQL using asynchronous methods to open a new connection and execute a command that retrieves a resultset and materialize a collection of objects to be used in your business logic. While tons of other things are happening behind the scenes when you execute a simple operation like this, and many best practices and guidance are available to optimize your data access layer, you will find yourself writing similar code in most of the database interactions you'll have in your applications. Let's address the same exact scenario using Java now, one of enterprise developers' most favorite programming languages.

Listing 3-2. Data access method in a Java application

```
public List<Order> getOrders() {

    List<Order> order = new ArrayList<>();

    String connectionString = "jdbc:sqlserver://<servername>.database.
    windows.net:1433;" + "database=WideWorldImporters-Full;user=<username>
    @<servername>;" + "password=<password>;loginTimeout=30;";

    try {
        try (Connection conn =
                DriverManager.getConnection(connectionString)) {

                String sql =
                "SELECT TOP 5 "
                    +"[o].[OrderID],"
                    +"[o].[OrderDate],"
                    +"[c].[CustomerName]"
```

```
            +"FROM [Sales].[Orders] AS [o]"
            +"INNER JOIN [Sales].[Customers] AS [c] "
            +"ON [o].[CustomerID] = [c].[CustomerID]";

        try (Statement stmt =
            conn.createStatement();
                ResultSet rs =
                stmt.executeQuery(sql)) {
            while (rs.next()) {
                order.add(new Order(
                    rs.getInt(1),
                    rs.getString(2),
                    rs.getString(3)));
            }
        }
        conn.close();
    }
} catch (Exception e) {
        System.out.println();
        e.printStackTrace();
    }
    return order;
}
```

Java code sample is very similar to previous .NET Core one. Once we create an initial code skeleton through Maven for the application type we're looking for (Console app, REST service, etc.), we need to reference JDBC driver library in the *pof. xml* file to download it from central package repository and then use it in your code. *DriverManager* class represents the entry point for all JDBC drivers loaded in the application, and the *jdbc:sqlserver* prefix in the connection string is indicating what specific driver to use. *Connection, Statement,* and *resultset* are again the main classes used to encapsulate underlying connection management, command execution, and resultset iteration. These three classes will be the foundation for most of your database interactions.

Python is a language that gained a lot of traction over the years for writing data access and management applications. Let's see how to use it to connect to an Azure SQL database instance.

Listing 3-3. Create a simple Python application

```
@app.route('/order')
def getorders():
    cnxn = pyodbc.connect("DRIVER={ODBC Driver 17 " \
    "for SQL Server};" \ "SERVER="+server+";DATABASE="+database+"" \
    ";UID="+username+";PWD="+ password)

    cursor = cnxn.cursor()

    tsql = "SELECT TOP 5 " \
            " [o].[OrderID], [o].[OrderDate]," \
            " [c].[CustomerName]" \
            " FROM [Sales].[Orders] AS [o]" \
            " INNER JOIN [Sales].[Customers] AS [c]" \
            " ON [o].[CustomerID] = [c].[CustomerID]"

    rows = cursor.execute(tsql).fetchall()

    order_list = []
    for row in rows:
        d = collections.OrderedDict()
        d['orderID'] = row.OrderID
        d['orderDate'] = str(row.OrderDate)
        d['customerName'] = row.CustomerName
        order_list.append(d)

    return json.dumps(order_list)
```

In this Python Flask function (you can find the complete app in the companion GitHub repo), *pyodbc* module plays a central role. It provides a wrapper around ODBC driver and higher-level abstractions like connection, cursor, and row, which let you both execute commands and iterate on results. Rows are then transformed into a list of ordered dictionaries and returned as a JSON fragment to function callers. In pure Pythonic spirit, *pyodbc* represents a pretty efficient and straightforward method for accessing Azure SQL database instances from your Python programs.

As we mentioned previously, *tedious* is the driver you can use to connect to Azure SQL from Node.JS applications. Let's take a look at a simple function that executes a query and converts a resultset into a JSON array that can be returned, for example, as REST API result.

Listing 3-4. Node.JS function returning JSON array from database

```
exports.getorders = function(req, res) {

  const { Connection, Request } = require("tedious");

  const config = {
    server: "<servername>.database.windows.net",
    options: {
      database: "WideWorldImporters-Full",
      encrypt: true},
      authentication: {
        type: "default",
        options: {
          userName: "username",
          password: "password",
        }
      }
  };

  const connection = new Connection(config);

  connection.on("connect", err => {
    if (err) {
      console.error(err.message);
    } else {
      getOrders();
    }
  });

  function getOrders() {
    var data = []
```

```
const request = new Request(
  `SELECT TOP 5 [o].[OrderID],
  [o].[OrderDate], [c].[CustomerName]
  FROM [Sales].[Orders] AS [o]
  INNER JOIN [Sales].[Customers] AS [c]
  ON [o].[CustomerID] = [c].[CustomerID]`,
  (err, rowCount) => {
    if (err) {
      console.error(err.message);
    }
    else {
      res.send(data)
    }
  }
);

request.on("row", function(row) {
  data.push({
    orderid: row[0].value,
    orderdate: row[1].value,
    customername: row[2].value
  })
});

connection.execSql(request);
  }
};
```

As seen in previous examples for other programming languages, the Connection and Request objects play a central role for opening a new connection to the database, executing a command, and retrieving results (you can find the complete working example in the companion GitHub repo). These two objects offer all properties and capabilities to cover most common scenarios, from defining parameterized queries to transaction management or bulk loads.

This section doesn't cover all available drivers and libraries but provides a representative overview of how applications are typically connecting with Azure SQL and can definitely be applied to other drivers not mentioned here. Moving forward, we will focus on advanced and specific scenarios that are critical for your application's data access layer.

Connectivity aspects

As briefly mentioned in Chapter 2, network connectivity is another fundamental aspect of interacting with Azure SQL from your applications. Although more related to infrastructure design and network security than pure app development, you'll need to consider various options and components that play a role in this process to successfully connect with your database instances. Both single database and managed instance deployment models for Azure SQL Database support two main connectivity options for applications:

- Private VNET

- Public connectivity

While a managed instance is automatically associated with an Azure Virtual Network at creation time, and public connectivity is optional, for individual Azure SQL Database instance is actually the opposite, and you should rely on Azure Private Link capability to connect your application deployed on one of the Azure services that support VNETs via a private endpoint and on a completely isolated network traffic path.

For those scenarios where public connectivity is required, there are still some options that can be considered to govern network traffic between your application and Azure SQL:

- Server- and database-level firewall

- VNET Service Endpoint

- VNET Network Security Group (NSG)

Server- and database-level firewall rules are designed to define what ranges of IP addresses (coming from public Internet connectivity or from within various Azure services) can establish a connection with Azure SQL Database single instances. If database-level firewall rules exist (today, these can be created through T-SQL commands only), those will be evaluated to understand if a client connection is coming from an allowed range; otherwise, server-level rules (valid for all database instances associated with that virtual server and defined through T-SQL, PowerShell/CLI, or Azure Portal) will be checked. If you decide to trust all network connections coming from an Azure service, then there's a check box option on the portal to "Allow Azure services and resources to access this server" to simplify your settings.

VNET Service Endpoint is a feature designed to guarantee that network connections targeting a given Azure SQL server will be accepted only if they come from one or more VNET/Subnet pairs where your applications are deployed.

On the application side of the connection, a VNET Network Security Group can be created and associated with a Virtual Machine's NIC or an entire Subnet to make sure they can only connect with a given range of IP addresses and ports where your Azure SQL instances reside.

Network security is not the only aspect that can affect database connectivity; network latency is the other critical one. Connection policy determines how your database connections will interact with the back-end node hosting your databases in Azure SQL and can be one of these two options:

- Proxy

- Redirect

With Proxy, you have maximum flexibility to connect to your instance from anywhere using FQDN server name and just port 1433, but these connections will always go through a Gateway front-end layer that will increase network latency (usually not good for chatty applications).

Redirect policy instead establishes connections directly to the node hosting the database, reducing latency, and improving application throughput, but it does require specific port ranges (11000–11999) to be open between your application host and the database.

Default connection policy is *Proxy* for all connections coming from *outside* Azure service IP ranges and *Redirect* for those *within* Azure, but you can change the default through PowerShell and Azure CLI. More details on Azure SQL connectivity architecture can be found at the following URLs:

> Azure SQL Database single instances – `https://aka.ms/sdca`

> Azure SQL Database managed instances – `https://aka.ms/ sdmica`

Resilient connection and query execution

Building distributed systems on cloud architectures requires a specific approach regarding service-to-service interactions to increase resiliency and availability. This is generally true for all kinds of cloud services and interactions, from transactional solutions to batch processing.

In a traditional on-premises solution, database and application servers are usually sitting next to each other with physical networking devices like switches and routers dedicated to providing stable and fast connectivity. When hardware or software failures are happening, despite proper redundancy and high-level device quality in place, chances are that these are going to be quite impactful and persisting until someone will physically fix the problem and bring the system back online again.

In a cloud environment, everything is virtualized and completely automated, so you'll have many more moving parts potentially introducing some transient connectivity blips that application developers should consider to make their application more reliable overall. As an example, Azure SQL will automatically manage hardware or software failures, or planned maintenance operations, to the database node service application requests at any point in time, but, as fast as the failover operation to a secondary node can be, data access code may face an exception for the very few seconds after that event happened (on average around 8 seconds, at most in less than 60 seconds) before being able to respond to requests regularly.

Other examples of transient connectivity issues could be related to reaching maximum limits in Azure SQL instances based on the service tier and size selected. As we're referring to a multitenant service, it is absolutely critical to preserve the overall system's stability. In case of such event, applications temporarily won't be able to connect to Azure SQL until resource utilization decreases to within given thresholds.

Retry logic

To make your applications more reliable, a common approach is to introduce proper retry logic capabilities in database access code. Retry logic usually refers to a technique that

a. Intercepts application errors provoked by a transient condition

b. Retries the original operation for a certain amount of times, introducing a delay period that can be fixed or incremental, to make sure you won't flood instances with requests that are going to fail anyway usually creating a convoy effect

This logic can be as simple as just retrying opening a connection, after a previous tentative has failed returning a certain exception, for a fixed amount of times and with some delay between retries.

A trickier use case for retry logic is when an operation ultimately modifies database state, like inserting a new record or updating one or more existing ones. If a transient error happened while this command was under execution, the application will be responsible for deciding if the previous attempt failed before or after the database was effectively modified. In this case, in fact, client applications cannot just blindly re-execute previous commands, as there's no guarantee data wasn't already modified (think about a bank account's transaction as an example). Retry logic needs to ensure that either the previous transaction was completely committed or that the entire operation was rolled back; otherwise, the database could remain in an inconsistent state. Basically, retry logic for transactional database code can be quite complex and will typically only apply for those use cases where your data modification code is completely idempotent (i.e., can be executed multiple times without necessarily modifying database state).

If correctly modeled, the database will help you in making sure data is consistent: for example, an order with an already existing number will not be allowed to be inserted. That said, you will still need to handle the returned error, and thus implementing solid retry logic will significantly improve your application reliability and stability.

Transient and persistent errors

A key aspect of implementing a robust retry logic mechanism is to intercept and decode what errors the application should interpret as transient and what are instead permanent (and retry logic won't be able to help).

As mentioned previously, there are several categories of conditions and events that could be categorized as transient, from underlying hardware failures and automatic reconfigurations to temporary resource exhaustion. Transient issues could also happen at different layers in the stack: think about a temporary glitch in software defined networking! While these episodes can be rare and very short in time, it's very important to proactively address them by adopting proper coding practices. A comprehensive explanation of typical connectivity issues at different layers is offered in Azure SQL's public documentation at this link: https://aka.ms/tciasb.

Custom code or reusable libraries

Let's see how to implement in practical terms a simple retry logic mechanism for database access as described in previous sections. The following code is quite straightforward and only provides basic retry functionalities by wrapping database interaction method in a for loop and intercepting potential exceptions that can be thrown during its execution.

Listing 3-5. Create custom retry logic in a C# application

```
bool success = false;
int retryCount = 3;
int retryInterval = 8;

List<int> RetriableCodes =
    new List<int> { 4060, 40197, 40501, 40613,
            49918, 49919, 49920, 11001,208 };

for (int retries = 1; retries <= retryCount; retries++)
{
    try
    {
        if (retries > 1)
        {
            Thread.Sleep(1000 * retryInterval);
            // Retry interval increases by 50% every retry
            retryInterval = Convert.ToInt32 (retryInterval * 1.5);
        }
        await MyDatabaseOperation();
        success = true;
        break;
    }
    catch (SqlException se)
    {
        if (RetriableCodes.Contains(se.Number) == true)
        {
            // Retriable error - log and continue
            continue;
        }
```

```
    else
    {
    // Non-retriable error - exit the loop
        break;
    }
  }
  catch (Exception e)
  {
    // Generic exception - exit the loop
    break;
  }
}
```

As you notice, a lot of "plumbing" and complexity is required for a quite simple database operation to make it resilient to transient errors. Imagine if this should be repeated for every method and interaction that your application has with its data layer! Plus, this lacks any option for consistently configure parameters like number of retries, fixed or incremental delays, or even what exceptions should be considered transient vs. permanent.

Luckily, over the years, a number of reusable libraries have been created covering pretty much every programming language and framework to encapsulate that plumbing code into configurable mechanisms that developers can use to make their applications more reliable.

For .NET applications, one of the most known retry logic libraries is Transient Fault Handling (TFH) Application Block, originally part of Microsoft Enterprise Library framework, that has been recently ported to .NET Core and is freely available on NuGet for downloads at this URL: https://aka.ms/eltfhc.

It is a fully configurable and comprehensive set of classes that let you define your own *RetryStrategy* (e.g., FixedInterval, Incremental, ExponentialBackoff) and use a standard (out of the box) or a custom transient error detection logic. These two components combined define a *RetryPolicy* which is the class you use to wrap database access activities. Let's look at a practical implementation using this framework.

Listing 3-6. Use a retry logic library in a C# application

```csharp
public async Task<IEnumerable<Order>> GetOrders()
{
    // Get retry strategy
    RetryStrategy retryStrategy =
        config.GetRetryStrategies<FixedInterval>()
            ["MyFixedStrategy"];
    // Create retry policy
    RetryPolicy retry = new
        RetryPolicy<MyTransientErrorDetection>(retryStrategy);

    // Wrap database interaction with retry policy
    await retry.ExecuteAsync(async () => {

    List<Order> orders = new List<Order>();
    using (SqlConnection cnn =  new SqlConnection(
                _config.GetConnectionString
                        ("DefaultConnection")))
    {
        SqlCommand cmd = new SqlCommand
            (@"SELECT TOP 5
                    [o].[OrderID],
                    [o].[OrderDate],
                    [c].[CustomerName]
                FROM [Sales].[Orders] AS [o]
                    INNER JOIN [Sales].[Customers] AS [c]
                    ON [o].[CustomerID] = [c].[CustomerID]",cnn);
        await cnn.OpenAsync();
        SqlDataReader dr = await cmd.ExecuteReaderAsync();
        while (dr.Read())
        {
            orders.Add(new Order()
            {
                OrderID = Convert.ToInt32(dr[0]),
                OrderDate = Convert.ToDateTime(dr[1]),
                CustomerName = Convert.ToString(dr[2])
```

51

```
            });
        }
    }
    return orders;

    });
}
```

In this fragment (you can find the complete example in the companion GitHub repo), we configure retry strategies' details in a configuration file, essentially defining all the parameters like number of retries, retry intervals, and so on.

You may want to define more retry strategies in your applications and use them depending on the kind of database operation you want to retry. For example, for less frequent data retrieval operation, you may want to define a more aggressive retry strategy with higher number of retries, while for a different use case, you may want to step back and quickly return the error to the end user so that he or she can make a different decision based on that.

Next step is to define what error detection strategy you want to use. TFH provides out of the box a class called *SqlDatabaseTransientErrorDetectionStrategy* which encapsulates the logic for detecting the most common error codes that Azure SQL will emit when facing a transient error. In this example, we instead created a custom strategy by creating a class that implements *ITransientErrorDetectionStrategy* interface, as we wanted to test our retry logic with some non-transient errors.

You then create a *RetryPolicy* instance by combining your retry strategy and transient error detection class, and that will provide the *ExecuteAction()* or *ExecuteAsync()* method to effectively wrap database access code.

Retry policy class also exposes a *Retrying* event that you can subscribe to and be notified when retry logic is intercepting a transient error and retrying an operation.

Another popular library in the .NET space is Polly (`https://aka.ms/avnp`) which also provides features that cover other app reliability aspects by implementing resiliency patterns like Circuit Breaker, Timeout, Bulkhead Isolation, and Fallback in addition to just Retry.

Similar implementations also exist in most other programming languages and frameworks. In Python, a common one is called Tenacity (`https://aka.ms/tenacity`) and provides similar capabilities. Tenacity comes as a generic decorator (*@retry*) for the methods you will want to retry automatically. You can specify several parameters, like number of attempts (stop condition) and delay between attempts (referred as wait condition), and of course customize what exception types should be considered retriable. This implementation is quite simple to use; let's see it in practice in the next example.

Listing 3-7. Implement retry logic in a Python application

```python
import pyodbc
import random
from tenacity import *
import logging

def is_retriable(value):
    # Define all retriable error codes from https://docs.microsoft.com/
      en-us/azure/sql-database/troubleshoot-connectivity-issues-microsoft-
      azure-sql-database
    RETRY_CODES = [1204,1205,1222,49918,49919,49920,4060,4221,40143,40613,
    40501,  40540,40197,10929,10928,10060,10054,10053,233,64,20,0]
    ret = value in RETRY_CODES
    return ret

@app.route('/order')
@retry(stop=stop_after_attempt(3), wait=wait_fixed(10), after=after_
log(logger, logging.DEBUG))
def getorders():
    cnxn = pyodbc.connect("DRIVER={ODBC Driver 17 " \
    "for SQL Server};" \ "SERVER="+server+";DATABASE="+database+"" \
    ";UID="+username+";PWD="+ password)

    try:

    cursor = cnxn.cursor()

    tsql = "SELECT TOP 5 " \
            " [o].[OrderID], [o].[OrderDate]," \
            " [c].[CustomerName]" \
            " FROM [Sales].[Orders] AS [o]" \
            " INNER JOIN [Sales].[Customers] AS [c]" \
            " ON [o].[CustomerID] = [c].[CustomerID]"
```

```
    rows = cursor.execute(tsql).fetchall()

    order_list = []
    for row in rows:
        d = collections.OrderedDict()
        d['orderID'] = row.OrderID
        d['orderDate'] = str(row.OrderDate)
        d['customerName'] = row.CustomerName
        order_list.append(d)

except Exception as e:
    if isinstance(e,pyodbc.ProgrammingError) or
        isinstance(e,pyodbc.OperationalError):
            if is_retriable(int(e.args[0])):
                raise
pass

return json.dumps(order_list)
```

In this example, we use Tenacity to decorate a Flask method interacting with our database called *getorders()*, and we retry three times with a fixed interval of 10 seconds in case of an exception. Instead of specifying in decorator's attributes what exception to retry with, we're instead wrapping *pyodbc* methods with a *try/except* block and checking if the exception has anything to do with database access. In that case, we're checking if underlying database error code is contained in the list we're maintaining for retriable error and, if that's the case, we're just raising that exception so that the *@retry* decorator can do its job of automatically retrying the method until it succeeds or it should stop trying as the max number of attempts has been reached.

Even in Java, there are again multiple options to achieve the same result. One of the most commonly used is called Failsafe (`https://aka.ms/jnfs`) and is very similar to the Transient Fault Handling library we mentioned previously. Without the need for demonstrating it in another complete application, the following code fragment shows how to quickly use Failsafe's main classes:

```
// Define a retry policy instance with familiar parameters
RetryPolicy<Object> retryPolicy = new RetryPolicy<>()
    .handle(ConnectException.class)
```

```
.withDelay(Duration.ofSeconds(1))
.withMaxRetries(3);

// Wrap your database interaction code with that retry policy
Failsafe.with(retryPolicy).run(() -> connect());
```

Connectivity best practices

Let's start from a very basic one: in a database application, latency matters! This means that, for performance reasons, it's important to make sure your application code runs as close to your database as possible, no matter what Azure service it will be deployed on. This is especially true for applications that are executing a lot of database interactions or roundtrips, where this latency can easily become more impactful than real processing time.

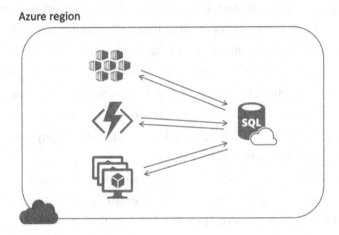

Figure 3-1. *Roundtrips to database*

At the very least, you should make sure your application gets deployed in the same region as where your database instance is. This may also have some architectural implications in case, for example, you're designing a highly reliable, cross-region solution. This means that you need to plan for failing over not only your data layer but also your application tier accordingly to minimize latency impact in case of a malfunctioning of your primary site.

Along the same line, it's also important to understand overall Azure SQL connectivity architecture (explained in the official docs: https://aka.ms/sdmica) and make sure that, if your application tier is running in an Azure service like Virtual Machine, App

Service, or Azure Kubernetes Service, as an example, it is leveraging the Redirect connection policy, which means that your application will communicate directly with the node hosting your database instance instead of passing through the Gateway layer for every single interaction. If your app is executing anything more than only a few queries every minute, this option will make a significant difference from a performance perspective, and the trade-off required is just to make sure that ports in the range of 11000–11999 are open in networking configuration where your client code resides.

While it may sound trivial, another recommendation related to connectivity is to make sure your code is effectively opening a connection with an Azure SQL database instance as late as possible before executing some meaningful command, and it's closing that connection as soon as results are consumed. Most driver libraries are, in fact, designed to leverage Connection Pooling, a mechanism that will help you balance between the cost of opening a brand-new physical connection (e.g., a TCP socket) with a remote service, which always comes with a given millisecond overhead, and the cost of keeping too many connections always open as that will increase the amount of resources (memory, worker threads, etc.) consumed on the service side.

Connection pooling works at the process level and keeps a physical connection opened for a certain amount of time even if in your application code you explicitly called a close or dispose method, so that if a new request to open a connection with the same connection string parameters will be executed later, the existing physical connection will be reused instead of opening a brand new one.

Thanks to this approach, in a canonical web application or web API scenario, it's not uncommon that, even if thousands of users are accessing a given page, only a few tens of real database connections are kept open at any given time, significantly reducing the overhead generated for Azure SQL database instances.

Generally speaking, in most scenarios where a multi-threaded application is executing a conventional database workload (queries, transactions, etc.) against an Azure SQL instance, it is recommended to leverage Connection Pooling for performance reasons. The only exception to this general rule is where your application really needs to carefully control how specific operations are executed against the database. A good example for that are Data Definition Language (DDL) commands (CREATE, ALTER, DROP that will be discussed later, that work on data structures instead of data itself) that your application may issue against the database, where usually one connection at time is executed and commands are serialized on that same connection.

As mentioned, most existing drivers are providing this capability out of the box and even enabling it by default, like .NET Data Provider for SQL Server, but there's an important exception. In the Java space, historically, connection pooling has been a separate implementation from JDBC drivers so SQL Server's one doesn't provide functionality.

Thankfully, there are many external packages offering that capability for your Java application, and one of the most known is certainly HikariCP (`https://aka.ms/hikaricp`), as mentioned before. It's important to notice though that, generally speaking, Java drivers have some challenges in detecting what are usually referred as "stale connections" or client-side connection objects that have lost underlying connectivity with a database instance due to a transient issue, without trying to execute a test command (by explicitly invoking *java.sql.Connection.isValid()* which pings the database every time to make sure the connection is opened). In other drivers, this is usually performed at a lower level by checking the state of a TCP socket, but Java native APIs have issues with that. A similar problem could happen while a command is executed, and a resultset is under consumption by your application code. The recommendation here is to carefully configure both your JDBC driver and your connection pooling classes with proper timeouts to avoid that the application can hang forever if a transient error happens at the wrong time. All the details about these configurations are further explained in an article at this URL: `https://aka.ms/jdbc-connection-guidance`.

Other high-level languages and frameworks like Python and pyodbc may be suffering from the same transient connectivity issues, and the same approach and guidance is also recommended.

Handling exceptions

Opening of a connection to a data source and the execution of commands are operations naturally subject to the occurrence of errors, which can range from the lack of network connectivity to the server up to the violation of some rules for maintaining data integrity, coded within the database (primary key, relationships, etc.) or even concurrency management (e.g., locking/blocking) within your application or during maintenance operations (complete list of database engine error codes is available here: `https://aka.ms/eaerde`). It is therefore necessary to provide, for your application code performing database interactions, an adequate interception mechanism and management of error conditions.

Most programming languages and frameworks implement exception handling through the try/catch (or except) approach. In the try block, you generally put the instructions that are presumed to generate exceptions, such as opening the connection, executing a command, or calling a component which in turn can generate an application exception. If one of these operations fails, application control passes to the first catch/except block which specifies an exception type compatible with the one that occurred. Generally, those exception types provide all the information concerning the specific operation failed; this information is then made available in the catch block so you can code a proper logic on how to manage it.

In T-SQL language (e.g., within a Stored Procedure), in addition to errors potentially generated by command interacting with database objects (e.g., a primary key constraint violation), you can also generate exceptions that represent a logical error in your procedure through the *RAISERROR* or *THROW* functions, so that your application can behave accordingly.

You can pass an error message, severity level, and code to the RAISERROR function, and depending on the severity, client providers will act accordingly:

- Level 10 or below, connection is not interrupted, and no exceptions are generated. Messages can still be collected from the client driver.

- From 11 to 19, the connection remains open, but an exception is thrown.

- Beyond 19 are considered fatal errors, an exception is thrown, and connection is terminated.

For Azure SQL, errors generated with a severity level equal or less than 10 do not really generate an exception but are considered as a simple informational or warning message. Driver libraries are capturing this information through specific classes (e.g., *InfoMessage* for *.NET Provider for SQL Server*) together with proper exception collection.

At the very minimum, you'll also want to use these details about the error condition as part of your logging strategy for further analysis from the operations team in charge or running your application. Other than that, you'll have to decide what option between just retrying the operation (as described in the retry logic section) and returning the information back to the caller is the most correct, so that one can take appropriate decisions on the best course of action for each specific use case.

Frameworks, ORM, and MicroORM

So far, we mentioned that client drivers are generally providing base abstractions to connect, query, and consume results from Azure SQL database instances. That said, application developers in most cases are typically looking at higher-level abstractions to help them be more productive and eliminate recurring and potentially error-prone data access tasks, like representing and interacting with data entities in their application logic.

To achieve higher productivity, a number of data access frameworks have been created of the last 20 years or such that could be grouped in two main buckets:

- Helper classes that just wrap those base abstractions and simplify common tasks

- Object-Relational Mappers (ORM), providing rich data modeling and mapping capabilities to reduce the impedance mismatch between relational structures and object-oriented programming

The following table represents a (non-exhaustive) list of some of the most popular libraries in the market by programming language:

Language	Recommended/popular libraries
.NET	• Datasets • Entity Framework (Core) • Dapper
Java	• Spring Data • Hibernate
PHP	• Doctrine • Eloquent
Node.js	• RxDB • TypeORM • Sequelize
Python	• SQLAlchemy • Django • pandas
Ruby	• ActiveRecord
Go	• Gorm

In the next sections, we'll dig deeper into some of them.

Data access frameworks

Although basic abstractions will generally take control of every possible aspect of your database interactions, they may require a lot of boilerplate code in your application to transform objects and structures representing higher-level entities in your logic into rows and columns within your database structure.

Over the years, a number of libraries and frameworks have been created to simplify this issue while still letting you control how your code interacts with your data. As a practical example, in the .NET space, ADO.NET Provider for SQL Server provides from the very first release, together with *SqlConnection*, *SqlCommand*, and *SqlDataReader* classes (representing what is usually referred to as the "connected" portion of SqlClient library), a number of other classes are provided to interpret and navigate through query results in a more "object-oriented" fashion, but also to take care of persisting back to the underlying database whatever change has been made to original data. I'm referring to classes as *SqlDataAdapter* and *DataSet* (typed or untyped). *DataSet* is an in-memory representation of resultsets populated from the scratch in your code or returned from one or more queries to the database and provides additional logic around offline change tracking, data validation, and relationship management between entities. *SqlDataAdapter* acts as a "connector" between *DataSets* and database objects and can both automatically generate T-SQL commands that take changes applied to in-memory data and persist them in the back-end database or leverage existing commands and Stored Procedures to control all aspects of these database operations for performance or concurrency reasons. DataSets can also be automatically generated from a database schema and become fully typed objects exposing internal resultsets as named collections (e.g., Customers, Orders, etc.) instead of rows and columns. To discover more about these options, you can find complete coverage at this link: https://aka. ms/dnfado.

Similar helper classes are very popular on other programming frameworks as well. Examples can be Spring Data Access for Java (https://aka.ms/sfrda) or SQLAlchemy Core classes for Python.

Listing 3-8. Using SQLAlchemy in a Python application

```python
def getorders():

    # create a SQLAlchemy engine using SQL Server dialect
    engine = create_engine("mssql+pyodbc:///?odbc_connect=%s" %
    connectionString)

    # initialize metadata repository
    metadata = MetaData()
    # define metadata for result sets
    orders = Table('Orders', metadata,
        Column('orderid', Integer, primary_key=True),
        Column('customerid', Integer),
        Column('orderdate', Date),
        schema='Sales'
    )

    customers = Table('Customers', metadata,
        Column('customerid',Integer,primary_key=True),
        Column('customername',String),
        schema='Sales'
    )
    # define our query using a SQL-like syntax
    s = select([orders.c.orderid,orders.c.orderdate,customers.c.
        customername]).\
            select_from(orders.join(customers, orders.c.customerid==
            customers.c.customerid)).\
                limit(10)

    try:
        # open the connection to the database
        cnn = engine.connect()
        # execute SQLAlchemy command
        res = cnn.execute(s)
        # iterate on results
        for row in res:
            print(row)
```

```
    # close the connection
    cnn.close()
except Exception as e:
    print (e)
    pass
```

In this simple example, you can see how SQLAlchemy lets us define in-memory representation of our application entities and how they map to database tables. Using an app-level SQL-like syntax, we can then specify our query containing advanced operations like joins, filters, aggregations, projections, and so on, and SQLAlchemy classes will translate this into a SQL syntax specific for Azure SQL, but you could easily port the same code to connect to other supported database systems as well. While SQLAlchemy can do much more (we've just scratched the surface here), its most advanced features more than just a data access framework belong to the realm of Object-Relational Mappers, which is the topic of the next section.

ORMs

The purpose for an ORM is to mediate between the relational and object-oriented worlds and let developers to write applications that interact with data stored in relational databases using typed objects that represent the application's domain and reducing the need for data access redundant (or "plumbing") code that they usually need to write. The following table recaps various ORM libraries you can use to connect with Azure SQL:

Language	Platform	ORM(s)
C#	Windows, Linux, macOS	Entity Framework
		Entity Framework Core
Java	Windows, Linux, macOS	Hibernate ORM
PHP	Windows, Linux, macOS	Laravel (Eloquent)
		Doctrine
Node.js	Windows, Linux, macOS	Sequelize ORM

Language	Platform	ORM(s)
Python	Windows, Linux, macOS	Django
Ruby	Windows, Linux, macOS	Ruby on Rails

One of the first and most successful libraries in this space is Java's Hibernate (`https://aka.ms/horm`) appeared in the early 2000s, with the goal of providing a better experience than Enterprise Java Beans entities to persist data into databases without necessarily using SQL commands. Over the years, these libraries became much more powerful and complex (for some people, even too complex, so that alternatives like "micro-ORM" libraries have been created) to cover other aspects of the data access tier like modeling, security, and scalability.

Microsoft's own ORM for .NET world is Entity Framework (EF), and its more recent release is EF Core (`https://aka.ms/ghdnefc`). EF Core works with several back-end database stores like SQL Server, Azure SQL Database, SQLite, Azure Cosmos DB, MySQL, PostgreSQL, and other databases through a provider plug-in API. It's the result of 10+ years of development in this space and provides features like LINQ queries, offline change tracking, batched updates, and database schema management through a feature named "migrations."

The core of this library is the *DbContext* class that developers can use to create their database interaction context and model how database tables will be mapped to entities and collections and how operations against these entities will be transparently transformed into SQL code to read, create, or update records within a database.

Listing 3-9. Using Entity Framework Core in a C# application fragment

```
using(var dbctx = new WWImportersContext())
{
    var res = dbctx.Orders
        .Include("Customer")
        .Select (o => new
        {o.OrderID,o.OrderDate,o.Customer.CustomerName})
        .ToList().Take(10);
```

```
    foreach(var o in res)
    {
        Console.WriteLine("OrderId: {0} - OrderDate: {1} -
        CustomerName: {2}",o.OrderID,o.OrderDate,o.CustomerName);
    }
}

class Order
{
    public int OrderID {get;set;}
    public DateTime OrderDate {get;set;}
    public int CustomerID {get;set;}
    public Customer Customer {get;set;}
}
class Customer
{
    public int CustomerID {get;set;}
    public String CustomerName {get;set;}
}
class WWImportersContext : DbContext
{
    // Model building deliberately omitted in this fragment
    public DbSet<Order> Orders {get;set;}
    public DbSet<Customer> Customers {get;set;}
}
```

Let's focus on the three key aspects of this simple example:

- First, the two POCO (plain old CLR objects) classes *Order* and *Customer* that represent the business entities managed by our application.

- *WWImportersContext* class, inheriting from *DbContext*, which represents the context our app is using to connect and query the database. Specifically, it does contain the two *DbSet* collections that are mapped to database tables.

- The LINQ query that interacts with the database context and expresses what entities we want to retrieve.

As you can notice in the complete example (see GitHub repo for that), it's interesting to see how our *WWImportersContext* class overrides the *OnConfiguring* and *OnModelCreating* methods of its base class to do exactly what their names imply: configuring the way our context communicates with the database and defining a model where our entities map to respective database tables. We also configured the logging infrastructure to show how the resulting T-SQL code automatically generated by the context looks like. Pretty straightforward, isn't it?

Entity Framework Core can do much more, and you can start familiarizing with all these capabilities through this free Microsoft Learn online course (`https://aka.ms/lmpsefc`).

"With great power comes great responsibility," so there are some basic good practices that you should always keep in mind to get the most out of ORM tools like EF Core:

- First of all, make sure you're pulling from the database only the data you really need and making your resultset as efficient as possible.

- If your application only needs to materialize objects based on query results and display them on a screen, but will never modify and update them, switch change tracking off. This will avoid wasting lots of application resources to track object state information you will never use.

- If instead your application will create or update many entities within your database context, make sure you're leveraging batching (e.g., calling the *AddRange()* method on your *DbSet* collections). EF Core will then behind the scenes create a Table-Valued Parameter (TVP) and use it in a MERGE statement to insert multiple rows in a single database roundtrip. This is providing many benefits for Azure SQL both in terms of reduced latency and minimizing transaction log pressure. For very large bulk operations (in the >10,000s rows ballpark), you may want to perform them outside of Entity Framework (e.g., using ADO.NET's SqlBulkCopy class) or use a nice EF Core extension called EFCore.BulkExtensions (`https://aka.ms/efcbe`).

- Where possible, turn on logging and validate T-SQL syntax generated by EF Core.

- In case of complex database interactions, using raw SQL commands or Stored Procedures through EF Core can solve performance and flexibility issues.

MicroORMs

For those scenarios where you don't need the complexity of a full ORM library, a new class of simplified tools emerged over the last years, and they're usually referred as MicroORMs. One of the most successful is probably Dapper from StackExchange (https://aka.ms/ghsaed). Basically, Dapper provides a fast and efficient way of materializing objects based on a SQL query, and it's a great solution for application scenarios where you don't necessarily need to track disconnected changes and manage full persistence for your objects into the database. Dapper extends existing *IDbConnection* interface (as available in various ADO.NET Data Providers) and provides helper methods to execute T-SQL queries and map results to collections of POCO objects or execute commands that modify database state in a performant manner. The following example shows how to use Dapper to retrieve a resultset.

Listing 3-10. Using Dapper in a C# application

```
class Program
{
    static void Main(string[] args)
    {
        using (SqlConnection cnn =
            new SqlConnection(
            "Server=tcp:<servername>.database.windows.net,"+
            "1433;Initial Catalog=WideWorldImporters-Full;"+
            "User ID=<username>;Password=<password>;"))
        {
            var orders = cnn.Query<Order>("SELECT TOP 10 OrderID,
            OrderDate, CustomerID FROM Sales.Orders;");
            foreach (var o in orders)
```

```
            {
                Console.WriteLine("OrderId: {0} - OrderDate: {1} -
                CustomerId: {2}",o.OrderID,o.OrderDate,o.CustomerID);

            }
        }
    }
}
class Order
{
    public int OrderID {get;set;}
    public DateTime OrderDate {get;set;}
    public int CustomerID {get;set;}
}
```

This example shows how MicroORMs like Dapper can be a good compromise between using base *SqlConnection*, *SqlCommand*, and *SqlDataReader* classes and a more sophisticated, but complex, solution like Hibernate or Entity Framework for your data access layers.

Using read-only replicas

One benefit provided by Azure SQL Premium, Business Critical, and Hyperscale database instances is that, as part of their high-availability architecture, several secondary replicas are deployed and are maintained in sync with primary replica at minimal latency by the underlying infrastructures. *Read Scale-Out* feature, by default enabled on Premium and Business Critical tiers, gives you the ability to run read-only workload against one of these secondary replicas without impacting performance of your primary, read-write, replica at no extra cost.

From a data access perspective, this is extremely easy to use as it only requires you to add the ApplicationIntent=ReadOnly; attribute to your connection string, and all traffic for that connection will be automatically redirected to a read-only replica of the database. Hyperscale performance tier also provides such capability, but you have to explicitly create at least one secondary replica for your database in order to be able to benefit from it.

Your application can make sure it's connected to a read-only replica by checking that this command SELECT DATABASEPROPERTYEX(DB_NAME(), 'Updateability') effectively returns READ_ONLY as result. It's worth remembering that, while read-only replicas are in a transactionally consistent state, in some rare cases there may be some small latency compared to data in the primary replica. Also, at the time of writing these notes, certain features like Query Store, Extended Events, and Audit are not yet supported on read-only replicas, although there are ways of monitoring them using traditional DMVs like *sys.dm_db_resource_stats* or *sys.dm_exec_query_stats*, *sys.dm_exec_query_plan*, and *sys.dm_exec_sql_text* that work as expected. For additional details on this interesting feature, please refer to the official documentation at https://aka.ms/sqrso.

If you want to know more

This chapter provided you with a comprehensive overview on how to connect to Azure SQL database instances from a variety of traditional and modern programming languages using conventional drivers and more advanced data access frameworks. It provided some best practices on how to effectively increase connection reliability and make your application more resilient to transient connectivity issues that may happen when you design and implement distributed systems in cloud-based environments. To dig deeper into some of these topics, we recommend to take a look at these links:

- Quickstarts: Azure SQL Database connect and query – https://docs.microsoft.com/en-us/azure/sql-database/sql-database-connect-query

- Azure SQL Transient Errors – https://docs.microsoft.com/en-us/azure/sql-database/sql-database-connectivity-issues

- Dapper.NET – https://medium.com/dapper-net

- How to use batching to improve SQL Database application performance – https://docs.microsoft.com/en-us/azure/sql-database/sql-database-use-batching-to-improve-performance

CHAPTER 4

Developing with Azure SQL – Foundations

Now that you know how to create an Azure SQL database, how to connect to it, and how to restore a sample database, it's now time to start to see what Azure SQL offers to a modern developer.

In this chapter, we will see all the major features that can help you to create modern applications, using the sample database WideWorldImporters as our playground.

As usual for this book, we'll keep a very pragmatic approach, assuming that you have a basic idea of a table: an entity composed of columns, each one with its name and own data type, that contains rows of data. Columns define the shape, the *schema*, of data. To be stored in a table, data must adhere to its schema, meaning that column data types and constraints must be observed; otherwise, the database will reject the data. This approach has been recently defined as *schema-on-write*: consistency with the schema is checked when data is written into the database. This ensures data is coherent with what the applications using it are expecting. Some other databases offer a *schema-on-read* approach, where all data can be stored, and schema is checked only when someone tries to read the data. Both approaches have, as usual, pros and cons; since data is useful only when coherent and meaningful, no matter what is the approach you choose, you still must be sure that served data is logically correct and sound. With a schema-on-write approach, Azure SQL works with you to make sure this happens, as it will check for you that data is always consistent with the defined schema. If not, it will return an error. This behavior may be seen as a bit rigid, and sometimes it is, so that's why Azure SQL also supports schema-on-write to some extent, by allowing natively to store and manipulate JSON documents. Keep in mind that with a schema-on-read, it's up to you to write code right inside your application to validate data before using it. In most of the common cases, that's quite a big incumbency that would be better taken care of by a specialized entity, like Azure SQL, alleviating a lot of your work as a developer and, again, helping to have a good separation of concerns. Data consistency and integrity is mainly a matter for a database that can take care of it in a centralized way for all solutions accessing its data.

A deeper discussion on tables will come in Chapter 6, but given that is pretty common for a developer to start to work on an existing database, we felt it was better to start understanding what we can do with the data we already have.

And there are lots of things we can do! For this reason, this chapter aims to give you a full overview of all the features you should know to make sure you are really using all the potential that Azure SQL has.

As there are so many features for developers packed in Azure SQL, in this chapter you'll find just the tip of the iceberg. Make sure you use the code samples included with the book to get more details on features and to see them in action. Use the referenced resources to dive deeper into all the features and their options.

Remember, this book is like a diving board that aims to give you a boost to better dive in the data ocean!

Pushing compute to data

I strongly recommend pushing as much of the computation needs you have to the data instead of bringing data to you. Moving data is a heavy, complex, resource-consuming task. Moving computing logic is much easier, as it is way more compact and lightweight. Also, with the usage of Views, Functions, or Stored Procedures that we will discuss in a moment, you don't even have to move source code or compiled binaries around.

But the main benefit of pushing compute to data is that you can really take advantage of all the money you are paying for using a database like Azure SQL. If you would have had to implement all the querying, filtering, and optimization logic in your code, then why use a database at all? Just use a much cheaper file storage and you would have saved a lot of money.

Well, that could be the impression, but in reality, you would still have to spend time to actually implement those features you are renouncing when not using Azure SQL. So, it wouldn't really be that much cheaper.

It turns out it would actually be much more expensive if you also take into account that you would probably need to maintain and evolve those features. And it will be just one or a few of you, while for Azure SQL, there are literally hundreds of engineers working on it every day, with just one objective: improve its performance and capabilities as much as possible. By pushing compute to data, you can get the benefit of all those engineers working behind the scenes. This can affect you and the performance of your application: let me give you a very practical sample of that.

If you need to find distinct values in a table that holds 50 million rows of data, until not so many years ago, you would have had to wait something like 5 seconds. Not bad, right? Still, 5 seconds, if you are creating an API to serve a mobile app, is a lot in today's world. In the last few years, the engine powering Azure SQL has been improved by adding columnstore table and vector (or batch) executions by taking advantage of SIMD CPU instruction set and some advanced optimization techniques like the *Grouped Aggregate Pushdown*. With all these improvements, the same query now takes a single-digit millisecond – single digit – from 5000 milliseconds originally.

Can you imagine how much effort and costs you would have had to go through if instead of pushing the calculation to the database, you would have moved the data to the application to reach the same improvement? Instead, you could use all those resources for something unique to your use case or business problem, something that the database cannot solve for you.

Push compute to data: it's really the best approach to have a scalable, modern, performant solution.

Declarative vs. imperative

Azure SQL allows you to use a different approach to create solutions to manipulate data, as opposed to the language you are used to work with every day. If you are using C#, Java, Python, or NodeJS, in fact, you are most probably used to work following the *imperative* paradigm. With the imperative paradigm, you tell the system exactly how you want a process, more precisely, an algorithm, to be applied. For example, if you have a list of numbers and you want to count how many distinct values there are in that list, you may implement the solution using a loop, iterating over the values, where you compare the current value to a list of values you have already seen before, and adding the current value to that list only if it is not yet there.

If you use a *declarative* approach instead, you only tell the system what you want, not how you want to have it done. Basically, you describe where you want to be, using the data structure you already have as a starting point. It's really not much different, conceptually, than setting your navigation system to bring you from point "A" to point "B."

So, using the same sample mentioned before, with Azure SQL (and any relational database), you would write something like

```
SELECT DISTINCT Number FROM Values;
```

We'll discuss the details of the preceding line of code in the next sections, but you can already understand intuitively what it is doing.

Python and C# provide some declarative support. C# supports Language-Integrated Query (LINQ), and Python uses List Comprehensions, so you may have some experience, and that will help you a lot in using Azure SQL. On the other hand, if you don't have experience with that yet, by reading this book, you'll get familiar with the power and beauty of the declarative paradigm.

Relational databases, and Azure SQL in particular, bring the idea of the declarative approach to the next level. Azure SQL will not only take care of the implementation details for you, so that you can focus on what you want and not how you can get it, but it will do so by taking into account an impressive number of additional factors. For example, how much data is in a table, how much memory it will need to manipulate it, if existing indexes can help, and even how data is distributed within a table.

If you think about it, a modern navigation system works exactly in the same way: it not only allows you to specify the start and the destination, but it will also take into account real-time traffic, roadblocks, and other conditions so that it can try to give you the *best* solution within a given finite amount of time, not just *a* solution.

In modern development, this is vital to make sure your application is always responsive, even if the data it uses keeps changing in value and size: adapting to changes is a key factor also for applications, not just for developers.

Query and data manipulation

The language you will use to interact with data in an Azure SQL database is, as one could guess, *SQL* (*Structured Query Language*). SQL is a standard that is adopted across many relational and non-relational databases. Learning it well is useful both to use Azure SQL and to take advantage of many other systems like Apache Spark, just to name another very well-known data platform. Every database usually implements the ANSI/ISO SQL standard to a certain extent, with some variations to exploit specific features available in the platform. The implemented SQL is therefore called a *dialect*. For Azure SQL, the dialect is the same used for SQL Server: *Transact-SQL* or *T-SQL* for brevity.

To manipulate data, all you need is a handful of commands, usually referred to as *DML – Data Manipulation Language* – that cover all the needed functionalities:

- SELECT

- INSERT

- UPDATE

- DELETE

- MERGE

As you can recognize, if you are familiar with the *CRUD – Create, Read, Update, Delete* – set of functions common in application development, only the first four SQL commands are really needed to implement CRUD operation; a fifth, MERGE, has been added so that insert, update, and delete can be done all together in just one command, simplifying code by leaving a lot of the details to the query engine and thus making it more understandable and in many cases also more performant.

Retrieving data

The SELECT command allows you to get a set of data back from the database. It requires the list of columns you want to get, the table name, and optionally, but almost always used, a filter to limit the returned rows to only those you are interested in, for example:

```
SELECT
    InvoiceID,
    InvoiceDate,
    DeliveryInstructions,
    ConfirmedDeliveryTime
FROM
    Sales.Invoices
WHERE
    CustomerID = 998
ORDER BY
    ConfirmedDeliveryTime;
```

This query will look into `Sales.Invoices` table, return all the rows that have the value "998" in column `CustomerID`, and limit the results to contain only columns `InvoiceID`, `InvoiceDate`, `DeliveryInstructions`, and `ConfirmedDeliveryTime`.

Even such a simple `SELECT` statement is quite interesting. First, it is worth noting that there is no inherent or natural order. If no `ORDER BY` is specified, data is returned without any specific order.

For performance reasons, the data will likely be returned in the order Azure SQL accesses it, which is something that may change over time; if you rely on data to be in a specific order, you must specify the order by clause. Second, unless specified otherwise with an option called `COLLATION`, database objects are not case sensitive. This also applies to data within a table. It's always possible to change this, but it may have performance implications: a bit more discussion on this will be done in the next Chapters.

Let's move to a more complex sample now. Let's say that our customer 998 is browsing her order history to look for a specific item that she received in the first quarter of 2016. By using a set of filters on a fictitious mobile app, this could be the T-SQL statement we need to execute:

```
SELECT
      il.InvoiceLineID AS LineID,
      i.InvoiceID,
      il.[Description],
      il.Quantity,
      il.UnitPrice,
      il.UnitPrice * il.Quantity AS TotalPrice,
      i.ConfirmedDeliveryTime
FROM
      Sales.Invoices AS i
INNER JOIN
      Sales.InvoiceLines AS il ON i.InvoiceID = il.InvoiceID
WHERE
      i.CustomerID = 998
AND
      il.[Description] LIKE N'%red shirt%'
AND
      CAST(i.ConfirmedDeliveryTime AS DATE) BETWEEN '2016-01-01' AND '2016-
      03-31';
```

When executed in the WideWorldImporters database, the result will be the one visible in Figure 4-1.

Results Messages

	LineID	InvoiceID	Description	Quantity	UnitPrice	TotalPrice	ConfirmedDeliveryTime
1	199437	61516	"The Gu" red shirt XML tag t-shirt (Black) XL	36	18.00	648.00	2016-01-06 07:25:00.0000000
2	207169	63948	"The Gu" red shirt XML tag t-shirt (Black) S	60	18.00	1080.00	2016-02-17 08:20:00.0000000
3	209948	64834	"The Gu" red shirt XML tag t-shirt (White) 3XS	48	18.00	864.00	2016-03-02 08:15:00.0000000
4	211586	65349	"The Gu" red shirt XML tag t-shirt (Black) XXS	84	18.00	1512.00	2016-03-10 08:40:00.0000000
5	211723	65392	"The Gu" red shirt XML tag t-shirt (White) M	12	18.00	216.00	2016-03-11 07:20:00.0000000

Figure 4-1. *Sample SELECT result*

In the sample query just used, even if simple, there are a few notable things that are very common in day-to-day use.

Caution Instead of specifying the columns you want to have as result, you may use the star character * to include all the columns in the table automatically. While this may be useful while executing queries to just take a look at the data or to do some data exploration, it is not a best practice when creating something that will be used by an application. Column's order may change at any time, and columns may be added or removed, if someone changes the table definition. Always specify the column you want to be returned, so that you will have a deterministic result. If you don't need all the columns, you will also avoid wasting network bandwidth and improve transfer speed.

Two-part names

Objects, like tables, have their own names like the `Invoices` table. Since the same name could be used in a different context, it is a good practice, though not required, to always qualify the object name with the *schema* it belongs to. A schema is a way to organize objects that belong to the same group, for example, `Sales`. All objects related to Sales would be placed in the same schema. Besides removing any ambiguity, schemas also help to simplify management especially from a security perspective, as permissions can be given to schemas, and they will affect all objects belonging to the same schema.

Aliasing

You have the ability to *alias* the name of the tables using the AS keyword, so that if a column is present in more than one table, you can just use the *alias* to prefix the column name and specifically decide from which table it must be taken from. Some column names will repeat quite frequently (think of, for example, Name, ID, Description, and so on), so a way to eliminate ambiguity is needed. An alias allows you to do that, also removing the need to use the full table name as a column prefix. Less code, nicer results.

Besides tables, columns can also be *aliased*. You may want to change the column name when returned to you, as it happens for the column InvoiceLineID which is returned as LineID instead. As you may have noticed, that column has been prefixed anyway with the alias of the table where it exists. It was not needed as there are no other columns with the same name in the tables used in the query, but prefixing also helps to quickly understand where a column is coming from. It is just a good practice to make the code more understandable and human-friendly.

Columns *must be* aliased when they would not have a name at all. For example, when a resulting column is created from an expression, as it happens for the column TotalPrice. In the sample, the expression is really simple, but keep in mind that they can be much more complex and apply complex data transformations to column values.

Quoted identifiers

Objects may have almost any name you like (well, there are some naming rules: https://aka.ms/rdddi), but if you use a name that may clash with a keyword, you just have to use the square brackets to make sure the query engine can understand that you are referring to a column or a table and not to something else, like a system function.

Joins

The sample also shows how you can return values from different tables. Using the INNER JOIN statement, we're saying that for each value that exists in table Sales.Invoices, column InvoiceID, we want to get all the rows with the same value in the same column but in table Sales.InvoiceLines. Invoice data has been saved into two different tables to avoid data duplication and to create easier access to each invoice line, but since the CustomerID is available only in the Sales.Invoices table, a join operation is needed to return the desired data.

Choosing if it is better to keep everything in fewer tables and then deal with data duplication challenges or if it is better to decompose data into different tables to avoid duplication and then have to put data together when needed is quite an important topic to understand and falls under the definition of database modeling, and more specifically, is a process called *normalization*. There are entire books dedicated to this discussion and what are the pros and the cons of normalization and *de*normalization, so you'll find more references at the end of this chapter. Keep in mind that the normalization process is about organizing data to minimize redundancy. Having duplicated information in a database brings a lot of not-so-obvious effects and a lot of challenges, and therefore is absolutely important to understand, even if you're using non-relational databases: all the normalization concepts will apply anyway. It's not by chance, in fact, that normalization is a concept that you can find also in NoSQL manuals.

There are different kinds of joins that allow you to exactly define what are the rows that must be returned in the results. Let's say, for example, that you want to have a list of all customers with all their related invoices and, as you can guess, you have two separate tables to hold the two different sets of data: Customers and Invoices. It could happen that you have a new customer that hasn't received any invoices yet. With an *inner join*, such a customer would not be included in the result of our hypothetical query. If you want *all* customers, no matter if they have an invoice or not, you need to use a *left* join. If instead you want to return all Invoices, even those that do not belong to any customer, you would have to use a *right* join. The terms left and right refer to the position of the table with respect to the JOIN clause (Figure 4-2).

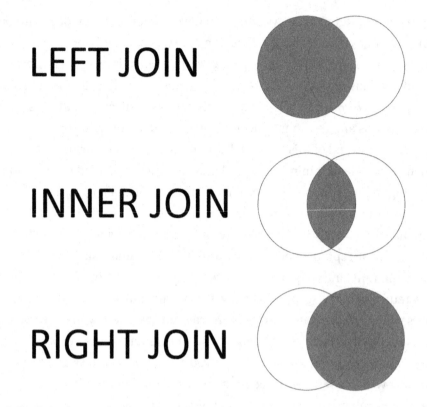

LEFT JOIN

INNER JOIN

RIGHT JOIN

Figure 4-2. *Join types*

The *Full Join* is all the three kinds together. You'll get rows from both the tables participating in the join.

Joins can be used along with other joins, so that you can represent complex relationships. If we would like to expand the original code sample to return also customers' data, we would have to change it so that Customers, Invoices, and InvoiceLines would be joined together:

```
SELECT
    c.CustomerName,
    il.InvoiceLineID AS LineID,
    i.InvoiceID,
    il.[Description],
    il.Quantity,
    il.UnitPrice,
    il.UnitPrice * il.Quantity AS TotalPrice,
    i.ConfirmedDeliveryTime
```

```
FROM
      Sales.Customers AS c
INNER JOIN
      Sales.Invoices AS i ON i.CustomerID = c.CustomerID
INNER JOIN
      Sales.InvoiceLines AS il ON i.InvoiceID = il.InvoiceID
WHERE
      i.CustomerID = 998
AND
      il.[Description] LIKE N'%red shirt%'
AND
      CAST(i.ConfirmedDeliveryTime AS DATE) BETWEEN '2016-01-01' AND
      '2016-03-31';
```

And the result would be the following:

CustomerID	CustomerName	InvoiceID	LineID	Description	Quantity	UnitPrice	TotalPrice
8	Tailspin Toys (Bow Mar, CO)	62518	202655	"The Gu" red shirt XML tag t-shirt (White) 7XL	84	18.00	1512.00
8	Tailspin Toys (Bow Mar, CO)	65562	212274	"The Gu" red shirt XML tag t-shirt (Black) M	72	18.00	1296.00
8	Tailspin Toys (Bow Mar, CO)	66042	213818	"The Gu" red shirt XML tag t-shirt (White) 3XL	120	18.00	2160.00
8	Tailspin Toys (Bow Mar, CO)	66042	213819	"The Gu" red shirt XML tag t-shirt (White) S	120	18.00	2160.00
9	Tailspin Toys (Netcong, NJ)	62000	200989	"The Gu" red shirt XML tag t-shirt (Black) 3XL	84	18.00	1512.00
9	Tailspin Toys (Netcong, NJ)	65163	211003	"The Gu" red shirt XML tag t-shirt (White) S	108	18.00	1944.00
9	Tailspin Toys (Netcong, NJ)	65163	211006	"The Gu" red shirt XML tag t-shirt (Black) S	60	18.00	1080.00
10	Tailspin Toys (Wimbledon, ND)	62467	202507	"The Gu" red shirt XML tag t-shirt (Black) XL	60	18.00	1080.00
11	Tailspin Toys (Devault, PA)	61820	200416	"The Gu" red shirt XML tag t-shirt (Black) 5XL	24	18.00	432.00

As you can see, the CustomerName and CustomerID are repeated for each row of
Sales.Invoice related to that customer, which is in turn repeated for each Sales.
InvoiceLine related to that invoice.

This allows you to have the full set of information needed by your application on
each line, but without having to store duplicate data in the database. While this may
seem complex at the very beginning and maybe also counterproductive as you may have
instead saved all the data into just one JSON document per line, so that you wouldn't
even need to put the pieces together when needed, it actually helps a lot to *simplify*
things.

By deconstructing complex data in smaller pieces, you allow each piece to be used and
reused together with some other set of data. It's the same concept of code reuse just applied
to data.

As mentioned before, the process of decomposing data into smaller pieces without
losing information is called *normalization* and is not specifically tied to relational
databases. On the contrary, it is helpful in many different areas and technologies, as it

is nothing more than a process that helps to avoid duplication of information, which usually brings more challenges than what it solves. Not surprisingly, it is referenced both in NoSQL documentation and even Object Modeling documents. Learning it will be helpful in a variety of cases, which goes from development to data science: you'll find several resources to dive deeper into these concepts and the end of this chapter.

Filtering

Quite often you'll want to get only a few rows, or even just one, from the database. To filter out the rows you don't need, the WHERE clause is what you must use. As you have seen in the sample query, the WHERE clause can contain one or more filter *predicates* that allow you to specify what are the values you are interested in for any column available to the query. Any column from tables specified in the FROM clause or the JOIN can be used.

Values used in the WHERE clause can be literals, variables, sets of data coming from other queries, or results of a function call. This allows you to exactly target the data you want to work on.

Subqueries

A subquery is a query that is nested within another query. As it happens for the Linux shell or Windows PowerShell, where you can pipe the result of one command into another one to easily build complex transformations, Azure SQL allows you to do something conceptually similar:

```
SELECT
    OrderId,
    OrderDate,
    (SELECT COUNT(*) FROM Sales.[OrderLines] AS ol
WHERE
    ol.[OrderID] = o.OrderId) AS OrderSize
FROM
    (SELECT * FROM Sales.[Orders] WHERE SalespersonPersonID = 2) AS o
WHERE
    o.[CustomerID] IN
    (
        SELECT
            c.CustomerID
```

```
FROM
        Sales.[Customers] AS c
    WHERE
        [CustomerName] = 'Daniel Martensson'
    )
AND
    OrderDate >= '2015-01-01'
ORDER BY
    [o].[OrderID];
```

In the preceding sample, there are three subqueries. The first one is used in the FROM clause, and it is used to limit the orders to only those generated by a specific salesperson. Then there is another subquery in the WHERE clause that limits the orders only to those done by a specific customer. And, finally, the third subquery is in the SELECT list, used to enrich the result with the count of lines in each order.

If you already have some experience with the SQL language, you may recognize that the sample query could have been written also using some joins, instead of using the subqueries in the FROM and in the WHERE clause. The Azure SQL Query Optimizer is smart enough to realize that too, and usually, there are no performance differences if a query is written in one way or the other.

Common Table Expressions

Common Table Expressions, or CTEs for short, are an improved alternative to subqueries. As you may have guessed, if you have a very complex SQL statement with many subqueries, it becomes very hard to read.

What happens, also, if the same subquery should be used twice in the same query? You'll end up duplicating code. But, as we strive to be better developers, we don't want to have any code duplication, if possible.

CTEs are exactly what we need to organize our code so that it can be more easily understood and, above all, changed and maintained. A CTE is a temporary query definition that will exist only for the duration of the SELECT, INSERT, UPDATE, or MERGE statement that uses it.

Here's the same code showed in the subquery paragraph, rewritten so that it can use CTEs instead of subqueries (where it makes sense to do so):

```
WITH cteOrders AS
(
    SELECT * FROM Sales.[Orders] WHERE SalespersonPersonID = 2
),
cteCustomers AS
(
    SELECT
        c.CustomerID
    FROM
        Sales.[Customers] AS c
    WHERE
        [CustomerName] = 'Daniel Martensson'
)
SELECT
    OrderId,
    OrderDate,
    (SELECT COUNT(*) FROM Sales.[OrderLines] AS ol WHERE ol.[OrderID] =
    o.OrderId) AS OrderSize
FROM
    cteOrders AS o
INNER JOIN
    cteCustomers c ON [c].[CustomerID] = [o].[CustomerID]
AND
    OrderDate >= '2015-01-01'
ORDER BY
    [o].[OrderID];
```

As you can see, after the WITH statement, two CTEs are defined, one named cteOrders and the other one cteCustomers. Each time in the query where we reference one of those names, it would be like if we would have put a subquery there. The difference is that code is much easier to understand. I personally like to think of CTEs as a nice way to clearly define what are the sets of data I'll need to work with in my main query: I can define these sets on the top, so that it will also be easier understanding how they operate on data, and then I can refer to them as much as I need and wherever I need without having to type the same code twice.

> **Remember**   CTE lifetime is scoped to the execution of the query that has
> defined them. If you need to reuse the query encapsulated into the CTE with
> other queries, you may want to create a VIEW or a FUNCTION. More on this in the
> next chapters.

CTEs can also refer to CTEs so you can create very complex queries while keeping
code very clean and easy to read. Also, CTEs can even refer to themselves so that you
can create recursive queries. This can become quite handy when you have to work with
data structured in an hierarchical way, a tree, for example, and you want to traverse the
entire tree, but you don't know how deep the tree is, so you need to have some "smart"
algorithm that will stop only when there is no more data to process, not just after a
certain amount of iterations.

A recursive CTE sample is available in accompanying code.

Union

In case you have two queries and you want to concatenate their results to return just one
resultset to the user, you can use UNION statement:

```
WITH cteContacts AS
(
    SELECT
        [CustomerID],
        [PrimaryContactPersonID] AS ContactPersonId,
        'Primary' AS [ContactType]
    FROM
        Sales.[Customers]
    UNION
    SELECT
        [CustomerID],
        [AlternateContactPersonID],
        'Alternate' AS [ContactType]
    FROM
        Sales.[Customers]
)
```

```
SELECT
    [ContactPersonId],
    [ContactType]
FROM
    [cteContacts] c
WHERE
    c.CustomerId = 42
```

The code will return the result of the two queries on Sales.Customer as a single result. To work without errors, the UNION requires that the two resultsets must have compatible schema.

Keep in mind that UNION will also remove any duplicate values from the resulting resultset, so it could be quite an expensive process. If you already know in advance that you can't have any duplicate values or you don't care about duplicate values, then you can use UNION ALL instead, which is more lightweight as it doesn't have to look for duplicates and remove them from the result.

Semicolon

All Azure SQL statements should be terminated by a semicolon. Though this is not mandatory now, it is a best practice as it's part of the standard ANSI-SQL 92 and it will be required in future versions. Already today, in fact, some commands require it to function correctly. For example, the WITH statement of a CTE must be the first statement of the line. In other words, this means that the previous command *must be* terminated by a semicolon.

Unicode strings

You may have noticed that the string N'%red shirt%' is prefixed with a capital N. This prefix tells Azure SQL that string is a Unicode string.

Adding data

INSERT INTO is the command used to add data into a table. It's very easy to use as it needs only three things to work: the table where you want data to be added, the columns you'll be targeting, and the values to be added.

The following code, for example, will add two rows to the table Warehouse.Colors:

```
INSERT INTO [Warehouse].[Colors]
     ([ColorID], [ColorName], [LastEditedBy])
VALUES
     (50, 'Deep Sea Blue', 1),
     (99, 'Out of space', 1);
```

The table may or may not have other columns, but we must provide values for the columns we specify. As you'll learn later, a table may have some specific constraints in order to make some columns mandatory, for example, the email for a User table; if no constraints are in place, for all the columns existing in the table but not specified in the INSERT statement, a default or a NULL value will be used.

In addition to specifying the values manually, as I did in the previous sample, INSERT can also take values from a SELECT statement, for example:

```
INSERT INTO
     [Warehouse].[Colors]
     ([ColorID], [ColorName], [LastEditedBy])
SELECT
     ColorID, ColorName, LastEditedBy
FROM
     [External].[Colors]
```

In this case, you may have data in another table, named External.Colors that you want to move into Warehouse.Colors. By using INSERT FROM … SELECT, you can move data with just one command.

Modifying data

To change existing data in a table, you can use the UPDATE command. Similarly to the INSERT command, you have to specify the table that contains the data you want to update and the new values for each column you want to update. Here's an example:

```
UPDATE
     [Warehouse].[Colors]
SET
     [ColorName] = N'Unknown',
```

```
        [LastEditedBy] = 2
WHERE
        [ColorID] = 99;
```

The WHERE part is optional but almost always specified, as it allows you to limit the scope of the changes that would otherwise be applied to all rows in the table. As explained in the "Retrieving data" section, the WHERE clause will make sure that you can exactly target only the rows you want to update.

The N character tells Azure SQL that the text being used to update the table is a Unicode text. You'll notice that if you don't specify it, everything will work fine. This happens because Azure SQL performs an *implicit conversion*, automatically casting the string to be a Unicode string. While in this case there is no harm done, implicit conversion can badly impact performances, so make sure data types are correct, especially when using WHERE predicates or JOIN clauses.

Removing data

To remove data from a table, you can use the DELETE command. For this command, only the table must be specified: DELETE will remove the entire row from the specified table, so there is no need to specify the columns as it happens for the other DML commands.

The WHERE clause is also, obviously, supported, and with that, you can make sure you remove only the rows you want to remove by specifying a predicate that targets only those.

Without a WHERE clause, all rows will be deleted. Be aware! No warning will be issued, and the table will be wiped out:

```
DELETE FROM
        [Warehouse].[Colors]
WHERE
        [ColorID] = 99;
```

Azure SQL automatically performs backups of your data, and it allows you to restore it to any point in time within the last 7 up to 35 days, depending on the offer you are using. There is no additional cost for this. Even if you delete everything by mistake, you'll be able to easily restore it right before the unwanted action happened.

Merging data

Merge is a command that allows you to execute inserts, updates, and deletes at the same time, so that one set of data can be *merged* into an existing one. The table that contains the data you want to merge into another table is your *source* table, while the other one is the *target* table. By merging a *source* table into a *target* table, this is what may happen, depending on what you specify in the MERGE command:

- All rows that exist in the source but not in the target will be inserted in the target table.

- All rows that exist in both tables will be updated in the source table.

- All rows that exist in the target table and not in the source will be deleted from the target table.

I said "may" as you are in total control of if and how the insert, update, and delete operations will happen and if they will happen at all:

```
MERGE INTO
    [Warehouse].[Colors] AS [target]
USING
    (VALUES
        (50, 'Deep Sea Blue'),
        (51, 'Deep Sea Light Blue'),
        (52, 'Deep Sea Dark Blue')
    ) [source](Id, [Name])
ON
    [target].[ColorID] = [source].[Id]
```

```
WHEN MATCHED THEN
    UPDATE SET [target].[ColorName] = [source].[Name]
WHEN NOT MATCHED THEN
    INSERT ([ColorID], [ColorName], [LastEditedBy]) VALUES ([source].Id,
    [source].[Name], 1)
WHEN NOT MATCHED BY SOURCE AND [target].[ColorID] BETWEEN 50 AND 100 THEN
    DELETE
;
```

After the MERGE INTO, there is the target table. USING tells what the source is. In this case, the code is using a *Table-Valued Constructor* to create a table on the fly and aliasing it with the name source. As such, a table is completely volatile and will be gone once the statement has completed the execution; it also requires you to have the names of its columns specified, as there is no metadata available anywhere to figure out how those are named. Data types will be automatically inferred from the provided values.

The ON part is very similar to how JOIN uses it, and it defines the rules needed by Azure SQL to understand how to match rows coming from the source with rows in the destination. In the sample case, we are using Id from source and ColorId from the destination. After that, you have to tell MERGE what to do when there is match and also when there isn't one:

- WHEN MATCHED – If there is a match between rows in source and target table, the code will update the ColorName column in the target table using the related value from the Color column in the source table.

- WHEN NOT MATCHED – If the target table doesn't have any rows with a ColorID that exists also in the source table, those rows will be taken from the source and inserted into the target.

- WHEN NOT MATCHED BY SOURCE – If the target table contains some rows with a ColorID that doesn't exist in the source table, those will be deleted from the target. The sample is adding an additional predicate to better define the scope. Not only must there be ColorID in the target that doesn't exist in the source, but also the ColorID values must be between 50 and 100. This means that all rows in the source table that have ColorID values from 0 to 49, for example, will *not* be deleted as outside the scope of the defined rule.

Additional useful features

So far, the basic concepts have been discussed. They are more than enough to start to create great solutions, but there are a few more features that you want to start to use right away, as they can be helpful in several different scenarios to simplify code and to improve performances and concurrency of your solution.

Output clause: inserted and deleted virtual tables

Returning to the application the result of an INSERT, UPDATE, or DELETE (or MERGE) operation is a very common requirement. For example, let's say that in the API solution you're creating, you accept updates to your entities via an HTTP PUT method. The API you created will apply the new data received via PUT to the database using an UPDATE or MERGE statement. To follow an established good practice, you want to return the full entity as a result of the PUT request, so that the caller can have the fully updated entity without the need to issue a dedicated GET request.

This would mean to do something like the following:

```
UPDATE
    [Warehouse].[Colors]
SET
    [ColorName] = 'Unknown'
WHERE
    [ColorID] = 99;

SELECT
    [ColorID],
    [ColorName],
    [LastEditedBy],
    [ValidFrom],
    [ValidTo]
FROM
    [Warehouse].[Colors];
```

The problem with the preceding code is that, on a highly concurrent system, it could happen that between the UPDATE and the subsequent SELECT, another connection could apply some changes to the data, which is a behavior that in general you want to avoid. A deeper discussion on this will be done in the chapter dedicated to transactions, but in the meantime, you can see that the problem comes from the fact that we have two different commands that we want to execute one after the other, without anything in between, just like if they were just one logical operation.

A very elegant, scalable, and performant way to solve this issue is to ask the UPDATE command to also generate an output, so everything will be executed as *one* command and the problem would be solved right at the root.

The OUTPUT statement does exactly this:

```
UPDATE
    [Warehouse].[Colors]
SET
    [ColorName] = 'Unknown'
OUTPUT
    [Inserted].[ColorID],
    [Inserted].[ColorName],
    [Inserted].[LastEditedBy],
    [Inserted].[ValidFrom],
    [Inserted].[ValidTo],
WHERE
    [ColorID] = 99;
```

The result will be the equivalent of the code with the separate UPDATE and SELECT statement, but without the described potential issue.

Inserted is a virtual table that exists only for the duration of the statement that uses it. The Inserted virtual table gives access to the data as it is as *after* it has been modified; there is also a Deleted virtual table that gives access to data as it was *before* the modification took place.

As an UPDATE statement can be thought of as a logical pair of DELETE/INSERT statements, the UPDATE allows you to use both virtual tables. An INSERT statement will give you access only to the Inserted virtual table and, of course, the DELETE statement only to the Deleted virtual table. The MERGE statement, obviously, will give access to both Inserted and Deleted virtual tables too.

Identity and sequences

When you need to create an Id number to be assigned to an entity or a row, usually to easily uniquely identify it, you may do it in your application or you can rely on the database to do it. Using the database will make sure that by default no two equal Ids can be generated simplifying your code a lot.

In Azure SQL, there are two ways you can use to achieve this. One is using the IDENTITY feature, which exists mostly for backward compatibility purposes. When you create a table, you can elect one integer column to be an identity column. This means that Azure SQL will generate values for that column automatically for you, every time a new row is inserted:

```
CREATE TABLE dbo.SampleID
(
    Id INT IDENTITY(1,1) NOT NULL,
    OtherColums NVARCHAR(10) NULL
);
```

IDENTITY(1,1) means that numbers will be generated starting by one and incremented by one.

While it worked nicely for many years, it has two main disadvantages. The first is that you *cannot* manually provide a value for that column when executing an INSERT command, unless you temporarily disable the identity behavior using a specific SET option. Not exactly user-friendly. The second, more importantly, is that if you have more than one table with an identity column (and this could be pretty common), they won't be aware of the existence of each other and thus different tables will have rows with the same Id values. This may not be a big deal, but sometimes you want to have rows that could be uniquely identified throughout all the database or at least among a group of logically related tables.

A *sequence* is exactly what you need to overcome old limitations and to get all the flexibility you need. A sequence is created at the database level and can be used anywhere you need:

```
CREATE SEQUENCE dbo.BookSequence
AS BIGINT
START WITH 1
INCREMENT BY 1;
```

```
CREATE TABLE dbo.SampleID
(
  Id INT NOT NULL DEFAULT(NEXT VALUE FOR dbo.BookSequence),
  OtherColums NVARCHAR(10) NULL
);
```

With this approach, you can decide if you want to use the automatically generated value or provide one of your own when writing your INSERT statement, without having to set any specific option before executing it.

Sequences also offer in general better performances and more control on how numbers are generated. You can even *reserve* numbers if you need to.

So, if you are starting to create a new database, the recommendation is to use one or more SEQUENCE to generate your Ids. Just keep in mind that neither IDENTITY nor SEQUENCE will give you any guarantee that no duplicate numbers will be generated: you can always reset the number generator and start from an already generated number. The SEQUENCE command even allows you to automatically restart from the beginning once a certain value has been reached, as sometimes this ability to cycle among a set of defined numbers could be very useful.

A sequence can be dropped using the DROP SEQUENCE command:

```
DROP SEQUENCE dbo.BookSequence;
```

Top and Offset/Fetch

Sometimes, especially if you are just exploring data, you don't really need to get all the data in a table. This is particularly true on big tables and even more as we're talking about a database in the cloud. There is no point moving around huge amounts of data if you're not really using it. Just the first 100 rows, for example, could be good enough to peek at the data you have to work with.

Another reason you want to limit the number of rows returned to a specific amount is because you want to paginate the data. For example, supporting pagination would be a common requirement if you are implementing a REST API that must expose an ODATA endpoint.

In Azure SQL, you have two options to make sure that only the requested number of rows are returned: TOP and the pair OFFSET/FETCH.

TOP is the easiest to use but also the most limited one. OFFSET/FETCH is a bit more complex but gives you more flexibility and makes pagination very easy to implement:

```
SELECT TOP (50)
    *
FROM
    [Sales].[Orders]
ORDER BY
    [ExpectedDeliveryDate] DESC;
```

The preceding code will return the first 50 ordered by ExpectedDeliveryDate in descending order.

The next code sample will do the same, but thanks to the offset option, it will skip the first 50 rows and will return the next 50. Basically, if you have a page size set to 50 for the pagination feature you're implementing, the code is effectively returning the second page of data. If OFFSET would have been set to 0, the would have produced the same results as TOP, but as you can see, OFFSET/FETCH provides a bit more flexibility. From a performance point of view, they are exactly the same:

```
SELECT
    *
FROM
    [Sales].[Orders]
ORDER BY
    [ExpectedDeliveryDate] DESC
OFFSET
    50 ROWS
FETCH
    NEXT 50 ROWS ONLY
```

Aggregations

Azure SQL offers extensive support for aggregations so that you can efficiently write queries that can aggregate and analyze datasets using the most advanced optimization techniques. You can get great performance while keeping the complexity of the code you need to write at the lowest level possible.

Grouping data

The GROUP BY clause can be used in a SELECT statement to apply an aggregation function, for example, COUNT or MAX (but there are many more) to all the groups that exist in a table. A group is defined as a set of rows that have the same value for the specified columns. For example, the following code returns which and how many products a warehouse has in stock, grouped by SupplierID and ColorID:

```
SELECT
    [SupplierID],
    [ColorID],
    COUNT(*) AS ProductsInStock,
    SUM(QuantityPerOuter) AS ProductsQuantity
FROM
    [Warehouse].[StockItems]
GROUP BY
    [SupplierID], [ColorID]
ORDER BY
    [SupplierID], [ColorID]
```

Here's a sample result.

	SupplierID	ColorID	ProductsInStock	ProductsQuantity
1	1	NULL	8	180
2	2	NULL	3	3
3	4	NULL	16	60
4	4	3	22	165
5	4	4	11	11
6	4	12	8	52
7	4	18	4	48
8	4	35	13	156
9	5	3	21	21
10	5	35	21	21
11	7	NULL	55	917
12	7	3	1	1
13	7	4	10	91
14	7	28	1	1
15	10	NULL	4	4
16	10	3	6	6
17	10	4	2	2
18	10	28	4	4

Figure 4-3. *Data aggregated by Supplier and Color*

Of course, you may want to JOIN the resulting data with other tables to return not only the IDs but also the name of the supplier and the color.

You can easily do that by starting to put together what you have learned so far, using a Common Table Expression and couple of JOIN to elegantly solve the problem and return to your application one resultset with all the data needed for doing its job.

A fully commented code that shows such a query is available in the code accompanying the book.

Multiple grouping

A very interesting feature that Azure SQL provides is the ability to perform aggregations on *different groups* at the same time. It may sound confusing, so an example will help. Using the same sample done before, let's now make it more realistic. You need to return data that can be used to create a matrix report where the end user can analyze how many products there are in the warehouse per supplier and per color. The rows and columns will contain suppliers and colors, respectively. At the intersection of a row and a column, one can find the number of products, with that color and from that supplier, in stock. Since it is a matrix report, the user expects to have the total number of products per supplier on the rightmost column and the total number of products per color on the last row.

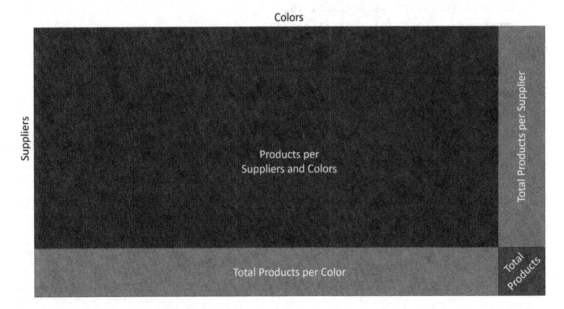

Figure 4-4. *A typical matrix report*

This means that you must group data using four different settings:

- Products and Suppliers

- Products

- Supplier

- All (count all products)

This would usually mean four different queries: on large datasets performances will be affected for sure as you must read and aggregate data four times.

I'm sure as a developer you are already thinking of using some caching to avoid this waste of resources, and move some calculations within your code so that you don't have to read the same data four times – clever, but that would increase the complexity of your code. If possible, we would like to avoid that. Luckily, such additional complexity is not needed, and you can keep your code simple and lean. All you need to do is ask Azure SQL to do this multiple concurrent aggregation for you, using the GROUPING SET feature:

```
SELECT
    [SupplierID],
    [ColorID],
    COUNT(*) AS ProductsInStock,
    SUM(QuantityPerOuter) AS ProductsQuantity,
    GROUPING(ColorID) as IsAllColors,
    GROUPING(SupplierID) as IsAllSuppliers
FROM
    [Warehouse].[StockItems]
GROUP BY
    GROUPING SETS
    (
            ([SupplierID], [ColorID]),
            ([SupplierID]),
            ([ColorID]),
            ()
    )
ORDER BY
    TotalPerColorID, TotalPerSupplierID
;
```

The result of the preceding query will contain data grouped by all the four defined *grouping sets*, so that you will have all the needed data without any added complexity – and with much better performances.

SupplierID	ColorID	ProductsInStock	ProductsQuantity	IsAllColors	IsAllSuppliers
7	28	1	1	0	0
10	28	4	4	0	0
4	35	13	156	0	0
5	35	21	21	0	0
10	36	2	2	0	0
NULL	36	2	2	0	1
NULL	35	34	177	0	1
NULL	28	5	5	0	1
NULL	18	4	48	0	1
NULL	12	9	53	0	1
NULL	4	23	104	0	1
NULL	3	51	203	0	1
NULL	NULL	99	1177	0	1
1	NULL	8	180	1	0
2	NULL	3	3	1	0
4	NULL	74	492	1	0
5	NULL	42	42	1	0
7	NULL	67	1010	1	0
10	NULL	18	18	1	0
12	NULL	15	24	1	0
NULL	NULL	227	1769	1	1

Figure 4-5. *Grouping Sets in action*

The function GROUPING present in the SELECT list is used to help the end user to understand if a row is representing the total for a specific value. For example, a row with IsAllColors equal to one is a row that must be used in the rightmost part of the matrix, as it represents the total product available for a specific supplier, no matter the color.

Windowing Functions

Windowing Functions and all the related features are probably one of the most powerful constructs that you can use in Azure SQL to manipulate data. The amount of problems that can be elegantly solved with them is amazing, and there are entire books dedicated only to explaining their usage in detail. The goal of this section is to make you familiar with their usage so that you can start to take advantage of their power right away.

While extremely powerful, Windowing Functions are quite easy to understand. In very simple terms, they allow you to access data that sits before and after the row you are currently processing.

The easiest practical example is provided by the calculation of a *running total*. A running total is defined as "a total that is continually adjusted to take account of items as they are added."

Here's an example.

	OrderLineID	Description	Quantity	RunningTotal
1	127	20 mm Anti static bubble wrap (Blue) 10m	10	10
2	128	Ogre battery-powered slippers (Green) M	9	19
3	129	USB rocket launcher (Gray)	8	27
4	130	DBA joke mug - SELECT caffeine FROM mug (Black)	1	28
5	131	USB food flash drive - hamburger	1	29

Figure 4-6. *Calculating the Running Total for an Order*

To calculate the running total for the third line, which equals to 27, Azure SQL, from a logical perspective, has to get all the values of all the previous rows for the Quantity column and sum them together. Same goes for when it has to calculate the Running Total value for the fourth row and so on.

These additional rows that are needed to be taken into consideration for the calculation represent the *window* of data on which Azure SQL is operating. For the Running Total, that window starts at the very first line of the table and ends at the current row.

Once the window is defined, you can tell Azure SQL which function you want to use on the data available in the window. Aggregate functions like SUM are common. And in fact, SUM is exactly what you need to implement a running total. The code needed to generate the result shown in the previous picture is the following:

```
SELECT
     [OrderLineID],
     [Description],
     [Quantity],
     SUM(Quantity) OVER (ORDER BY [OrderLineID] ROWS BETWEEN UNBOUNDED
     PRECEDING AND CURRENT ROW) AS RunningTotal
```

```
FROM
    [Sales].[OrderLines]
WHERE
    [OrderID] = 37
```

Another common aggregation function is the AVG that will give you an easy way to calculate moving averages. You just need to define how big is the size of the window you want to use for calculating the average, for example:

```
AVG(Quantity) OVER (ORDER BY [OrderLineID] ROWS BETWEEN 2 PRECEDING AND
CURRENT ROW) AS MovingAvg
```

The size of the window is called a *frame*. Besides aggregates, you can also use *analytical functions* that increase the power of windowing functions incredibly. For example, you can use the function LAG to access a value existing in a row that is preceding the current one. Again, a practical sample will make this very easy to understand. Let's say you want to calculate how much time passes between two consecutive orders for a specific customer.

	OrderID	OrderDate	ElapsedDays
1	1	2013-01-01	NULL
2	45	2013-01-01	0
3	495	2013-01-09	8
4	1318	2013-01-25	16
5	1387	2013-01-28	3
6	2550	2013-02-21	24
7	2840	2013-03-01	8
8	4079	2013-03-21	20
9	6020	2013-04-27	37
10	7122	2013-05-16	19

Figure 4-7. *Calculating elapsed days between orders*

For each row, you would need to access the previous row, take the order date, and compare it with the one in the current row. Thanks to windowing functions, this is very easy:

```
SELECT
    [OrderID],
    [OrderDate],
```

```
DATEDIFF(
        [DAY],
        LAG(OrderDate, 1) OVER (ORDER BY [OrderDate]),
        [OrderDate]
    ) AS ElapsedDays
FROM
    [Sales].[Orders]
WHERE
    [CustomerID] = 832
ORDER BY
    [OrderDate]
```

This is a very simple and elegant code that can also be nicely optimized by the Azure SQL engine; it also saves you from a huge amount of code that you would have had to write otherwise.

So far, we focused on usage of just one specific Customer Id or Order Id. But, going back to the running total sample, what if we want to calculate the running total for all the orders in the entire table? Of course, we don't want to mix lines of Order Id 37 with Order Id 39. Windowing function can take care of this for us too. We just need to specify how to *partition* the calculation process. In this context, partitioning allows us to tell Azure SQL when it should start a new calculation from scratch. You can think of it as something like "as long as you are processing values that belong to the same group, keep accumulating values." Let's modify the running total sample to use two orders instead of only one.

	OrderID	OrderLineID	Description	Quantity	RunningTotal
1	37	127	20 mm Anti static bubble wrap (Blue) 10m	10	10
2	37	128	Ogre battery-powered slippers (Green) M	9	19
3	37	129	USB rocket launcher (Gray)	8	27
4	37	130	DBA joke mug - SELECT caffeine FROM mug (Black)	1	28
5	37	131	USB food flash drive - hamburger	1	29
6	39	136	Furry gorilla with big eyes slippers (Black) XL	1	1
7	39	137	Developer joke mug - fun was unexpected at this...	10	11
8	39	138	Animal with big feet slippers (Brown) S	4	15
9	39	139	Dinosaur battery-powered slippers (Green) L	6	21

Figure 4-8. *Partitioning calculations per order*

As you can see, the running total must start from scratch again once the Order ID changes from 37 to 39, since we want to calculate the Running Total for each order.

The code to do so is very similar to the original one, just with the addition of PARTITION BY [OrderID], that tells Azure SQL to keep accumulating values as long as the value in the OrderID column doesn't change. When it changes, then Azure SQL must start a new calculation:

```
SELECT
    [OrderID],
    [OrderLineID],
    [Description],
    [Quantity],
    SUM(Quantity) OVER (
        PARTITION BY [OrderID]
        ORDER BY [OrderLineID] ROWS BETWEEN
            UNBOUNDED PRECEDING AND
            CURRENT ROW
    ) AS RunningTotal
FROM
    [Sales].[OrderLines]
WHERE
    [OrderID] in (37, 39)
```

Windowing functions can help a lot in both simplifying your code and having great performances, and we just have seen a very small part of what they can do, so make sure to check them out and to use them whenever appropriate.

Bulk operations

If you need to load *a lot* of data into Azure SQL, where a lot means hundreds of thousands, millions, or even billions of rows, you need to use a specific API called Bulk Copy API. As it allows only to insert data into a destination table, it is sometimes also referred to as Bulk Insert API or Bulk Load API.

This API is directly called by client libraries, and it allows you to massively load data with extreme speeds, easily loading tens of thousands of rows, and more, per second. Of course, I'm talking of performances within Azure, from a Web API application or a VM to the Azure SQL database being used in the back end. If the API or the application is in another cloud or running on premises, the speed at which you can load data will depend on the local network speed.

To run a bulk load, .NET provides the SqlBulkCopy class, while Java has the SQLServerBulkCopy class. Here's an excerpt of a sample written using .NET:

```
using(var conn = new SqlConnection(Environment.GetEnvironmentVariable("CS_
AzureSQL")))
{
    conn.Open();
    var bc = new SqlBulkCopy(conn)
    bc.DestinationTableName = "dbo.BulkLoadedUsers";
    bc.BatchSize = 10000;
    bc.WriteToServer(userDataTable);
}
```

Just to give you an idea of how fast this is, and you can test it yourself as the sample is part of code accompanying the book, if executed from an Azure VM in the same region of the database you are loading data into, it will load 100,000 rows in 0.91 seconds or 110,000 rows per second, even using a small BC_Gen5_2 database. Guess we can call it *fast*, right?

If you want to know more

In this chapter, you learned a lot, providing you the foundations to understand why pushing compute to data is important, along with the knowledge needed to do it efficiently, starting from understanding the declarative approach power up to manipulating data using Windowing Functions.

We also discussed briefly about normalization and why that is important and how that idea is useful not only to relational databases. Here's a list of resources to get deeper into everything you have just learned:

- Query Processing Architecture Guide – https://docs.microsoft.
  com/sql/relational-databases/query-processing-architecture-
  guide

- Intelligent Query Processing – `https://docs.microsoft.com/sql/relational-databases/performance/intelligent-query-processing#batch-mode-on-rowstore`

- Finding Distinct Values Quickly – `https://sqlperformance.com/2020/03/sql-performance/finding-distinct-values-quickly`

- Class Normalization – `www.agiledata.org/essays/classNormalization.html`

- Normalized Data Models – `https://docs.mongodb.com/manual/core/data-model-design/#normalized-data-models`

- T-SQL Fundamentals – `www.amazon.com/T-SQL-Fundamentals-3rd-Itzik-Ben-Gan-dp-150930200X/dp/150930200X`

- T-SQL Querying Developer Reference – `www.amazon.com/T-SQL-Querying-Developer-Reference-Ben-Gan-dp-0735685045/dp/0735685045/`

- Windows Functions Developer Reference – `www.amazon.com/T-SQL-Window-Functions-Developer-Reference/dp/0135861446`

- An Introduction to Database Systems – `www.amazon.com/Introduction-Database-Systems-8th/dp/0321197844`

- Pro SQL Server Relational Database Design and Implementation – – `www.amazon.com/Server-Relational-Database-Design-Implementation-ebook/dp/B01MR14K06`

- Practical Issues in Database Management: A Reference for the Thinking Practitioner – `www.amazon.com/Practical-Issues-Database-Management-Practitioner/dp/0201485559`

- Database Design and Relational Theory: Normal Forms and All That Jazz – `www.amazon.com/Database-Design-Relational-Theory-Normal-ebook/dp/B082X1B6WP`

## CHAPTER 5

Developing with Azure SQL – Advanced

After having discussed the foundational aspects of querying and manipulating data, it's now time to focus on more advanced and development-oriented features that you can use in Azure SQL. If you already took a peek at the chapter content, you may be surprised to find a full section on security. Don't be. Security is not something that can be added later, like an afterthought, that is a nice to have but not so core. On the contrary, security *is* important as much as performances and maintainability and must be taken into consideration from the ground up. Therefore, the options Azure SQL offers you to keep your data secure are a must-known for everyone who wants to create a modern application – modern because it is not only scalable and modular, but because it is also secure.

Programmability

As a developer, you already know how important it is to be able to reuse and encapsulate existing code. Azure SQL provides a wide range of options that you can use to make sure your SQL code is clean, legible, easy to maintain, and reusable.

Variables

There are two types of variables in T-SQL: Scalar and Table. A scalar variable is just a normal variable as the one you are used to work with in other programming languages. Variables must be explicitly declared, have a name that starts with the character "@", and must be typed:

```
DECLARE @i INT = 42;
DECLARE @name NVARCHAR(50) = N'John';
SELECT @i AS FamousNumber, @name AS CommonName;
```

© Davide Mauri, Silvano Coriani, Anna Hoffman, Sanjay Mishra, Jovan Popovic 2021
D. Mauri et al., *Practical Azure SQL Database for Modern Developers*,
https://doi.org/10.1007/978-1-4842-6370-9_5

T-SQL doesn't support arrays, lists, or dictionaries, but if you need to store more than one value in a variable, you can use a Table Variable:

```
DECLARE @t AS TABLE (
    [Id] INT NOT NULL,
    [Name] NVARCHAR(50) NOT NULL
);
INSERT INTO @t VALUES (42, N'John');
SELECT * FROM @t;
```

One behavior that may surprise at the beginning, and that is quite different from variables in other programming languages, is how Azure SQL manages the variable's scope. A variable is scoped to a *batch* or to an object. In the case of an object, understanding the scoping is easy, as T-SQL behaves exactly like any other programming language. A variable defined within a Stored Procedure, Trigger, or Function will be scoped to that object only.

Variables defined outside an object, instead, are scoped to the batch. A batch is a group of T-SQL statements executed together. In the preceding code sample, you must execute all three statements (DECLARE, INSERT, and SELECT) all together; otherwise, the code would not work. If you try to execute the DECLARE statement alone, that will work, but once done, the variable will be gone. If you would try to execute the INSERT statement, then you'll get an error telling you that the variable @t is not defined.

Table Variables are generally used in very niche places as they may have a quite heavy impact on performances, and usually they should not contain too many rows. Be aware that this has nothing to do with memory consumption or anything related to that: the issue is that Table Variables are something in between two worlds – Variables and Tables – and for this reason, the Azure SQL engine cannot optimize access to their data as much as it would with regular table instead. If you want to learn more details about this, look at the end of this chapter so that you can learn more. In general, if you need to have a temporary place where to store some of your data, use Temporary Tables instead.

Temporary Tables

Especially if creating analytical solutions, it could happen (even pretty frequently) that you need to temporarily store processed data somewhere, so that you can work on it at a later time. Sometimes it is also helpful to split a very complex query in several smaller queries, and you'll need a place to store the result of a query so that it can be picked up from another one for further processing.

Temporary Tables will help you exactly in those cases. You can create a temporary table using the regular CREATE TABLE command. As long as the table name starts with the hash character (#), that table will be temporary:

```
CREATE TABLE #t
(
    [Id] INT NOT NULL,
    [Name] NVARCHAR(50) NOT NULL
);
```

Temporary means that it will exist until manually destroyed with the DROP command or until it goes out of scope. For a Stored Procedure or a Trigger, the scope is the lifetime of the Stored Procedure or Trigger that created the temporary table. Once the Stored Procedure or Trigger has finished executing, the temporary table will be destroyed.

A quick way to *create and fill* a temporary table with the result of a query is the SELECT INTO statement:

```
SELECT
    [OrderLineID],
    [Description],
    [Quantity]
INTO
    #Order37
FROM
    [Sales].[OrderLines]
WHERE
    [OrderID] = 37;
```

A Temporary Table named #Order37 will be created, automatically inferring the column names and types, and it will be filled with all the rows from the table Sales. OrderLines related to the specified order.

Temporary Tables benefit from special optimizations that Azure SQL can do, as it knows such tables are ephemeral by definition. If you need to park your temporary data somewhere, make sure you use them in place of regular tables.

Views

Views are probably the simplest option available to reuse code and encapsulate data processing logic. A view is nothing more than a query definition, labeled with name, and usable as a table. In fact, views are also known as *virtual tables*, even if this name is seldomly used.

Views are useful for code reuse but also for securing access to your data and to keep backward compatibility with existing applications, by abstracting access to underlying tables.

The first point is quite obvious: instead of writing a complex query with JOINs, Windowing Functions, and all the goodness that Azure SQL provides, you can just save the query definition as a view and then call it later by executing simpler code. For example, let's create a view to encapsulate the logic to calculate a Running Total:

```
CREATE OR ALTER VIEW [Sales].[OrderLinesRuninngTotal]
AS
SELECT
    [OrderID],
    [OrderLineID],
    [Description],
    [Quantity],
    SUM(Quantity) OVER (
        PARTITION BY [OrderID]
        ORDER BY [OrderLineID] ROWS BETWEEN
            UNBOUNDED PRECEDING AND
            CURRENT ROW
    ) AS RunningTotal
FROM
    [Sales].[OrderLines];
GO
```

Now you can execute the same query using this simpler code:

```
SELECT
    OrderID,
    [OrderLineID],
    [Description],
    [Quantity],
    [RunningTotal]
FROM
    [Sales].[OrderLinesRuninngTotal];
```

The query executed will be *exactly the same* as if you would have executed the query code directly without using the view. More precisely, the view body is "expanded" and merged with the query's body. For example, in fact, if you write something like this:

```
SELECT
    OrderID,
    [OrderLineID],
    [Description],
    [Quantity],
    [RunningTotal]
FROM
    [Sales].[OrderLinesRuninngTotal]
WHERE
    [OrderID] IN (41, 42, 43);
GO
```

GO is not a T-SQL command or keyword. GO is a keyword recognized by a tool, like SQL Server Management Studio or Azure Data Studio, that notifies the tool that two sets of T-SQL statements, usually called batches, must be executed *separately* and *independently* (but not in parallel though!). This is needed by some commands, many CREATE statements, for example, so that you can tell the tool you're using when a view's body is finished and when another command, potentially even unrelated to the created view, is starting.

Azure SQL will behave like it could *push* the WHERE clause into the view and apply the filter so that the running total will be calculated only on the requested Orders. More precisely, what really happens is that the view is *expanded* and merged with the query that is using it. This allows Azure SQL to optimize the query as a whole and avoid, for example, to just follow the precedence order which would require to calculate the Running Total for *all* orders and then remove all the rows that are not in the query's scope. As you can imagine, that would be extremely inefficient. By following this optimization process instead, the view can take advantage of all the filters used in outer queries (when it makes sense) so that it can reduce as much as possible the number of rows on which it has to operate, providing better performance and less resource usage.

Security is another reason why views are useful: you can grant someone access to a view while denying that user access to the table used by the view. This means that you can be sure a user can only see the result of the query, but not the values stored in the underlying tables used to create that result.

Last reason for taking advantage of views is that they help to abstract access to tables by creating an indirection layer, so that your application and the database can stay loosely coupled, giving you the flexibility to make changes to your database without necessarily breaking any working application: views can used as a backward-compatible interface to existing applications. You are free to refactor your database and evolve its design to some new direction you want it to take, with the peace of mind that you won't introduce any breaking changes.

Views can be dropped using the DROP VIEW command:

```
DROP VIEW [Sales].[OrderLinesRuninngTotal];
```

Functions

Functions in Azure SQL are of two types: functions that return a table and functions that return a scalar value. Besides this difference, they are very similar to what you probably already expect, given the fact that they are, as the name implies, *functions*. They allow you to encapsulate and reuse code and processing logic and can accept parameters and return a result.

As Azure SQL has many system-provided functions built in, for example, STRING_ SPLIT, the functions created by the user are generally called *User-Defined Functions* or *UDFs*.

UDFs that return a table are usually referenced to as *Table-Valued Functions* or *TVF* for short; as such, they can be used anywhere a table could be used too, for example:

```
SELECT
      [OrderID],
      [OrderDate],
      [TotalQuantity],
      [TotalValue]
FROM
      dbo.[GetOrderTotals](40, 42);
```

If a TVF is made only of one SELECT statement, it becomes very similar to a view with the exception that it supports parameters. As a view, such function can be expanded and merged (this process is usually referred to as *inlining*) with the query that is using it and thus can take advantage of better optimization. For this ability to be *inlined*, those TVFs are called *Inline Table-Valued Functions*:

```
CREATE OR ALTER FUNCTION dbo.GetOrderTotals(@FromOrderId AS INT, @ToOrderID
AS INT)
RETURNS TABLE
AS
RETURN
WITH cte AS (
    SELECT
          [OrderId],
          SUM([Quantity]) AS TotalQuantity,
          SUM([Quantity] * [UnitPrice]) AS TotalValue
    FROM
          [Sales].[OrderLines]
    WHERE
          [OrderId] BETWEEN @FromOrderId AND @ToOrderID
    GROUP BY
          [OrderId]
)
```

```
SELECT
     o.[OrderId],
     o.[OrderDate],
     ol.[TotalQuantity],
     ol.[TotalValue]
FROM
     cte ol
INNER JOIN
     [Sales].[Orders] o ON [ol].[OrderID] = [o].[OrderID];
GO
```

A Table-Valued Function that is made of more than one single SELECT statement is called *Multi-Statement Table-Valued Function*, and while it provides more flexibility than an Inline TVF, it cannot be optimized as much when called by other queries. For this reason, it should be used only if there are no other options available as it may have a tangible impact on performances.

On the other side of the spectrum, there are the Scalar Functions. They return just a single value. The code used in their body can be as complex as you want and even include several SELECT statements, but at the end of its execution, one and only one scalar value must be returned.

While Scalar Functions could give the impression of something you would use as much as possible, especially if you are used to imperative programming languages, you should instead think twice when you want to create and use a new one. The reason is simple and is related to the fact that applying one operation to a set of data is usually much more efficient than executing that operation for each data point (rows in case of a relational database) in your set. If you create a Scalar function and use it to process the values returned by a query, you are forcing Azure SQL to execute that function for each row returned. Each call to a function has its own overhead, which adds up to the fact that Azure SQL Query Optimizer is working with his hands tied as it doesn't have much space to optimize your code, as the function must be executed for every row. Performance will suffer a lot. And it is not by chance, in fact, that every time a database is forced to work processing single rows instead of a set of data, people refer to it as *RBAR* (*Row-By-Agonizing-Row*). So, use Scalar UDFs sparingly. On the bright side, in the last few years, Microsoft research found some clever methods to take the code inside the Scalar

Function and *rewrite* it as more optimizable code, but still, if you can write the code in such a way RBAR is not needed from the start, you will help the optimizer right away, without having to wait for Microsoft Research, and in turn you'll get better performance immediately.

Functions can be dropped using the DROP FUNCTION command:

```
DROP FUNCTION dbo.GetOrderTotals;
```

Stored Procedures

Stored Procedures are exactly what the name says: procedures stored in the database that can be executed by calling them by name. Stored Procedures can have parameters, can return a single scalar value, and can return zero one or more resultsets.

They offer an extremely powerful way to encapsulate complexity, reuse code, and create an abstraction layer: they can be used to create an API interface – a contract – that can shield the user from any changes or evolution that happens during a database's lifetime. In addition to that, Stored Procedures offer other interesting benefits.

Like many other programmability features used to easily secure access to data, Stored Procedures can also be used for that purpose. A user can be authorized to execute a Stored Procedure but could be denied to access the underlying tables or views directly. This, especially if you are creating public facing applications, like an API or web app, is vital as you can be sure that, no matter what, a user accessing the database through that solution will only be able to access data via the procedures you have created for that purpose. Even if for some reason a user could gain direct access to the database, bypassing your middle tier or your web app, he or she won't be able to do anything else apart from what the Stored Procedures would allow him or her to do. That's a pretty important point and a huge help in keeping your data secure.

Stored Procedures also have another important benefit. Azure SQL, once the Stored Procedure is invoked for the first time, will cache the *execution plan*, also known, in other database systems, as a *DAG* (*Directed Acyclic Graph*), which is a list of steps that Azure SQL will execute in order to generate the result of your query. You will learn more about this later in the book, but as you can imagine, especially for complex queries, generating an execution plan can be expensive and resource-intensive, so caching it will help Azure SQL to save CPU and time, giving you better overall performances and freeing resources for higher scalability without incurring into additional costs.

As a developer, Stored Procedures will be something you will love to use as they really help you in creating a very clear separation of concerns, keeping the code clean and polished, facilitate a clear definition of an interface between database and application, and ultimately favor a good loosely coupled architecture.

A Stored Procedure can contain all the code you need to implement, even the most complex data manipulation processes, and they are called using the EXEC (or EXECUTE if you like to be verbose) command:

```
CREATE OR ALTER PROCEDURE dbo.GetOrderForCustomer
@CustomerInfo NVARCHAR(MAX)
AS
IF (ISJSON(@CustomerInfo) != 1) BEGIN
    THROW 50000, '@CustomerInfo is not a valid JSON document', 16
END

SELECT [Value] INTO #T FROM OPENJSON(@CustomerInfo, '$.CustomerId') AS ci;

SELECT
    [CustomerID],
    COUNT(*) AS OrderCount,
    MIN([OrderDate]) AS FirstOrder,
    MAX([OrderDate]) AS LastOrder
FROM
    Sales.[Orders]
WHERE
    [CustomerID] IN (SELECT [Value] FROM #T)
GROUP BY
    [CustomerID];
GO
```

In the preceding code, the Stored Procedure requires a string parameter. After a simple validation, the JSON document received in input is read and, just to simulate an intermediate step, the relevant content is saved into a temporary table. After that, the results are retrieved and returned to the user. The created Stored Procedure can be executed just by using the EXEC command:

```
EXEC dbo.GetOrderForCustomer N'{"CustomerId": [106, 193, 832]}';
```

The code inside the Stored Procedure will be executed, and one resultset, the one generated by the SELECT ... FROM Sales.[Order] query, will be returned.

You may be wondering, at this point, when you should use Functions and when Stored Procedures. Good question! As a general guidance, keep in mind that while functions are quite powerful, especially the Inline Table-Valued Functions, they also have quite a lot of limitations and constraints. For this reason, unless you have some specific use case that is perfectly suited for a Function, the recommendation is to use Stored Procedures: they offer better performances and don't have all the limitations that Functions have.

A Stored Procedure can be dropped using the DROP PROCEDURE command:

```
DROP PROCEDURE dbo.GetOrderForCustomer;
```

Triggers

Triggers are special Stored Procedures that get executed when something happens. There are two types of Triggers: *DML* (*Data Manipulation Language*) Triggers and *DDL* (*Data Definition Language*) Triggers.

The first type, DML Triggers, gets executed when an INSERT, UPDATE, or DELETE (or MERGE) command is executed. The latter, DDL Triggers, is instead executed when CREATE, ALTER, or DROP commands, which are used to define data structures, are invoked.

In both cases, you will have access to special objects that will allow you to interact with the event that sparked the Trigger execution.

For DDL Triggers, you have access to the Inserted and Deleted virtual tables so that you can access the data as it was before and after the change. You can decide to do whatever you want with that data. For example, you can store the deleted data into another table to provide an easily accessible log of changed rows. You can also instruct the Trigger to prevent that change to happen at all: for example, you may want to be sure that some configuration data is not removed from a core table that your application needs to work properly.

In DML Triggers, you have access to an EVENTDATA function that returns an XML containing all the details about the statement being executed. For example, in this case, you can save that information to keep track of when, how, and who altered a table or dropped an object. Also in this case, you can also prevent that modification from happening.

Triggers are part of the transaction being executed, which means that you can decide if that transaction should be allowed to successfully complete or not. A situation where this could happen, for example, is when only a set of selected users are authorized to make changes to the discount rates applied to your products for selected customers. In a Trigger, you may check that the user making the change has the authorization to do it, maybe even logging that operation in another table to keep track of that. If the user doesn't have that authorization, you can roll back the transaction right within the Trigger, meaning the change won't happen at all:

```
CREATE OR ALTER TRIGGER [Warehouse].[ProtectAzure]
ON [Warehouse].[Colors]
FOR UPDATE, DELETE
AS
BEGIN
    IF EXISTS(
            SELECT * FROM [Deleted]
            WHERE [ColorName] IN ('Azure')
            )
    BEGIN
            THROW 50000, 'Azure is here to stay.', 16;
            ROLLBACK TRAN;
    END
END
```

If you try to DELETE or UPDATE a value in the Warehouse.Colors table so that the color "Azure" will be removed or changed to something else, the Trigger will roll back that action, leaving the "Azure" color intact:

```
DELETE FROM [Warehouse].[Colors] WHERE ColorID = 1
```

This capability is very powerful but also quite expensive: since Triggers are part of an active transaction, they can roll it back, but from a resource usage perspective, it would be better to prevent it in the first place. Preventing it would have avoided using IO, CPU, and memory resources just to discover, right at the end of the process, that all the work done must be undone – such a waste of precious resources.

Besides the impact on resource usage, Triggers can also have a big impact on performances. Their performance will be as good as the code you write and as fast as the logic you built into the Trigger could be. If in the Trigger you're trying to aggregate data of a billion rows table, chances are that performance won't be exactly stellar. And this will happen *every time* the Trigger is executed.

That's why, more and more frequently, Triggers are replaced with natively supported features. For example, as you'll learn in the next sections, keeping track of all changes done to a table can be done more efficiently and easily using a feature called Temporal Tables, or that securing access to specific rows and values can be done with Row-Level Security.

So, in general, try to keep Triggers' usage as low as possible. You should do all the checks upfront before making any changes to your data, so that you don't have to undo anything. It will favor performance, concurrency, maintainability, and scalability.

Triggers can be dropped using the DROP TRIGGER command:

```
DROP TRIGGER [Warehouse].[ProtectAzure]
ON [Warehouse].[Colors];
```

Non-scalar parameters

As you just learned in the previous sections, Stored Procedure and Functions, as expected, support parameters. In all modern programming languages, parameters can be anything, from scalars to complex objects. In Azure SQL, this is true too, albeit with some differences, since there is no concept like an *object*, given that SQL is not an object-oriented language. In the next sections, you'll find the options available to achieve what passing an object would do in other languages.

Table-Valued Parameters

As the name implies, parameters can be tables. Yes, you can pass an entire table into a Function or a Stored Procedure. This is by far the best option you have when you need to pass quite a lot of data from your application to Azure SQL. I've written *quite* a lot because, as a rule of thumb, this option is good when you have up to some thousand rows to pass. If you are in the realms of hundreds of thousands, millions, or even more, then you should look at the "Bulk operations" section discussed in the previous chapter for *really good* performance.

Also keep in mind that the Table-Valued Parameter (TVP) feature needs to be supported by the client library, as it needs to be aware of that option to be able to use it. Common languages like .NET, Python, Node, and Go all support TVPs.

How to use the TVP depends on the language you are using, but the common idea is that you can load data into an object that can be enumerated, making sure that the data structure is compatible with the schema of the table *type* you'll use as a parameter, and then pass that object to the Stored Procedure you are calling.

You start creating the table type:

```
CREATE TYPE dbo.PostTagsTableType AS TABLE
(
    Tag NVARCHAR(100) NOT NULL UNIQUE
);
```

And then you reference it into your Stored Procedure:

```
CREATE PROCEDURE dbo.AddTagsToPost
@PostId INT,
@Tags dbo.PostTagsTableType READONLY
AS
INSERT INTO dbo.PostTags SELECT @PostId, Tag FROM @Tags
```

As you can see, the parameter @Tags is really a table so you can use it as a regular table with the only limit that it is read only. Then, with .NET, for example, you can use the TVP as shown in the following code:

```
var p2 = new SqlParameter("@Tags", SqlDbType.Structured);
p2.TypeName = "dbo.PostTagsTableType";
p2.Value = tags;
cmd.Parameters.Add(p2);
```

where the object tags is a .NET DataTable:

```
var tags = new DataTable("PostTagsTableType");
tags.Columns.Add("Tag", typeof(string));
tags.Rows.Add("azure-sql");
tags.Rows.Add("tvp");
```

Table-Valued Parameters are heavily optimized for performances, and also by sending a batch of rows to Azure SQL, your application will do the roundtrip to the database only once, instead of as many times as you have rows to pass. As every call to resources external to application has small overhead, by keeping the number of times you call the database as low as possible – also referred to as a less or not chatty application – you'll make sure to give the end user the best experience possible, creating applications that are scalable and provide great performance.

JSON

Sometimes passing an object as a table will not be possible. For example, when we have an object representing something like a post, with its own tags, categories, author details, and so on. We could surely find ways to turn such objects into some Table-Valued Parameters, but it would hardly be elegant. So why not just pass the object serialized as JSON as a whole? Azure SQL is perfectly capable of doing complex JSON manipulations, as you'll learn in Chapter 8. You can write a Stored Procedure that can accept JSON as a parameter; you can use it then to read the needed JSON sections so that you can fill the appropriate tables or pass the extracted values, or even the JSON document, to other procedures:

```
CREATE PROCEDURE dbo.AddTagsToPost
@PostId INT,
@Tags NVARCHAR(MAX)
AS
INSERT INTO dbo.PostTags
SELECT @PostId, T.[value] FROM OPENJSON(@Tags, '$.tags') T
GO
```

And the Stored Procedure can accept JSON in @Tags:

```
EXEC dbo.AddTagsToPost 1, '{"tags": ["azure-sql", "string_split", "csv"],
"categories": {}}';
```

As JSON is passed a regular string, this technique will work with any language as there is no special knowledge required by the client libraries to take advantage of this option.

CSV

What about if you just need to pass a small array of values? Or if the language you are using does not support TVPs and JSON feels just overkill for the goal? One way to elegantly solve the problem would be to use good-old, but always present *CSV* (*Comma-Separated Values*). Note that the comma is not really mandatory, as you can use the divider you prefer, like a pipe or a dash. Azure SQL gives you the Table-Valued System Function STRING_SPLIT to use for this purpose:

```
CREATE PROCEDURE dbo.AddTagsToPost
@PostId INT,
@Tags NVARCHAR(MAX)
AS
INSERT INTO dbo.PostTags
SELECT @PostId, T.[value] FROM STRING_SPLIT(@Tags, '|') AS T
```

And then you can just use the Stored Procedure like this:

```
EXEC dbo.AddTagsToPost 1, 'azure-sql|string_split|csv'
```

Same as with JSON, this option doesn't require any special handling on the client side, so you can use this technique with any development language that supports regular ODBC connections.

Monitoring data for changes

Finding what data has changed from the last time an application, or a user, accessed it can be extremely helpful to increase application efficiency and scalability. Much fewer resources, in terms of CPU, network, and IO, would be needed, for example, to exchange only the changed data instead of a full set of data with a target application. In addition to such an already important point, since the burden of tracking changes can be left to Azure SQL, you'll have your code leaner and solely focused on the specific business case you need to take care of. As a result, you will have more time to take care of it, removing from your plate the need of having to deal with other complexities that are anyway needed and expected in modern applications – like efficiency in data transfer.

Change Tracking

Change tracking is a simple, yet effective technology to understand what data has changed since a specific moment in time. The idea behind this feature is that every time a user accesses a table, he or she can ask for the version number active at that moment. The user must keep that version number safely stored somewhere so that the next time he or she tries to access that table again, the user can also ask Azure SQL to only get the *changed* data starting from that version number and on. Azure SQL will return all the changed data from that version number along with the operation – insert, update, or delete – that the user should do on its own dataset to update it to the current status, along with the new version number that the user must use next time, to get a new set of changes.

This feature is really powerful as it completely removes all the complexity from the client side, as the only thing that the client must do is to preserve the version number and present it to Azure SQL.

Change Tracking must be enabled on the database:

```
ALTER DATABASE WideWorldImportersStandard
SET CHANGE_TRACKING = ON
(CHANGE_RETENTION = 2 DAYS, AUTO_CLEANUP = ON)
```

And on the table you want to track

```
ALTER TABLE [Warehouse].[Colors]
ENABLE CHANGE_TRACKING
```

From that moment on, you can use the system scalar function `CHANGE_TRACKING_CURRENT_VERSION()` to get the current version number:

```
SELECT CHANGE_TRACKING_CURRENT_VERSION()
```

The version number is calculated and automatically updated at the database level – that's why it doesn't require any parameter – and will change every time some data is changed in one of the tracked tables. Let's say, for example, that I've just read the table `Warehouse.Colors`, and after doing that, I asked the current version number. In addition to the resultset, Azure SQL returned the value 42 to me, which represents the number associated with the *current* version, which means that the values I just read are associated with that version number.

Now let's say that someone, maybe even including myself, makes some changes to the Warehourse.Colors tables. After a while, let's say 3 hours, I need to get the data again from the same table, but now, instead of getting the full dataset, I'd like to have only the changes from when I last saw it, so that I can avoid having to read and transfer all the rows that haven't been changed in the meantime and that, most probably, would be the majority.

CHANGETABLE is the function I need to use for this purpose:

```
SELECT
    SYS_CHANGE_OPERATION, ColorID
FROM
    CHANGETABLE(CHANGES [Warehouse].[Colors], 42) C
```

The query will return a table like the following:

	SYS_CHANGE_OPERATION	ColorID
1	U	10
2	D	30
3	I	100
4	I	101

where you can see the operation done on a row and the value of the column for the Primary Key of that row. With the Primary key – that uniquely identifies rows in a table – we can join that result with the original table, Warehourse.Colors, and get all the data we need. We can now run the CHANGE_TRACKING_CURRENT_VERSION() function again to get the current version; let's say now it is equal to 50, and we keep the value somewhere, so that the next time we query for changes again, we'll be using that value to get the new changes happened from that moment on – and so on for the next syncs.

Easy and extremely efficient – and helpful to keep your client-side code very clean and easy to understand.

To disable Change Tracking on a specific table, you use the ALTER command on the table where you want to disable Change Tracking:

```
ALTER TABLE [Warehouse].[Colors]
DISABLE CHANGE_TRACKING
```

To disable it on the entire database, you use the ALTER command on the whole database:

```
ALTER DATABASE WideWorldImportersStandard
SET CHANGE_TRACKING = OFF
```

Change data capture

Change data capture is an even more sophisticated technology that uses the internal immutable transaction log to read all the changes done on data and save it into a specified table. It resembles very closely the idea of a Change Feed that some other databases provide. It reads from the transaction log using an asynchronous process and thus is perfect to consume changes without affecting performance of the table where those changes happened. At the moment, it is not yet fully available on all Azure SQL offerings, but keep an eye out for it. With solutions like Debezium, it will easily allow the creation of near real-time ETL solutions and integration with Kafka for a completely upgraded developer experience.

Protecting data assets

Aside from storing data and making it available upon request, a database also has the task of keeping the data secure. Azure SQL offers plenty of features to do that, ranging from permission management through data masking and up to encryption, so that you can choose exactly to which degree you want to expose your data and to whom.

In addition to the features that will be presented in the next sections, keep in mind that by default data is encrypted at rest automatically, thanks to a feature named *Transparent Database Encryption*. As the name implies, it is completely transparent and doesn't require any change to your code. Your data is secured by default once it is on Azure. Of course, that might not be enough for you, so read on.

Permissions

Managing permissions and thus data access authorization is typically a database administrator duty, but security is, as discussed already, a key point in every application, so it is always good for a developer to have at least a basic knowledge of the security principles of the tools and the system he or she needs to use, to make sure security can be taken care of from the ground up, avoiding future headaches and unpleasant surprises.

Azure SQL applies the principle of the least privilege, and as such, a newly created user cannot really do much in Azure SQL. Aside from the *administrative* user you defined when you created the Azure SQL Server or Azure SQL Managed Instance resource, which has all the possible authorizations as it is an administrative account, and should not be used to grant application access to the data, you should create a dedicated user for your application. For example, for an API service hosted in Azure Web API, you could create the WebAPI user:

```
CREATE USER WebAPI WITH PASSWORD = '94m1-2sx0_1!';
```

If you try to log in with this user, you'll discover that it doesn't have access to anything. To allow it to do a SELECT on a table, for example, you need to GRANT it the correct permission:

```
GRANT SELECT ON OBJECT::[Sales].[Orders] TO WebAPI;
```

There are lots of permissions in Azure SQL which allow you to fine-tune the security access of any user. To simplify the management of security, you can use *roles* or *schemas*. Roles allow you to group users together, so that a user can inherit the permissions given to the roles he or she has been assigned to. Roles can be created manually, or you can use pre-existing roles. For example, any user in the db_datareader role can read data from any table, but they won't be able to modify any data:

```
ALTER ROLE [db_datareader] ADD MEMBER [WebAPI];
```

If you want to give some permissions only to a specific set of objects, for example all the tables used by the Web API solution you are creating, you can target an object schema:

```
GRANT SELECT ON SCHEMA::[Sales] TO WebAPI;
```

Such code will allow you to use SELECT on any object that belongs to the Sales schema.

As Stored Procedures do not allow SELECT to be used, as you may have already guessed, you'll need to grant the EXECUTE permission to a user to make sure one can execute the desired Stored Procedure:

```
GRANT EXECUTE ON OBJECT::[dbo].[AddTagsToPost] TO WebAPI;
```

Every time a user tries to execute an action on an object for which he or she doesn't have the correct permission, an error will be raised, and the execution of the statement will be halted.

In order to test that a specific user has the correct permissions, you can *impersonate* that user if you have logged in using the administrative account:

```
EXECUTE AS USER = 'WebAPI';
```

From now on, you can execute all the T-SQL code you want to test, and it will be executed as if was the user WebAPI to invoke it.

To revert back to your administrative user, you just need to run

```
REVERT;
```

Also, keep in mind that if you want to make sure someone cannot access something, you can explicitly DENY to that user the permission to do something on an object:

```
DENY SELECT ON OBJECT::[Sales].[Orders] TO SampleUser;
```

A DENY will always win if there are several different and conflicting authorizations for the same object. This could happen if the user is part of one or more roles.

To completely remove a user from a database, so that he won't even be able to connect to it, one easy way is to delete the user:

```
DROP USER SampleUser;
```

In case you want to temporarily prevent the user from connecting, instead of dropping that user, you could just deny him or her the permission to connect if you want:

```
DENY CONNECT TO SampleUser;
```

Permissions and security are huge topics, but this is a good start. Remember to keep security in mind right from the beginning and you'll already be one step ahead.

If you're already a security-savvy person, you may be thinking that using a password for logging in into a system is something that's not really secure, and you are totally right. You can create an Azure SQL user that does not have a password stored in Azure SQL and that relies on Azure Active Directory instead. Your application can then use a Managed Identity to authenticate itself when connecting to Azure SQL.

A full tutorial on this topic is here: https://aka.ms/aswtcmsi.

Row-Level Security

With permissions, you can deny access to certain tables or even just to certain columns. But what if you want to deny access to some specific rows? In Azure SQL, you have a powerful feature called *Row-Level Security*, or *RLS* for short, that allows you to do exactly that.

With RLS, you can create a *policy* that will target one or more tables. Each time a read or a write operation is executed against those tables, the policy will kick in: it will evaluate if the rows affected by the requested operation are accessible to the user executing it or not.

To do the evaluation, the policy will apply a provided user defined Inline Table-Valued Function to each row touched by the active operation. If the function returns 1, that row will be accessible; otherwise, it won't.

Thanks to the Azure SQL Query Optimizer, the function will be *inlined*, and thus it won't really be executed for each row in scope; otherwise, performance would be horrible, but from a logical point of view, that's exactly what is happening.

Here's an example of a security policy definition:

```
CREATE SECURITY POLICY OrderSecurityPolicy
ADD FILTER PREDICATE [rls].LoginSecurityPolicy(SalespersonPersonID) ON
[Sales].[Orders]
WITH (STATE = ON);
```

As you can see, it uses the Function `rls.LogonSecurityPolicy` to check authorization for rows in `Sales.Orders` table. The function will receive the value of the column `SalespersonPersonID` for each row it needs to evaluate. The function is created as follows:

```
CREATE FUNCTION rls.LoginSecurityPolicy(@PersonID AS INT)
RETURNS TABLE
WITH SCHEMABINDING
AS
RETURN
SELECT
    1 As [Authorized]
```

```
FROM
     [Application].[People]
WHERE
     LoginName = SESSION_CONTEXT(N'Login')
AND
     PersonID = @PersonId;
GO
```

The code uses the system function SESSION_CONTEXT to retrieve the value of the Logon key. The function is incredibly useful as it allows a client to pass some information to Azure SQL as part of the connection data that can then be accessed anytime during the connection lifetime. This feature comes in handy when you are creating a solution that runs on a middle tier or as a microservice and cannot impersonate the calling user. In this way, you can still have a way to pass to Azure SQL the information you need, for example, the login name, so that you can use it to apply a security policy. If you are using OAuth2 to authenticate the user calling the solution you are working on, for example, this is absolutely a needed feature; otherwise, Azure SQL won't be able to know who is really trying to access the data, and you would have to find clever (and complex) way to solve the security challenge by yourself on the client side.

Once Azure SQL has the information on who is actually trying to access the data, as you can see in the code, it will check if that login exists in the Application.People table. It will also check that such person is the one assigned to manage the order he or she is trying to access by using the value injected into the @PersonId variable by the active security policy. If all these checks are true, then the row is allowed to surface to the user. If not, the row will simply be discarded, and the user won't even know it exists. In fact, when the security policy is active, if Miss Kayla Woodcock (that has PersonId = 2) tries to access the data via the solution we created, she will only see her rows:

```
27
28   SELECT * FROM [Sales].[Orders]
29   GO
```

	OrderID	CustomerID	SalespersonPersonID	PickedByPersonID	ContactPersonID	BackorderOrderID	OrderDate	ExpectedDeliveryDate	Cu
1	1	832	2	NULL	3032	45	2013-01-01	2013-01-02	1:
2	16	414	2	NULL	2027	57	2013-01-01	2013-01-02	1(
3	18	423	2	4	2045	NULL	2013-01-01	2013-01-02	1:
4	31	467	2	4	2133	NULL	2013-01-01	2013-01-02	1(
5	45	832	2	4	3032	NULL	2013-01-01	2013-01-02	1:
6	57	414	2	4	2027	NULL	2013-01-01	2013-01-02	1(
7	102	122	2	14	1243	NULL	2013-01-02	2013-01-03	1(
8	160	547	2	NULL	2293	213	2013-01-03	2013-01-04	1(

This is pretty amazing, as it really helps to simplify the code a lot, making sure that only the data a user is authorized to see will actually leave the database.

Other than filtering out rows, a policy can also be instructed to raise an error in case someone is trying to access rows for which he or she doesn't have the needed permissions. This can be useful, for example, to intercept INSERT commands that would insert non-authorized values. As the value doesn't exist yet, there is no way to use the filter predicate, but still you may want to block its execution: that's exactly what the BLOCK PREDICATE can do.

As usual, the security policy can be deleted with the DROP command:

```
DROP SECURITY POLICY OrderSecurityPolicy;
```

A video that goes into detail of RLS and shows how it can be used to create real-world application, along with a GitHub repo with working sample code, is available here: https://aka.ms/rlsvideo.

Dynamic Data Masking

Sometimes you can't prevent access to certain columns as the application expects them to work properly. For example, imagine you are creating a set of APIs that will allow the user to execute ad hoc queries on available data, so that one can have an ad hoc reporting or analytics solution to run even the most exotic analysis. A typical use case for this would be to connect Power BI to such API. Depending on the user accessing the data, you may want to mask some of the returned data, so that the unauthorized user, instead of getting an error, would simply see a predetermined pattern, protecting sensitive information. To do that, you need to add a *Mask* to the columns you want to obfuscate:

```
ALTER TABLE [Application].[People];
ALTER COLUMN EmailAddress ADD MASKED WITH (FUNCTION = 'email()');
```

After the preceding code is executed, anyone who doesn't have the UNMASK permission will see only masked data for the EmailAddress column.

	PersonId	FullName	EmailAddress
1	1	Data Conversion Only	NULL
2	5	Eva Muirden	eXXX@XXXX.com
3	16	Archer Lamble	aXXX@XXXX.com
4	21	Reio Kabin	rXXX@XXXX.com
5	22	Oliver Kivi	oXXX@XXXX.com
6	23	Hanna Mihhailov	hXXX@XXXX.com
7	24	Paulus Lippmaa	pXXX@XXXX.com
8	25	Kerstin Parn	kXXX@XXXX.com
9	26	Helen Ahven	hXXX@XXXX.com
10	27	Bill Lawson	bXXX@XXXX.com
11	28	Helen Moore	hXXX@XXXX.com
12	29	Penny Buck	pXXX@XXXX.com
13	30	Donna Smith	dXXX@XXXX.com
14	31	Madelaine Cartier	mXXX@XXXX.com
15	32	Annette Talon	aXXX@XXXX.com
16	33	Elias Myllari	eXXX@XXXX.com
17	34	Vilma Niva	vXXX@XXXX.com
18	35	Prem Prabhu	pXXX@XXXX.com

Figure 5-1. *Dynamic Data Masking in action*

This obfuscation happens right into the database, so no sensitive data is ever sent outside Azure SQL.

As data is only obfuscated, a user that is *already* in possession of some sensitive data can still use that information to query the database. Let's say that in the report you are creating, you need to analyze a specific user and that user gave you her own email. A query like this will work perfectly:

```
SELECT * FROM [Application].[People] WHERE EmailAddress = 'helenm
@fabrikam.com'
```

This gives you quite a lot of flexibility as you can be sure to protect data without limiting its usage for those who had access to that protected information in some other, legitimate way.

Of course, this is a double-edged sword as it also means that by executing brute force attacks, obfuscated data could be guessed by a malicious user. That's why Dynamic Data Masking should always be used along with other security features, like Row-Level Security, so that the possibility of allowing a data breach is minimal. Azure also offers a feature called Advanced Threat Protection that works with Azure SQL too and that raises alerts for potential threats by using sophisticated Machine Learning algorithms to monitor suspicious database access and anomalous query patterns, so that you can always be sure that any malicious attempt to access your data will be reported immediately.

Always Encrypted

Always Encrypted is a feature that will guarantee that your highly sensitive data, like Credit Card numbers or Social Security numbers, is encrypted with a set of keys that are not shared with the database engine. This means that even database administrators won't be able to decrypt that data, as the data will be encrypted directly by the application and sent to the database in its encrypted form.

```
CustomerName              CreditLimit
Daniel Martensson         0x013EF0A67897A28747DD83E999521025284466E17C543E42F95830A15A6E4B55F29F762C...
Philip Walker             0x01D8B6C1A8BE2DEECD0032ADA020F9799F8A85A2995D198DF35C6CC5242E5FFBB3AD904...
Marie LeBatelier          0x016D189DC39C402F4BF5AB7A89BB0043848CA0A33C7FC6CB774F7383C0BF815C2588CD0...
Leyla Siavashi            0x01D8B6C1A8BE2DEECD0032ADA020F9799F8A85A2995D198DF35C6CC5242E5FFBB3AD904...
Miriam House              0x01BB1E415E8E17AADEF18411896680E5A741FD1FC177F6597FBD232778CBEDB261FB7DE...
Jitka Necesana            0x019CEFE4C25C5F01C0B3918FA34E63891A38A1A8DE47B3D214E4B3B68B8B303258C2DE0...
Edmee Glissen             0x017A511AB391AC5550517E5DFA80E29FDC75F353387BFEA15BFB8A716999FC4C265B3C5...
Magdalena Michnova        0x016329DD4EA7F97C12DE735B3E3EC6104B123A30DFD08F9ED6B955C9AF1A510367952AD...
Maryann Huddleston        0x01D75E732A05BD4FC7CAA3D46F4208A13AE802F8980DA25D15C2CCCDE254B4B35D7700F...
Radha Barua               0x010670C2E6CF3FADBEA98F771EE6621B20B2A06A0CB6589A76A30AFC9663F84DA65A3A6...
Anindya Ghatak            0x018E30273F2D8C54F5C7EBD273D9C5A2B3B4C8F1AD3333DCB9DA3FA4D0E3CE987A5116E...
Chandrashekhar Dasgupta   0x01FA227E60B28407B43213E74795B04926153DC4BE75938B39759FBC4D040D9B1BBEE18...
Debbie Molina             0x015234D78BE74E059D5D9C6ECD0F2B257A12707DFAD2D155E18934074CC5E88FE5A896E...
Baran Jonsson             0x01D8A15E14366986B3D8A7985DCFFA2466A30D0CE8F7E6E63189E3F39A30403457D10CF...
```

Figure 5-2. *CreditLimit has been Always Encrypted*

The keys used for encryption can be stored in the local machine or in Azure Key Vault, and only those applications that have access to those keys can access the encrypted data. Trying to access Always Encrypted data without the correct key will result in an error:

```
Msg 0, Level 11, State 0, Line 0
Failed to decrypt column 'CreditLimit'.
```

To encrypt and decrypt the values, the client application must use a connection library that supports Always Encrypted, like

- Microsoft JDBC Driver 6.0 (or higher)

- ODBC Driver 13.1 for SQL Server

- ODBC Driver 17 for SQL Server

- Microsoft Drivers 5.2 for PHP for SQL Server

- Microsoft.Data.SqlClient

Those libraries will take care of everything, and encryption and decryption will be completely transparent for the developer.

If you want to know more

You now have a complete knowledge of all the supported programmability features that Azure SQL offers, as well as a very good base of security concepts and options. These capabilities are at your disposal to make sure your application is not only scalable and fast but also secure.

To know more about the topics mentioned in this chapter, you can start from these resources:

- SQL Server 2017 Developer's Guide – `www.amazon.com/SQL-Server-2017-Developers-Guide-dp-1788476190/dp/1788476190`

- What's the difference between a temp table and table variable in SQL Server? – `https://dba.stackexchange.com/questions/16385/whats-the-difference-between-a-temp-table-and-table-variable-in-sql-server/16386#16386`

- Working with Change Tracking – `https://docs.microsoft.com/sql/relational-databases/track-changes/work-with-change-tracking-sql-server`

- Debezium: Stream changes from your database – `https://debezium.io/`

- SQL Server Change Stream – `https://medium.com/@mauridb/sql-server-change-stream-b204c0892641`

- Transparent data encryption – `https://docs.microsoft.com/azure/sql-database/transparent-data-encryption-azure-sql?tabs=azure-portal`

- Always Encrypted – `https://docs.microsoft.com/sql/relational-databases/security/encryption/always-encrypted-database-engine`

- Always Encrypted Client Development – `https://docs.microsoft.com/sql/relational-databases/security/encryption/always-encrypted-client-development?view=azuresqldb-current`

## CHAPTER 6

Practical Use of Tables and Indexes

When people imagine a table, in most of the cases, this looks like an Excel spreadsheet. There are a bunch of cells organized in rows and columns, and there is usually one column that contains the identifiers of the rows.

Azure SQL enables you to use much more than a plain table. You can configure and optimize your table for some specific query patterns, complex analytics, or highly concurrent updates. You can also configure your tables to keep a full history of changes, implement some parts of domain data-integrity logic, and apply fine-grained security rules. In this chapter, you can find some practical advice that can help you leverage the features that Azure SQL provides to create a table that is best fit for your needs.

Designing good tables

As a first step, we need to understand some best practices for table design. Table design is tightly coupled with Domain-Driven Design (DDD) theory described in Eric Evans book. In DDD, we are defining Domain Model entities (objects or classes) that are divided into *Bounded Contexts*. A Bounded Context is a logical boundary where particular terms, definitions, and rules apply in a consistent way. There are also associations between Domain Model entities, as shown in Figure 6-1.

© Davide Mauri, Silvano Coriani, Anna Hoffman, Sanjay Mishra, Jovan Popovic 2021
D. Mauri et al., *Practical Azure SQL Database for Modern Developers*,
https://doi.org/10.1007/978-1-4842-6370-9_6

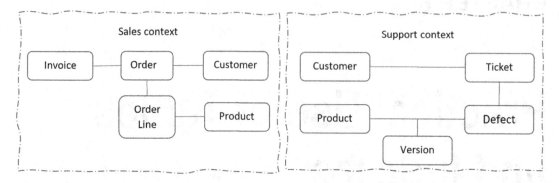

Figure 6-1. *Domain model of application*

Definition of entities in the Domain Model is known as a domain or logical design. Eventually, we need to decide how we should store Domain Model objects in the database. If you decide to store Domain Model entities in Azure SQL, there is a straightforward way to define your underlying tables. Every Bounded Context (`Sales` or `Support` in Figure 6-1) can be represented as a schema. In certain cases, the Bounded Contexts can be even represented by individual databases. Every Domain Model entity should be mapped to one or many tables in the associated schemas. Some high-level guidelines that you can use to map your Domain Model entities to database tables are:

- Every Domain Model entity should be mapped to one table with a column that uniquely identifies the domain object (so-called *Primary Key*).

- Every simple property of a domain object should be represented as a column in the table with a matching SQL type.

- Every collection, array, or list in the domain object should be represented as a separate table. This table should have a column (known as *Foreign Key*) that matches the primary key of the row that contains this collection.

- If there is a relationship from one domain object to another, the underlying table should have a column that contains a primary key of related objects. In some complex cases, there should be a separate mapping table with pairs of primary keys of related tables.

Looks complex? It might seem at the beginning. The process of rearranging complex domain objects into a set of tables with the minimum amount of redundancy is definitely a challenge. We already discussed a bit about this process, called normalization, as you may recall from Chapter 4.

Normalization enables us to avoid accidental mistakes and prevent data inconsistency. As an example, people use words like "inquiry" and "enquiry" interchangeably (some might consider "enquiry" to be a spelling mistake of "inquiry"). There are also lots of words in American and British English that are spelled with a slight difference (e.g., colour and color, center and centre). Let's imagine that you have an entity stored as a single row (or document in NoSQL document databases) that has type property with value "inquiry" and an array of tags where one tag is ".NET". Someone might insert another similar entity with type "enquiry" and "dotnet" as one of the tags. A functionality that searches entities by types and tags will return different results based on search criterion because clients will enter "inquiry" and "enquiry" or ".NET" and "dotnet" and you probably cannot implement sophisticated rules that understand these synonyms. In these cases, it might be a better idea to store values of types and tags in a separate table, assign them identifiers, and use these identifiers in entities. This way, someone might choose a standardized term that will be used, maybe a list of synonyms for that term, and searches will always return consistent results.

How can you do this correctly if you have never done it before? Luckily, creating a good model is an iterative application of the normalization rules, so we're not alone here. As normalization is all about avoiding potential data inconsistencies and redundancy, it is worth understanding why we absolutely try to avoid those at all costs.

Redundancy is not necessarily bad per se, but it surely brings challenges. Let's say, for example, that an Order Header shows that the order value is 100$, but then if you sum up all the items in the Order Details table for that specific order, you find a total value of 120$. Which one is correct? You don't know. Even worse, you *cannot* know the answer just by looking at the data you have, as data is inconsistent. Data is there, but information is lost. And this is just one example. There are several well-known *data anomalies* (for details, see https://aka.ms/sednda) that can be prevented by a correct normalization.

The normalization process will help you decompose objects into smaller pieces without losing any information. It is a "non-loss decomposition" process: it gives you the ability to always rebuild the original information when you need it. At the same time, it helps to avoid the perils of redundancy and thus inconsistency, favoring reuse of the smaller piece of information created as a result of its application.

We just have scratched the surface of this topic, and detailing the whole normalization process is beyond the scope of this book. You can start with the correct foot by keeping in mind that a good model is one where tables have scalar columns that depend *only* on the primary key and where foreign keys are used to reference and enforce relationships with other tables, so that information is never lost.

Normalization is an amazingly interesting topic, as is one of the few formal processes that can be applied to informatics: you can find more details about database design in the books referenced and at the end of this chapter.

So far, we focused on the logical aspect of database design: normalization and mapping of domain classes to a table are not the end of the process. To optimally design a table, you need to think about the following:

- What is the best way to define types and other properties for the columns in your table?

- How to optimize operations on your tables using indexes?

- What rules and constraints you want to define in your table to ensure that your data is valid?

- How to make your tables secure?

In the following sections, you will be presented some of the guidelines that can help you to answer these questions.

Creating tables

Azure SQL enables you to easily create a table without need to use graphical tools or generators. You can use a short CREATE TABLE statement to create a new table:

```
CREATE TABLE Customer (
    CustomerID tinyint,
    CustomerName varchar(max),
    LocationID bigint
);
```

Although it is easy to create a specification of a table with columns, this is still not table design. Proper table design is a process where you identify table characteristics that are the best fit for your application. By looking at the table definition in the previous example, we might ask ourselves few questions that would challenge the design:

- Could there be two customers with the same `CustomerID`? Do we need to ensure that no one might insert two customers with the same identifier?

- Is `tinyint` type a proper choice for ID of customer? `tinyint` column may contain only 256 different values, so would this be enough for all customers that we might have?

- `varchar(max)` type enables us to put strings with size up to 2GB; however, is this overkill? If we know that customer names cannot be longer than 100 characters, could we use some smaller type like `varchar(100)`?

- `varchar` types enable us to use most of the common characters from English and other Western languages. However, could we have some customer with some non-common Latin (e.g., Hungarian ű or ő or Slavic đ, č, or ć), Cyrillic (ђ, ч, or ħ), or Asian characters? In that case, `nvarchar` type might be a better choice.

- Should we ignore letter casing when we sort or compare customer names? Are there some other language rules that we need to apply?

- In `LocationID` column, we can store 2^{64} different locations, but do we really have so many locations? Could we use some smaller type?

- Is the `LocationID` value an identifier of some location in a separate table? In that case, how do we ensure that the value in `LocationID` exists in another table? How to ensure that location will not be deleted if there is still a customer that has an id of that location?

Proper table design should answer these questions and enable you to have the right solution for your table.

You may also have noticed that quite a few questions were around proper data type size. Today there is no shortage of space and resources, so spending time just to spare a bunch of bytes may seem a waste of time. Well, keep in mind that if your solution is successful, your database can easily contain literally billions of rows. Wasting space will not only mean wasting storage space but also more memory needs and higher CPU consumption. In the cloud, where you pay for what you use...well, I guess you figured it out already: more costs for exactly the same performance of an otherwise optimized model. Be a better developer!

Determine the right column types

When you design your table, you need to find a SQL column type for every data type from your application that you want to persist. You need to consider the following to effectively design your tables:

- Define column types that describe your data.

- Specify collations to define sorting and comparison rules for textual data.

- Use computed columns for pre-calculated expressions.

In the following sections, you will see some best practices and guidelines that you can use while you are defining your tables.

Define your column types

Most of the value types from application programming languages have a matching SQL type counterpart, from which you can quickly determine which SQL types to store the values from domain objects. There are also lots of tools that automatically generate table columns and their types based on the type of class properties (so-called Code First approach). Although you can use tools and deterministic mapping, it would be beneficial if you learn how to carefully examine and improve your table design. The main reason is the fact that you know more about the domain model than your tools, and you should not let an automatic generator create the most essential part of your application using a set of generic rules. Some examples of default mapping rules that might not be the best fit for your design are

- String types are by default mapped to NVARCHAR(MAX) type because it can contain any Unicode text with arbitrary string length (up to 2GB). The downside of this decision is that NVARCHAR(MAX) is a list of 4000-character strings, and therefore, it is suboptimal in many operations compared with the string types with the length less than

4000 characters. If you know that your text will have some length limit, try to use a more precise type like NVARCHAR(100), which might boost performance of your queries.

- Some languages, like C#, do not have fine-grained types for date and datetime. You might use DateTime type for dates even if you do not use time parts. These data values are mapped to datetime2. If you know that your DateTime values contain only dates without time, it would be more optimal to use the exact date type.

- Decimal numbers (float, real types) are mapped to decimal type. Instead of plain decimal type, in Azure SQL, you can explicitly specify how many decimal places it can have and that is the size. Size of decimal numbers might vary between 5 and 17 bytes per number depending on the precision. If you know that you are using a decimal number to store money where you have just two decimal places, and you know the maximal theoretical amount of money that your application will use, you can explicitly specify the size.

These examples are minor checks and adjustments that can make you a hero if you spend some time to validate the results of the default rules and improve them with your knowledge of the domain model.

General advice is to try to make your columns as small as possible and find the minimal SQL types for a given type. With appropriately sized smaller types, you can store the same amount of application data using a smaller amount of storage. Beyond storage savings, smaller types can positively impact query performances. Azure SQL database has an internal memory cache (known as SQL buffer pool) that contains a part of the data from persistent storage, increasing the speed of retrieval for that data. With unnecessarily large types, you waste the precious buffer pool space with unnecessarily padded data. Also, smaller types require fewer disk and network input/output operations which allows you to more quickly load or save data. Further, big columns can trick the Azure SQL query optimizer into reserving excess memory for the queries on those columns. The memory would not be leveraged, but since it is reserved for the queries, other queries may not get enough memory. In addition, data with a smaller memory footprint can be allocated to smaller and much faster memory cache layers. In some cases, you might find that query performance increases just because data does not have useless 0 values padded because someone chose a larger than necessary data type.

Some recommend to use globally unique identifier (GUID) values as the identifiers of your domain model objects to avoid dependency on databases that will generate object identifiers. The advantage of GUID is that you can assign the identity to the Model object in your app without consulting your database. However, the big disadvantage is the fact that GUID values are 16-byte long compared to `int` (4-byte) or `bigint` (8-byte). While storage consumption is not optimal, it is not the main concern here. Finding or joining the rows could be much slower if you unnecessarily used GUID values, as data is spread randomly everywhere, impacting a lot on cache efficiency, especially once your table grows after you go to production, especially if the solution is successful and it is used by a lot of users. Good design might prevent a lot of performance issues that might happen once your application faces a real scenario with millions of rows per table.

Collations

Collation is another important text property in Azure SQL. Differing collations enable you to define what linguistic rules should be used when Azure SQL compares or sorts the text values.

In standard programming languages, you use plain strings and you need to explicitly specify that you want to use case-insensitive comparison or sorting rules when you need it. For example, if you need to use some locale linguistic rules to sort strings in C#, you need to specify `CultureInfo` for the target language. In most programming languages, you need to specify case insensitivity or culture explicitly in some method. Azure SQL enables you to define language rules and case sensitivity, but it also enables some more advanced comparison and sorting rules like accent sensitivity, Kana sensitivity (to distinguish Japanese Hiragana and Katakana characters), or Variation selector sensitivity (to apply some fine-grained sorting rules in modern digital encodings).

You can easily set collation on any string column using a statement like the following one:

```
ALTER TABLE Warehouse.StockItems
    ALTER COLUMN Brand NVARCHAR(50)
    COLLATE Serbian_Cyrillic_100_CI_AI
```

This statement will specify that any string operation on the column will use Serbian linguistic rules and ignore casing (CI) and accents (AI) in strings. Changing the property of the column will automatically be applied on all sorting and comparison rules that use this column.

Azure SQL has collations for most of the world languages and enables you to turn on/off case, accent, or kana sensitivity rules for all of them. This is the huge benefit for you if you need to implement applications for global markets.

If you do not speak Japanese and you get a bug that some Japanese words in the application are incorrectly ordered, the last thing that you would like to do is start learning about the difference between Katakana and Hiragana just to fix the bug. This is the time when you would leverage the power of linguistic rules that Azure SQL provides and rely on the fact that Azure SQL can correctly sort results.

Another important property of text is encoding. Characters can be stored using different binary representations, and the rule that translates a character to its binary form is called encoding schema. Unicode standard assigned a unique numeric identifier (known as *code point*) to most of the relevant characters that are currently used (even emojis have their unique code points!). Encoding schema defines how to serialize characters or their code points as a series of bytes.

One of the simplest encoding schemas is ASCII that uses 7 bits to encode most common characters used in English language with one byte per character (e.g., code 0x5B is used for "]"). ASCII encoding supports only common characters used in English language, but not other characters used in Western or Latin languages such as ä, ö, ü, ñ, or ß. Windows-1252 and ISO-8859-1 are the extensions of ASCII that use 8 bits to encode a wider character set. These encoding schemas encode other common characters in Western languages. However, since these encoding schemas cannot represent characters used in the other languages, other nations derived their own 8-bit encoding schemas for national character sets. Examples of other national character sets are ISCII (India), VSCII (Vietnam), or YUSCII (former Yugoslavia). The single-byte national character sets use the code points in range up to 256 to represent common characters used in their national alphabets. Azure SQL uses varchar type to represent a character in some of the single-byte encoding schemas (although there are also some multi-byte codepages). To differentiate what national character set the encoded value belongs to some codepage, Azure SQL uses the column collation. If a binary value in the varchar column is 0xC6 and column collation is one of the Latin collations (codepage Windows-1250), Azure SQL will assume that this is character "Ć". If collation is one of the Serbian collations, Azure SQL will assume that this is character "Ж" (in `Serbian_Cyrillic` collations - codepage Windows-1251) or "Æ" (in `Serbian_Latin` collations - codepage Windows-1252). Identifying characters based on 8-bit code point and national character set is unnecessarily simplistic and error-prone, so Unicode standard uses multi-byte encoding space to encode characters from all languages with a different code point for every character. There are several encoding schemas for Unicode code points like UTF-8 where every character is represented using 1, 2, 3, or 4 bytes and UTF-16 where every character is represented using 2 or 4 bytes. Azure SQL uses a varchar type to represent Unicode characters with UTF-8 encoding, but these values must use a collation ending with UTF8. To represent UTF-16 encoding scheme Azure SQL uses `nvarchar` type, which is not dependent on collations.

Always use Unicode unless you are sure that characters in `string` columns have only limited known values. `nvarchar` type is a good choice in most of the scenarios. Although it uses 2 bytes even for common characters that can fit into one byte, Azure SQL has some optimization that automatically compresses these values. If you are really concerned about performance and want to optimize for common characters, you should use `varchar` type with a UTF-8 collation.

Computed columns

In addition to classic columns, you can use special computed columns that represent the named expressions. As an example, imagine that you have quantity of purchased products, price for each unit, and the tax rate. You could create a function that calculates the profit and provide the values of columns, but in some cases, it would be better to create an automatically re-calculated virtual column:

```
ALTER TABLE Sales.OrderLines
    ADD Profit AS (Quantity*UnitPrice)*(1-TaxRate)
```

An application that reads this table will get the profit value without need to know some function for profit calculation. For external applications, this value would look like yet another value in the table. This computed column does not occupy additional space, and it is dynamically re-calculated whenever some query uses it. This lightweight computed column is an ideal solution if the expressions can be quickly calculated. However, if you have some heavy calculation that requires string processing, you might want to permanently store calculated values until the base column changes. This way, you will use some additional space, but the queries will not wait for the calculation to finish for every row that should be returned. These types of computed columns are known as persisted computed columns and can be created by adding the keyword PERSISTED in the preceding example. The resulting code will be this:

```
ALTER TABLE Sales.OrderLines
    ADD Profit AS (Quantity*UnitPrice)*(1-TaxRate) PERSISTED
```

The values in persisted computed columns are automatically re-calculated whenever any of the base values is changed.

This may seem very similar to what you can get using a User-Defined Function, as you learned in the previous chapter: in fact, you could decide to use a User-Defined Function to create a calculated column if you want too. If you don't plan to use a User-Defined Function anywhere else, you may simply define the logic as an expression for a calculated column and you'll just save some code and effort.

Complex-type columns

Scalar-type columns are standard and the most used column types in relational databases. In most of the cases, you will be able to represent your domain model with normalized tables containing only scalar-type columns. However, in some scenarios, you would need to represent your application object with some non-scalar types. Azure SQL enables you to store the following types in the table columns:

- XML – Azure SQL enables you to store properly formatted XML documents in columns.

- Spatial columns contain some common elements that are used to represent geographical and geometrical concepts such as points, lines, polygons, and so on.

- CLR column – These columns contain serialized binary representation of .NET objects.

These types are not just a binary serialization of their application counterparts. Azure SQL enables you to apply some methods that are specific for these types. The following code example shows a Nearest Neighbor query that returns five cities that are closest to the given point:

```
DECLARE @g geography = 'POINT(-95 45.5)';
SELECT TOP(5) Location.ToString(), CityName
FROM Application.Cities
ORDER BY Location.STDistance(@g) ASC;
```

Spatial columns have methods such as STDistance that calculates the distance between the point and the location provided as an argument, making sure that correct calculations, for example, taking into account that the Earth is a spheroid and that there are several ways to project Earth surface on a map, are correctly applied. Not-so-easy trigonometric calculations are there for you to use for free!

Complex types in Azure SQL enable you to solve very specific problems that need some special handling that does beyond classic table types.

Azure SQL enables you to store JSON documents; however, there is no special JSON type. Azure SQL uses standard nvarchar type to store text in JSON format. This means that *any* programming language can support it without the need of special libraries.

Declarative constraints

One of the golden rules of application development is that the business rules should be implemented in the application layer. The purists may argue that pushing business logic to database Stored Procedures, Functions, and Triggers or on the client side might cause issues and maintenance nightmares. We discussed this a bit already, clearly describing the need to push compute to data, but let's set all the previously discussed reasons aside for a second, and let's focus on just Business Rules. Business Rules must stay in the application layer: is this always true? Let us look at some examples of business rules that you might need to implement:

- You must ensure that the email address or username of a person is unique. Are you going to query a table to check if there is another user with the same email before you create the new one?

- You must ensure that a product cannot be saved if it references some customer that does not exist. Are you going to read the customer table every time before you save the product just to ensure that nobody deleted the customer in the meantime?

- When you delete a customer from the system, all additional information (like documents) should be also deleted, except orders and invoices where you need to break the relationship with the customer and set a `null` value in the reference column. If the customer still has some active accounts, they should not be deleted. Are you going to query `Orders` and `Invoices` tables from the application layer to ensure that they will not return any result before you delete the product? This might be a non-trivial strategy that you need to implement and thoroughly test.

Although you can implement these rules in your application, it is arguable should you do it. The business rules that describe data state and behavior on some actions can be easily declared in the database. Those business rules, in fact, are closely tied to the data, up to the point that they really are more a kind of *data consistency* rules. Surely, it is always part of the big family of "business rules" definition, but, as always, generalizing too much can be more harmful than beneficial. In fact, by applying these rules at the database level, you can be sure that the data will be consistent with the business rules and that rules will be applied without a line of application code, following the golden principle of keeping things as simple as possible (but not simpler!) and also helping in establishing a good and clear separation of concerns. Data is definitely a database concern. In addition, there would be no additional performance impact on your action because you would not need to run additional queries within the main action just to validate additional rules or implement some side activities. So, you'll also get better performance. This should help you better understand up to which degree business rules should be applied in the application layer and which should be applied on the database.

Azure SQL enables you to enhance your tables and declaratively define the rules that will ensure that the data is valid using the following constraints:

- Primary keys enable you to specify that a column (or a set of columns) holds a unique identifier of the object.

- Foreign keys specify that an object (table row) logically belongs to some other object or it is somehow related to that object. This is known as *referential integrity,* and it guarantees that the relationship between the two rows bounded with foreign key and primary key cannot be accidentally broken.

- Check constraints are the conditions that should be checked on every object. These constraints guarantee that some condition would always be true on the data that is saved in the table. You can implement these checks as a last line of defense, so even if your application code fails to check some condition or you have multiple services that can update the same data, you can be sure the database will guarantee that the condition must always be true.

- Unique constraints guarantee that a value is unique in the column. They are almost like primary keys (a big difference is that they allow for null values) and can be used for values like usernames or email addresses.

Azure SQL enables you to declaratively specify these constraints without need to implement them. The following declarations describe relations between a customer and their invoices and orders. These declarations would also specify what the action should be taken on related data once a customer is deleted. When someone tries to delete the customer, this relationship would delete all customer invoices:

```
ALTER TABLE Sales.Invoices
ADD CONSTRAINT FK_Cust_Inv FOREIGN KEY (CustomerID)
    REFERENCES Sales.Customers (CustomerID) ON DELETE CASCADE;
```

The following declaration will stop the customer delete action if there is some order for the customer:

```
ALTER TABLE Sales.Orders
ADD CONSTRAINT FK_Cust_Orders FOREIGN KEY (CustomerID)
    REFERENCES Sales.Customers (CustomerID) ON DELETE NO ACTION;
```

With a few lines of code, you can easily implement business rules that might be hard to code (and especially test) in your application layer. Using these built-in constraints, you can rely on Azure SQL to maintain data integrity without any effort in your application logic.

Making your tables secure

Azure SQL enables you to associate fine-grained permissions to any user or login that can access your database. Let us imagine that you have a Sales microservice that manages information about the sales orders. This microservice accesses the Azure SQL database using the login `SalesMicroservice` that should be able to read or insert `Sales.Orders` table but not to update or delete data. It should just be able to read information about Customers and Invoices. For some custom actions, it might use only procedures that are placed in the Sales schema. A minimum set of permissions required for this microservice can be defined using the following rules:

```
GRANT SELECT, INSERT ON OBJECT::Sales.Orders TO SalesMicroservice
GRANT SELECT ON OBJECT::Sales.Customers TO SalesMicroservice
GRANT SELECT ON OBJECT::Sales.Invoices TO SalesMicroservice
GRANT EXECUTE ON SCHEMA::Sales TO SalesMicroservice
```

These are easy to write and review security rules that you can define in your database. This security model is important in the architectures such as Command Query Responsibility Segregation (CQRS) where you have separate processes that are allowed only to read or update data. Assigning the minimum required set of permissions would ensure that you are not vulnerable to various security attacks such as SQL Injection or unauthorized changes. The security rules in Azure SQL database are the last line of defense of your data that should prevent data breaches even if there is some security hole in your application layer.

If you need to examine permissions assigned to users, you can log in as the user or impersonate as user and check the permissions using `fn_my_permissions` function:

```
EXECUTE AS USER = 'SalesMicroservice';
SELECT * FROM fn_my_permissions('Sales.Customers', 'OBJECT');
REVERT;
```

In addition to manual inspection, there is a Vulnerability Assessment tool built into any Azure SQL that automatically inspects permissions assigned to the users and makes recommendations.

147

Improve performance with indexes

A table, unless you create a *clustered index* on it (you'll learn about this in a few pages; for now, just keep in mind that by default a primary key also creates a clustered index behind the scenes), is a set of rows physically stored in the area like the heap memory in .NET, Java, and other modern programming languages or runtime environments. That kind of table is called a *heap table* in Azure SQL terminology.

A classic heap table can be useful in an extremely limited set of scenarios (like scanning small tables or appending rows). However, the most expected operations in Azure SQL database would be finding the row by identifier (primary key), finding or updating a set by some criterion, and so on. These common operations are extremely inefficient on a plain set of rows organized as heaps. As you will soon learn, even a plain scanning of the entire table is more efficient if we use some special Columnstore format.

Azure SQL enables you to use *indexes* to enhance this basic structure and speed up the access to the rows in various scenarios. Indexes are the structures of row addresses that enable you to organize the rows in your table or build a structure that the queries can use more efficiently than a basic table. There are several kinds of indexes in Azure SQL:

- B-tree indexes that represent multi-level tree-like structures of pointers. These indexes enable you to easily locate one or a set or rows without scanning the entire table.

- Columnstore indexes organize data in columnar format instead of default row format. These structures, which will be described in the next chapter, are an excellent solution for speeding up reporting and analytic queries that scan large parts of the table.

- Domain-specific indexes are special types of indexes built to efficiently support some non-standard structures or data types. Azure SQL supports Spatial indexes, Full-text indexes, and XML indexes. These indexes enable you to run some non-standard filters like containment of the coordinate within the area, XPath expression, filtering based on proximity of two words in the text, and so on.

B-Tree indexes are the most common structure that you will find and use in any
Azure SQL database (and more generally in any database, relational or not). B-tree
indexes and tables are so tightly coupled that we cannot talk about them separately.
In Azure SQL terminology, they are called Hobits (HOBT – Heap or B-Tree), and they
represent the most common structures in most databases.

Columnstore and domain-specific indexes are advanced concepts that will be
explained in future chapters.

B-Tree indexes

A B-Tree index is a hierarchical structure of nodes divided by the values present in the
table columns. It's very common in all relational and non-relational databases, as it
is extremely efficient and computationally simple. This is a Composite design pattern
described in the famous *Design Patterns* book written by Erich Gamma et al. In the
B-Tree index, every leaf node has references to table rows, and non-leaf nodes have
references to other nodes. These multi-level tree-like structures enable you to easily
locate one or a set of rows. Every B-Tree index has a so-called key column(s). The values
from this column(s) are used to search the rows for the desired values.

Figure 6-2 shows an index that divides pointers to rows using Price column.

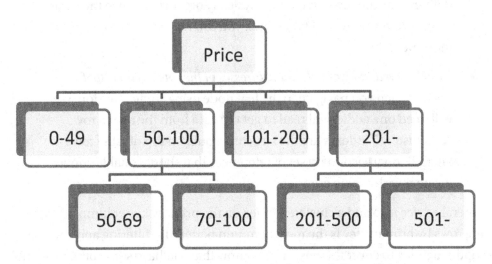

Figure 6-2. *Dividing rows into groups using index on Price column*

Under the root node, you have a set of groups representing the ranges of rows based on the value of the `Price` column. Each group might contain references to the rows with these values or references to other nodes with more granular ranges. Imagine that we need to find a set of rows with `Price` equal to 73. Starting from the root, we can locate the node that represents a range of references to the rows with `Price` values between 50 and 100. This node would lead us to the node that contains the references to the rows with `Price` column in the range between 70 and 100. This is the leaf node that contains the addresses of the rows, and we can search the list of references in this node to find the ones with desired value. The number of references in the leaf node is not big, so the rows are found quickly.

Leaf nodes in the index are lists of rows or row addresses, and these lists should not be big to make sure performance is always optimal. If the number of references goes above a defined limit, Azure SQL will split the node into two nodes (action known as page split).

Leaf nodes might contain the references (addresses) of table rows or the cells placed in actual table rows. Therefore, we have the following types of indexes:

- *Clustered indexes hold actual rows in their leaf nodes.* When you navigate to the leaf node using some criterion, you will find the actual row. Clustered indexes physically organize table rows. Their structure defines how the rows would be physically organized. Since there can be only one structure of table rows, you can have only one clustered index per table.

- *Nonclustered indexes hold the addresses of the rows in their leaf nodes.* When you navigate to the leaf node using some criterion, you will need one additional read to get the data from the actual row. Nonclustered indexes are the structures built on top of table rows as an additional secondary set of references that should enable you to locate rows by some criterion.

General advice is to add a clustered index on the primary key column because filtering rows by primary key is the most common pattern for filtering and you want the most optimal index to cover this case. If you know that you have some other dominant pattern, you can choose some other column for clustered index (e.g., foreign key or some date column).

Nonclustered indexes are additional utility structures that optimize the queries that are common but not dominant. You can add several nonclustered indexes, and the query optimizer will choose the one that is the best fit for the query.

Let's see in detail when to use what.

When to use B-Tree indexes?

B-Tree indexes are the most common type of the indexes that you will find in Azure SQL databases. Their structure can help us in the following scenarios:

- Index seeks operation that locates a single row or a set of rows with the specified values of columns.

- Range scans operation that locates a set of rows that have values in some range.

The indexes might be a helpful performance booster in the following queries:

```
SELECT c.CustomerName, c.CreditLimit,
       o.CustomerPurchaseOrderNumber, o.DeliveryInstructions
FROM Sales.Customers AS c
INNER JOIN Sales.Orders AS o
ON c.CustomerID = o.CustomerID
WHERE c.PostalCityID = 42
```

Azure SQL would need to read the Customers table to find all customers with PostalCityID value 42. Then, it would need to read the Orders table to find orders with values of CustomerID column that match the CustomerID values fetched from the first read. It might be very inefficient to scan the entire table just to fetch a few rows. Let us see what will happen if we create the following indexes:

```
CREATE INDEX ix_Customer_PostalCityID
       ON Sales.Customers(PostalCityID);

CREATE INDEX ix_Orders_CustomerID
       ON Sales.Orders(CustomerID);
```

With an index on the Customers table that has a PostalCityID column, Azure SQL would use the created index to quickly locate the Customers rows with the given PostalCityID. Then it will find the orders in the second index based on CustomerID values. As you can imagine, in large tables, this can be a huge performance benefit, not to mention less resource, CPU, RAM, and IO usage, which in turn means better scalability for lower costs.

When to create indexes?

People are sometimes tempted to optimize a database by adding various indexes whenever they believe that they might help. Some people even believe that automatic indexes created on every column might be the holy grail of database design. However, you need to be aware what the price of indexes is before you create them.

Indexes are not silver bullets that will always boost performance of your queries. They might be a perfect solution in read-only workloads because they give more choices for better execution plans, while the worst impact is just some additional space that they occupy. However, for write operations, they represent a burden because every index that contains the updated value must be updated together with the table. If you have a table with five indexes, there is a chance that every insert, delete, and many update statements would need to update not just the primary table but also all indexes.

You should not add indexes blindly on every column or foreign key because this might hurt your database performance. Some generic guidelines that you can use to choose where to add the indexes are:

- You can start by creating clustered indexes on primary key columns, because the most common operation on a table is finding a row by primary key value.

- Tables might need to have nonclustered indexes on foreign keys because you might expect that queries would need to read all rows with foreign key value.

- If you find some important query for your application that is slow, you might need to create an index on the columns that the query uses.

As the complexity of your database and solution increases, you may find that a very common query that returns all the orders done in the last day using the `OrderDate` column. In such cases, it may be useful to create the clustered index on that column, so all the orders done on the same date will be physically close together. Remember, in fact, that the clustered index holds rows in its leaf level and that rows are ordered by the columns on which the index is created. This means that Azure SQL can start to read from the first order placed in the day and can stop once the last is found, optimizing the reads to the minimum possible. Of course, as there is only one clustered index, you need to carefully evaluate this strategy based on your knowledge of how the application works and how users mostly use it.

As you can see, determining the correct indexes is not an easy task. For this reason, there are various tools like Performance Dashboard in SQL Server Management Studio, Database Tuning Advisor, or open source scripts like Tiger Toolbox or First Responder Kit (reference to both in the links at the end of the chapter) that can provide a list of indexes that you might need to create. Always use tools to prove that you need an index before you create it. Over-indexing and rarely used indexes are two of the most common causes of performance issues.

Azure SQL has a set of intelligent features like Automatic tuning that provides recommendations about the indexes that you might need to create. This is the best way to identify missing indexes because the recommendations are powered by machine learning algorithms trained on the substantial number of databases in Azure SQL. Even better, you can let the Azure SQL Automatic tuning capability automatically create indexes for you. The main benefit of the Automatic tuning capability is that it verifies that the created index would improve performance of your queries. Azure SQL has built-in machine learning models that measure performance of the database workload before and after index creation, identify the queries that are affected by the index, and check whether the query performance is improved or degraded. If the performance improvement is not big enough or if the new index degrades performance, the change will be reverted. In addition, Automatic tuning scans the usage of your indexes and recommends to you the indexes that should be dropped. Another important benefit is that Automatic tuning combines index recommendations to provide the best indexes. As an example, if there are two recommendations, one to create index on column A and another to create index on columns A and B, Azure SQL index recommendation will recommend only the second one, because it can also cover the queries that need only column A.

Maintaining the indexes

Indexes are updated whenever the data in the indexed columns is changed. Initially, the created index is a perfectly balanced tree that provides optimal performance. However, on an actively used database, the underlying data changes over time, making the index unbalanced and leaving some nodes half-populated. Index maintenance operations regenerate the indexes and return them in better state. There are two maintenance operations that you can perform on indexes:

- REBUILD is an operation that fully re-creates the index, drops the old structure, and re-creates a new perfectly balanced index. This operation guarantees that your index will be in the perfect shape at the cost of the resources that it uses.

- REORGANIZE is an operation that reshuffles the data in the parts of indexes trying to fill the unused space and balance parts of the indexes. This is a very lightweight operation that usually doesn't affect your application performances or consume a lot of resources, but on the other hand, it might not be able to fix all problems.

The SQL statement that re-creates the index is shown in the following example:

```
ALTER INDEX FK_Sales_Customers_DeliveryCityID ON Sales.Customers
    REBUILD WITH ( ONLINE = ON);
```

If you want to reorganize the index, you will just replace REBUILD keyword with REORGANIZE. One interesting optional option in this statement is the ONLINE option. There are two ways to rebuild the indexes:

- OFFLINE is the default option that is the fastest way to rebuild your index, but it will block any query that might touch the data in indexed columns.

- ONLINE enables your workload to change the data since it will pick up any changes that are made in the meantime. This is a more flexible operation, but it might consume more resources than OFFLINE version and might affect performance until it finishes.

These options are available only in REBUILD actions. REORGANIZE is always ONLINE.

The most important questions in index maintenance are what is the option that we should use and on what indexes. Rebuilding or reorganizing all indexes will just spend the resources that should be used for queries, and most of the indexes might not even need any maintenance. The criterion that is commonly used to determine the health state of the indexes is fragmentation. Fragmentation is the percentage of space in the index that contains indexed data.

The following query returns fragmentation of all indexes for a provided database and object where indexes should be scanned:

```
DECLARE @db_id int = DB_ID('Wide World Importers');
DECLARE @object_id int = OBJECT_ID('Sales.Customers');

SELECT index_id, partition_number, avg_fragmentation_in_percent
FROM sys.dm_db_index_physical_stats(@db_id, @object_id, NULL, NULL ,
'LIMITED');
```

In the result of the query, you can find index_id, partition_number, and fragmentation, so you can find the fragmented indexes using system views such as sys.indexes. Notice the last parameter in the function – LIMITED. Investigating fragmentation of indexes is not a lightweight operation especially on large indexes, and you can specify whether you would like to get approximate results by scanning a limited part of the index, calculate statistics from a sample, or analyze the entire index.

The action that you need to take on the index depends on the fragmentation. Some general rules of thumb are as follows:

- If fragmentation of the index is between 5% and 30%, use REORGANIZE operation.

- If fragmentation is greater than 30% and you can find some period where the table will not be used (a.k.a. Maintenance period), use OFFLINE REBUILD operation.

- If your table is frequently used and you cannot block the application workload, use ONLINE REBUILD operation.

You can also use proven open source scripts that can help you to identify candidates for maintenance and apply recommended actions. The most commonly used scripts for index maintenance are Ola Hallengren scripts and SQL Tiger Toolbox.

Resumability is another important index maintenance strategy. If you cannot avoid potentially expensive REBUILD action and you don't have a maintenance period, Azure SQL enables you to temporarily pause a rebuild and resume it later. This is an excellent choice in the cases where you find out that index maintenance affects performance of your application and need to hold off index rebuild, let your application finish some job, and then continue with maintenance without losing the work that is already done.

Retiring the indexes

Creating indexes is easy, but the more important question is "are they used or are they causing more harm than benefit?" Over-indexing might cause big performance issues. Even if you have an ideal set of indexes, your application patterns and database workload will change over time, and some of the indexes may need to be removed, as not used anymore. Eventually, you would need to retire and drop some indexes.

Experienced database administrators can easily identify the unnecessary indexes by looking at system views and query execution plans, or by examining the number of logical reads when setting STATISTICS IO option. If deep expertise in this area is not one of your career goals, you might again rely on the benefits that Azure SQL provides. In addition to index creation recommendations, Azure SQL provides drop index recommendations. Azure SQL scans usage of your indexes to identify unused indexes. It can also identify duplicate indexes that should be dropped. You can either take the scripts and drop the indexes or let Azure SQL clean up the indexes for you. Azure SQL will not just drop and forget the index. Automatic tuning will use the same algorithm that is used for index creation and monitor if the drop index operation decreased performance. Azure SQL will re-create the dropped index if it detects performance issues.

If you want to know more

The knowledge that you gained in this chapter enables you to professionally create proper database designs and understand the issues that you might find in databases. The concepts explained in this chapter represent the core knowledge required for database design. In the next chapter, we will go one step further – you will understand how to use some advanced concepts and types of tables and indexes that can improve the performance of your database.

To know more about the topics mentioned in this chapter, you can start from these resources:

- Database Design and Relational Theory: Normal Forms and All That Jazz – www.amazon.com/Database-Design-Relational-Theory-Normal-ebook/dp/B082X1B6WP

- Expert Performance Indexing in SQL Server – www.amazon.com/Expert-Performance-Indexing-SQL-Server/dp/1484211197

- Design Patterns: Elements of Reusable Object-Oriented Software – www.amazon.com/Design-Patterns-Elements-Reusable-Object-Oriented/dp/0201633612

- Domain-Driven Design: Tackling Complexity in the Heart of Software – www.amazon.com/Domain-Driven-Design-Tackling-Complexity-Software-ebook/dp/B00794TAUG

- Databases: Explaining Data Normalization, Data Anomalies and DBMS Keys – https://towardsdatascience.com/softly-explained-data-normalization-data-anomalies-and-dbms-keys-f8122aefaeb3

- Heaps & Indexes – https://docs.microsoft.com/sql/relational-databases/indexes/heaps-tables-without-clustered-indexes

- Tiger Toolbox – https://github.com/microsoft/tigertoolbox

- First Responder Kit – https://github.com/BrentOzarULTD/SQL-Server-First-Responder-Kit

- sp_WhoIsActive – https://github.com/amachanic/sp_whoisactive

CHAPTER 7

Scalability, Consistency, and Performance

Scalability, as generally defined, is the property of a system to handle a growing amount of work by adding resources to the system. In cloud platforms, where massive standardization and "economy of scale" principles are driving hardware design, the ability to just add resources to a single instance of a service may be limited. That is why, in addition to adopting scale-out architectures, an equally important aspect of scalability will be to design and tune your workload so that it can maximize resource utilization. If you are designing a brand-new application or have the chance to modify an existing one before migrating, this will also tangibly reduce your cloud bills.

While scalability is certainly a key attribute, consistency is another critical aspect that we should expect from a RDBMS solution. Transactional systems are making sure that data will remain in a consistent state after applications and users' interactions, and the underlying engine is responsible to govern how multiple concurrent activities from different users will access data to maintain this consistency, based on configurable attributes like the level of isolation between these transactional activities.

Consistency is really a key factor in application development, even if it is quite often overlooked: many developers still think that consistency is optional. In some edge cases, it may be true; in most cases, it is not. In fact, it is not by chance that lately RDBMS has become again at the center of the stage. In the famous paper "F1: A Distributed SQL Database That Scales," Google clearly stated that "Designing applications to cope with concurrency anomalies in their data is very error-prone, time consuming, and ultimately not worth the performance gains." And if consistency is not taken care of right into the database, guess who will be asked to write code to deal with it? Right, you, the developer. That's because your users will, instead, take consistency for granted. So, someone or

159

something must have to deal with it – at scale, of course. And database-level consistency at scale is the reason why a whole new generation of post-relational databases like Google Spanner, Amazon Aurora, and Azure SQL Hyperscale came to light.

Transactions

Transactions are units of work within a given application logic that it may be composed of multiple lower-level tasks. Transactions are known also as "Unit Of Work," a very well-known pattern that keeps track of changes and that logically commits or rolls back them as a whole, also described by Martin Fowler in his *Patterns of Enterprise Application Architecture* book. Database systems process transactions while maintaining what are known as *ACID* properties (*Atomicity, Consistency, Isolation*, and *Durability*) to guarantee data integrity and accuracy. Canonical examples of business logic for a transaction can be a money transfer between bank accounts or an ATM cash withdrawal, where you want to make sure a number of operations are happening following the "all or nothing" logic. A database platform helps enforcing these ACID properties without requiring complex implementations from an application standpoint: developers won't need to manually implement logic that reverts update actions if at least one update fails.

Now, you may be very familiar with this sample, and you may be thinking that you're not going to write a banking application, so you don't really need transactions. While this line of thought can be apparently correct, keep in mind that even in the simplest application, let's say a blog engine, you may have the need to use transactions. Let's say, in fact, that you want to keep track of how many people visit your blog, keeping the count both for the whole blog and for each post you have written. Since you want to be sure you can scale as much as needed, you have two counters, one for the whole blog and one for each article. Each time someone visits a page, you need to increment the counter for the whole website and the counter for that page. What happens if you don't implement and manage transactions properly?

It could happen that, for any reason, something crashes after the website counter has been updated but before the post counter is updated too. This means that now you have completely lost the information. Consistency is gone. If you try to sum up all the single counters, the result will be different than the site counter. Which value is correct now? You may be able to rebuild the information – maybe – with a lot of dedication, time, and effort. In many cases, you just can't. Now, for a blog counter, that's not a big deal (and even this is not true, what if you get paid by the number of visits to your blog?), but it gives you the importance of consistency, and thus transactions, even in places where maybe you haven't thought. Data consistency should be the cornerstone of every system. Without it, data is just noise.

Luckily for us, in modern database systems, ACID properties are usually achieved through write-ahead logging (WAL) which is a capability that provides atomicity and durability by recording changes in the transaction log at first and only later are written to the database by a recurring background process referred to as *checkpoint*. The log is usually storing both redo and undo information that will be used to recover whatever transaction was already committed, but not yet written in the database, in situations like recovering from a power loss or during a database restore.

Note   If you are an Apache Kafka user, you may find a lot of similarities between the WAL technique and the Immutable Log principle used by Apache Kafka. Everything is an event, stored in the log, in both cases. By reading the log forward or backward, you can redo or undo any action and even stop at a desired point in time. This is exactly why RDBMS like Azure SQL guarantees the end user that no data will be lost and everything can be recovered and the point in time they desire.

In Azure SQL, you can think of several use cases where using a transaction can help. As an example, you may want to insert, update, or delete multiple rows from a table as a single unit or batch process rather than going one by one. Similarly, you may need to modify the state of a table when, and only when, other tables in the same or in a different database (or even server) have been modified as well. As these systems can process multiple of these operations concurrently, Azure SQL engine will protect consistency, generally, by placing locks on various resources involved in these transactions (base tables, index keys, etc.), with a level of granularity that can span from a single row to the entire database, depending on how concurrency (also known as isolation) settings have been configured. These locks will be released once transactions will be committed or rolled back. Locks are just one of the options, probably the simplest, that Azure SQL can use to make sure data stays consistent. Another, much more sophisticated, is the ability to keep different versions of the same row active at the same time, serving the correct version to the requesting transaction, guaranteeing consistency even if other transactions are changing that very same row. Discussion of this technique, known as *row versioning*, is way out of the scope of this book: just keep in mind that Azure SQL will use a mix of the two to make sure you have the best possible experience and performance by default.

Tip   Keeping your transactions as short in duration as possible is a best practice that will help increase concurrency on your database objects and reducing system resources needed to maintain locks or row versions.

Applications can control transactions by specifying when a transaction starts and ends, successfully or not, through either Transact-SQL commands or API functions exposed by client drivers. Transactions are usually managed at the connection level: when a transaction is started on a connection, all Transact-SQL statements executed on that connection are part of the transaction until the transaction ends.

Note   An exception to this behavior is when you have a multiple active resultset (MARS) session. MARS is a feature that can be turned on through a connection string attribute and will let an application to execute a command on a connection while there is already an active resultset opened on the same connection. A typical scenario is while you are cycling over a series of rows retrieved by a SELECT query and you want to execute an UPDATE command using the same connection. In this case, a transaction will be scoped at the batch level (instead of at the connection level), and when it completes, Azure SQL will automatically roll it back if the transaction is not explicitly committed or rolled back.

Transactions in Azure SQL are defined **explicit** when you explicitly define start and end through an API function (e.g., BeginTransaction() method in .NET languages) or by issuing T-SQL statements like BEGIN TRANSACTION, COMMIT TRANSACTION, COMMIT WORK, ROLLBACK TRANSACTION, or ROLLBACK WORK.

When you do not explicitly initiate a transaction, but execute a single command against Azure SQL, then the default mode is called **auto-commit**. In this mode, every T-SQL statement is committed or rolled back when it completes. If a statement completes successfully, it is committed; if it encounters any error, it is rolled back. Auto-commit mode is also the default mode in which client drivers like ADO, OLE DB, ODBC, and DB-Library operate.

The third mode we have is called **implicit**. In this mode, Azure SQL starts a new transaction after the current transaction is committed or rolled back. There is nothing to do to start off a transaction; you only commit or roll back each transaction. This last mode is mainly implemented for compliance and backward compatibility reasons. In most use cases, your applications will use auto-commit when executing simple database commands, and controlling complex transactions is not strictly needed. Switch to explicit mode is recommended when some more complex specific transactional behavior needs to be managed. Transaction mode settings are controllable at connection level by issuing an explicit T-SQL statement. Different client drivers may have different transaction mode default settings and are invoking T-SQL statements for you when a new connection is established, so it's important to check in the documentation what's the behavior of the one you're using.

Local transactions

As an application developer, you will mostly interact with transactions executed within the context of a single Azure SQL database instance, and these are usually referred as *local transactions*, to differentiate from distributed transactions that we will discuss later on. In this scenario, local transactions are commonly used while wrapped in some more complex business logic inside a Stored Procedure, which is usually the recommended approach to keep transactions short in duration and avoid multiple roundtrips between application and database code. If, for whatever reason, you are not relying on Stored Procedures but are writing your database access command within your application code, you can control transactional behavior by invoking specific commands exposed through client drivers' APIs.

Here is an example of how to use explicit transactions within a T-SQL script like a Stored Procedure. In our system, there are two main tables: `Orders` and `Inventory`; every time a new order is placed for a given product, we need to decrement its quantity in stock. Business logic in our system must prevent placing a new order for an article that is running out of stock. Out of many ways of implementing such a logic, in our sample we're wrapping both new order's placement and decrementing the inventory for the same article in an explicit transaction:

```
-- Create table structures
CREATE TABLE dbo.Orders (ID int PRIMARY KEY, ProductID int, OrderDate
datetime);
```

```
CREATE TABLE dbo.Inventory (ProductID int PRIMARY KEY, QuantityInStock int
                            CONSTRAINT CHK_QuantityInStock CHECK
                            (QuantityInStock>-1));

-- Fill up with some sample values
INSERT INTO dbo.Orders VALUES (1,1,getdate());
INSERT INTO dbo.Inventory VALUES (1,100);

-- Begin an explicit transaction
BEGIN TRANSACTION mytran
-- Try executing the unit of work in app logic
BEGIN TRY
    INSERT INTO Orders VALUES (2,1,getdate());
    UPDATE Inventory SET QuantityInStock=QuantityInStock-1 WHERE ProductID=1
    -- If both commands are successful, commit the transaction
    COMMIT TRANSACTION
END TRY
BEGIN CATCH
    -- If there is an error, capture the details
    SELECT
            ERROR_NUMBER() AS ErrorNumber
          , ERROR_SEVERITY() AS ErrorSeverity
          , ERROR_STATE() AS ErrorState
          , ERROR_PROCEDURE() AS ErrorProcedure
          , ERROR_LINE() AS ErrorLine
          , ERROR_MESSAGE() AS ErrorMessage;
    -- Explicitly rollback the transaction
    ROLLBACK TRANSACTION
END CATCH

SELECT * FROM dbo.Orders
SELECT * FROM dbo.Inventory
```

In this script, after creating and filling a couple of tables, you can find the BEGIN
TRANSACTION statement followed by an (optional) name.

The BEGIN TRY block will try to execute all statements until the END TRY, and if they will all be executed without errors, the transaction will be permanently committed by the COMMIT TRANSACTION statement.

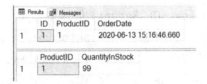

Figure 7-1. *Successful transaction results*

We now change the quantity in stock for our product and we set it to zero, as we want to test what happens when running out of stock, and then we try to run the transaction again:

```
UPDATE dbo.Inventory SET QuantityInStock=0 WHERE ProductID=1
```

	ErrorNumber	ErrorSeverity	ErrorState	ErrorProcedure	ErrorLine	ErrorMessage
1	547	16	0	NULL	6	The UPDATE statement conflicted with the CHECK constraint "CHK_QuantityInStock". The conflict occurred in database "WideWorldImporters-Full", table "dbo.Inventory", column 'QuantityInStock'.

	ID	ProductID	OrderDate
1	1	1	2020-06-13 15:16:46.660

	ProductID	QuantityInStock
1	1	0

Figure 7-2. *Transaction rollback results*

In this case, an error will be thrown while executing the UPDATE Inventory statement as we are violating the CHECK constraint placed on the QuantityInStock attribute. Control will pass from with the BEGIN TRY block to the BEGIN CATCH block. In that block, we're retrieving all the details related to the latest error happened in that session, but we're also explicitly calling ROLLBACK TRANSACTION to make sure that modifications made to other tables as part of the same transaction, in the sample INSERT INTO Orders command, will not be persisted, and system's state will be consistent.

Let's see how the same behavior can be achieved developing a sample application using Python.

Listing 7-1. Example of using transactions in Python

```
import os
import pyodbc
from decouple import config
```

```python
server = config('server')
database = config('database')
username = config('username')
password = config('password')
driver= '{ODBC Driver 17 for SQL Server}'
# Connecting to Azure SQL Database with autocommit=True
cnxn = pyodbc.connect('DRIVER='+driver+';SERVER='+server+';PORT=1433;
DATABASE='+database+';UID='+username+';PWD='+ password,autocommit=True)

def prepare_database():
    try:
        # Executing database preparation tasks
        cursor = cnxn.cursor()
        cursor.execute("""IF (EXISTS (SELECT *  FROM INFORMATION_
        SCHEMA.TABLES
                        WHERE TABLE_SCHEMA = 'dbo'
                        AND  TABLE_NAME = 'Orders'))
                        BEGIN
                            DROP TABLE [dbo].[Orders];
                        END

                        IF (EXISTS (SELECT *  FROM INFORMATION_
                        SCHEMA.TABLES
                        WHERE TABLE_SCHEMA = 'dbo'
                        AND  TABLE_NAME = 'Inventory'))
                        BEGIN
                            DROP TABLE [dbo].[Inventory];
                        END

                        CREATE TABLE [dbo].[Orders] (ID int PRIMARY KEY,
                        ProductID int, OrderDate datetime);
                        CREATE TABLE [dbo].[Inventory] (ProductID int
                        PRIMARY KEY, QuantityInStock int
                          CONSTRAINT CHK_QuantityInStock CHECK
                          (QuantityInStock>-1));
```

```
                            -- Fill up with some sample values
                            INSERT INTO dbo.Orders VALUES (1,1,getdate());
                            INSERT INTO dbo.Inventory VALUES (1,0);
                            """)
        except pyodbc.DatabaseError as err:
            # Catch if there's an error
            print("Couldn't prepare database tables")

def execute_transaction():
    try:
        # Switching to autocommit = False, our app can now control
          transactional behavior
        cnxn.autocommit = False
        cursor = cnxn.cursor()
        cursor.execute("INSERT INTO Orders VALUES (2,1,getdate());")
        cursor.execute("UPDATE Inventory SET QuantityInStock=Quantity
        InStock-1 WHERE ProductID=1")
    except pyodbc.DatabaseError as err:
        # If there's a database error, roll back the transaction
        cnxn.rollback()
        print("Transaction rolled back: " + str(err))
    else:
        # If database commands were successful, commit the transaction
        cnxn.commit()
        print("Transaction committed!")
    finally:
        cnxn.autocommit = True

prepare_database()
execute_transaction()
```

In this example, you can see how the *auto-commit* property plays an important role when controlling transactions with *pyodbc* in Python. We're opening the connection with *autocommit=True*, which means that each command will be automatically committed once executed. In the *prepare_database()* method in fact, we're executing some preparation activities in the database, and these will be executed as a single transaction. In the *execute_transaction()* method though, we're explicitly switching to *autocommit=False*, so that we can programmatically control when to commit or roll back our logical unit of work. Remember that our application logic is enforced with a CHECK constraint that prevents placing new orders when a given product is out of stock.

By executing this code sample, you will get back this error message and database tables will not be modified as the transaction is rolled back:

```
Transaction rolled back: ('23000', '[23000] [Microsoft][ODBC Driver
17 for SQL Server][SQL Server] The UPDATE statement conflicted with
the CHECK constraint "CHK_QuantityInStock". The conflict occurred in
database "WideWorldImporters-Full", table "dbo.Inventory", column
\'QuantityInStock\'. (547) (SQLExecDirectW)')
```

In this very simple example, we're reacting to the exception raised when we're getting an error executing a database operation, but there are other scenarios where our application logic requires to check on a specific state of a given entity in the database (by querying a table) and then decide whether commit or roll back the entire unit of work as a whole.

Naming a transaction can be a useful practice that improves code readability and, maybe more important, will be reflected in various transaction-related system views simplifying the debugging process. BEGIN TRANSACTION [transaction_name] starts a local transaction, but nothing is effectively written in the transaction log until further data manipulation actions such as INSERT, UPDATE, or DELETE are triggering an update to the log (although it may be that other activities like acquiring locks to protect the transaction isolation level of SELECT statements can happen).

An application or a script can begin, and even commit or roll back, a transaction where another transaction already exists. Azure SQL does not really provide direct support for nested transactions, and committing a transaction opened within another has absolutely no effect. Only outer transactions will effectively control what happens to various data manipulation activities executed on various transactions in between, committing or rolling back everything. As application developers, we should not really use this approach to avoid misleading behaviors and consequences.

So why are nested transactions allowed at all? Well, a common scenario where they can be used is when you are writing Stored Procedures containing transactional logic that can be invoked either stand-alone or from an outer procedure that may have itself already initiated a transaction. A good practice is always to check if there's already an open transaction on that connection using the @@TRANCOUNT system variable and then decide if to start a new one or just participate in the one started by the outer procedure and marking the start of the inner part of the transaction with a SAVE TRANSACTION savepoint_name.

Every time a new BEGIN TRANSACTION is executed, @@TRANCOUNT will be incremented by 1. Same will be decremented by 1 every time COMMIT TRANSACTION will be executed. In case of a ROLLBACK TRANSACTION, all transactions will be rolled back and @@TRANCOUNT will be reset to zero, with the single exception of the ROLLBACK TRANSACTION savepoint_name which will not affect @@TRANCOUNT counter in any way.

When more complex transactional logic is required in fact, developers can define a location in the transaction flow where to return if only a portion of the transaction is conditionally canceled or rolled back: this is usually referred as a *savepoint*. If a transaction is rolled back to a savepoint with a ROLLBACK TRANSACTION savepoint_name, then the control flow must proceed to completion, optionally executing more T-SQL statements if needed, and a COMMIT TRANSACTION statement to complete it successfully. Otherwise, it must be canceled altogether by rolling the transaction back to its beginning. To cancel an entire transaction, use the form ROLLBACK TRANSACTION transaction_name.

A T-SQL example that summarizes all these concepts is as follows.

Listing 7-2. Example of using transactions in a T-SQL script

```
USE AdventureWorks2012;
GO
IF EXISTS (SELECT name FROM sys.objects
          WHERE name = N'SaveTranExample')
    DROP PROCEDURE SaveTranExample;
GO
CREATE PROCEDURE SaveTranExample
    @InputCandidateID INT
AS
    -- Detect whether the procedure was called
    -- from an active transaction and save
    -- that for later use.
    -- In the procedure, @TranCounter = 0
    -- means there was no active transaction
    -- and the procedure started one.
```

```
-- @TranCounter > 0 means an active
-- transaction was started before the
-- procedure was called.
DECLARE @TranCounter INT;
SET @TranCounter = @@TRANCOUNT;
IF @TranCounter > 0
    -- Procedure called when there is
    -- an active transaction.
    -- Create a savepoint to be able
    -- to roll back only the work done
    -- in the procedure if there is an
    -- error.
    SAVE TRANSACTION ProcedureSave;
ELSE
    -- Procedure must start its own
    -- transaction.
    BEGIN TRANSACTION;
-- Modify database.
BEGIN TRY
    DELETE HumanResources.JobCandidate
        WHERE JobCandidateID = @InputCandidateID;
    -- Get here if no errors; must commit
    -- any transaction started in the
    -- procedure, but not commit a transaction
    -- started before the transaction was called.
    IF @TranCounter = 0
        -- @TranCounter = 0 means no transaction was
        -- started before the procedure was called.
        -- The procedure must commit the transaction
        -- it started.
        COMMIT TRANSACTION;
END TRY
BEGIN CATCH
    -- An error occurred; must determine
    -- which type of rollback will roll
```

```
            -- back only the work done in the
            -- procedure.
            IF @TranCounter = 0
                -- Transaction started in procedure.
                -- Roll back complete transaction.
                ROLLBACK TRANSACTION;
            ELSE
                -- Transaction started before procedure
                -- called, do not roll back modifications
                -- made before the procedure was called.
                IF XACT_STATE() <> -1
                    -- If the transaction is still valid, just
                    -- roll back to the savepoint set at the
                    -- start of the stored procedure.
                    ROLLBACK TRANSACTION ProcedureSave;
                    -- If the transaction is uncommittable, a
                    -- rollback to the savepoint is not allowed
                    -- because the savepoint rollback writes to
                    -- the log. Just return to the caller, which
                    -- should roll back the outer transaction.

            -- After the appropriate rollback, echo error
            -- information to the caller.
            DECLARE @ErrorMessage NVARCHAR(4000);
            DECLARE @ErrorSeverity INT;
            DECLARE @ErrorState INT;

            SELECT @ErrorMessage = ERROR_MESSAGE();
            SELECT @ErrorSeverity = ERROR_SEVERITY();
            SELECT @ErrorState = ERROR_STATE();

            RAISERROR (@ErrorMessage, -- Message text.
                       @ErrorSeverity, -- Severity.
                       @ErrorState -- State.
                       );
        END CATCH
GO
```

The logic here is checking if an existing transaction already exists before modifying the database. If that is the case, then it first creates a savepoint, and if the data modification fails, it rolls back only to that savepoint without involving any previous activities executed in the outer transaction.

Not all database drivers provide direct control over transaction names or savepoints: for example, *pyodbc* doesn't provide methods to invoke beginning of a transaction (with or without name) or savepoint, but you can always access these functionalities by simply executing the equivalent T-SQL statements.

In other languages like C# and .NET Core, you can instead control all aspects of your transactional logic, as demonstrated by the following example.

Listing 7-3. Example of using transactions in a .NET Core app

```
using (SqlConnection connection = new SqlConnection(connectionString))
{
    connection.Open();

    SqlCommand command = connection.CreateCommand();
    SqlTransaction transaction;
    // Start a local transaction.
    transaction = connection.BeginTransaction("SampleTransaction");

    // Must assign both transaction object and connection
    // to Command object for a pending local transaction
    command.Connection = connection;
    command.Transaction = transaction;

    try
    {
        command.CommandText =
            "Insert into Region (RegionID, RegionDescription) VALUES (100,
            'Description')";
        command.ExecuteNonQuery();

        transaction.Save("FirstRegionInserted");
```

```
        command.CommandText =
            "Insert into Region (RegionID, RegionDescription) VALUES
            (101, 'Description')";
        command.ExecuteNonQuery();

        // Rollback to a savepoint
        transaction.Rollback("FirstRegionInserted");

        // Only first insert will be considered
        // Attempt to commit the transaction.
        transaction.Commit();
        Console.WriteLine("Only first insert is written to database.");
    }
    catch (Exception ex)
    {
        Console.WriteLine("Commit Exception Type: {0}", ex.GetType());
        Console.WriteLine("  Message: {0}", ex.Message);

        // Attempt to roll back the transaction.
        try
        {
            transaction.Rollback("SampleTransaction");
        }
        catch (Exception ex2)
        {
            // This catch block will handle any errors that may have
            //  occurred
            // on the server that would cause the rollback to fail, such as
            // a closed connection.
            Console.WriteLine("Rollback Exception Type: {0}", ex2.
            GetType());
            Console.WriteLine("  Message: {0}", ex2.Message);
        }
    }
}
```

Azure SQL offers several Dynamic Management Views (DMVs) to monitor transactions running in a given database instance. They start with the `sys.dm_tran_*` prefix. The following example returns detailed information on open transactions at the database level:

```
SELECT * FROM sys.dm_tran_database_transactions WHERE database_id = db_id()
```

Distributed transactions across cloud databases

Relational database management systems have traditionally supported transactions across multiple databases and even multiple servers, usually referred as distributed transactions. These capabilities are enabled through specific components, like distributed transaction coordinators and monitors (like Microsoft Distributed Transaction Coordinator, or MS DTC), and two-phase commit protocols like XA. Generally speaking, these underlying technologies were designed to run within traditional data center environments, with low-latency, tightly coupled local connectivity and specific hardware configurations. In highly distributed systems and standardized cloud environments though, design patterns have evolved to remove dependencies on these traditional approaches, moving instead into more decoupled, asynchronous patterns like Saga which are usually managed outside of the database tier.

As per the time of writing, MS DTC is supported only in Azure SQL Managed Instance, and you are able to take full advantage of it. But what if you need distributed transaction support in Azure SQL Database? You'll be happy to know it is still possible to implement distributed transactions across multiple Azure SQL Database instances using Elastic Transactions, which are available for .NET-based applications.

With this approach, Azure SQL Database will effectively coordinate the distributed transaction on behalf of MS DTC, and applications can connect to multiple instances and execute a transaction controlled through *System.Transaction* classes, with mandatory requirement of .NET 4.6.1 or greater, while unfortunately this is not yet supported by .NET Core at the time we're writing this. The following picture visualizes how various components are interacting with each other to support this scenario.

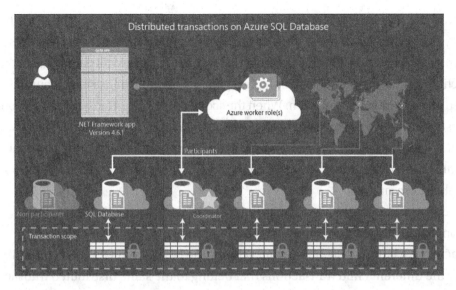

Figure 7-3. *Distributed transactions on Azure SQL Database*

Let's see how this can be implemented in our applications through a simple example:

```
using (var scope = new TransactionScope())
{
    using (var conn1 = new SqlConnection(connStrDb1))
    {
        conn1.Open();
        SqlCommand cmd1 = conn1.CreateCommand();
        cmd1.CommandText = string.Format("insert into T1 values(1)");
        cmd1.ExecuteNonQuery();
    }

    using (var conn2 = new SqlConnection(connStrDb2))
    {
        conn2.Open();
        var cmd2 = conn2.CreateCommand();
        cmd2.CommandText = string.Format("insert into T2 values(2)");
        cmd2.ExecuteNonQuery();
    }

    scope.Complete();
}
```

As you can see, usage is quite straightforward: `TransactionScope` is doing all the heavy lifting by establishing an *ambient transaction* (an ambient transaction is one that lives in the current thread), and all connections opened within that scope will participate in that transaction. If these are pointing to multiple databases, then the transaction is automatically elevated to a distributed transaction. When the scope is complete, transactions will commit.

Elastic Transactions can also involve databases belonging to multiple logical servers, but to enable that, these servers will need first to be entered into a mutual communication relationship by invoking the `New-AzSqlServerCommunicationLink` PowerShell commandlet.

We can monitor the status of a distributed transaction using the same DMVs mentioned for local transactions (e.g., `SELECT * FROM sys.dm_tran_active_transactions`), but for distributed transactions, the UOW (Unit Of Work) column will identify the different child transactions that belong to the same distributed transaction. All transactions within the same distributed transaction carry the same UOW value.

Locking and non-locking options

Database engines are generally multi-user systems, where operations performed by a given user may or may not affect tables and rows used by others concurrently. By specifying an isolation level for an individual transactional command, or as a default for a session or all sessions in a database, we can define the degree to which one transaction must be isolated from resource or data modifications made by other transactions. *Isolation levels* define which concurrency side effects, such as dirty reads (read data from a row that has been modified by another running transaction not yet committed) or phantom reads (rows added or removed by another transaction to the records being read), are allowed. They control things like whether locks are taken when data is read, what type of locks are requested, and how long the read locks are held. If locks are not used to provide consistency, isolation level helps the engine to understand when different versions of the same rows can be deleted as no other transactions are using it. When read operations are referencing rows modified by another transaction, isolation levels define if they get blocked until the exclusive lock on the row is freed; if locks are not used, they define which committed version of the row that existed at the time the statement or transaction started should be retrieved; if isolation is set low enough, you can even read *uncommitted* data. While this is permitted, you should almost never use this ability. Reading uncommitted data means that you are reading something that has the chance to be rolled back; this means that your application may start to do something based on the data that, for example, has been entered by mistake and thus undone.

An important concept to understand is that changing transaction isolation level does not affect how the locks are acquired to protect data modifications. Transaction always gets an exclusive lock on any data modified and holds that lock until the transaction completes, regardless of the isolation level set for that transaction. Locks are not only a synchronization mechanism but also carry metadata which is very useful to the database engine to know what's going on anytime it is needed. What can be changed is how locks are used. Luckily, we don't have to go into nitty-gritty details, as we can express the desired behavior we want, in terms of consistency and concurrency, and Azure SQL will use the correct locks for us.

For reads, isolation levels define the level of protection from modifications made by other transactions. Lower isolation levels increase the ability of more concurrent access to data at the same time but increase potential concurrency issues like dirty reads and inconsistency. Higher isolation levels increase consistency but increase the chance of blocking other transactions by using locks that will also consume system resources (i.e., memory). Application logic and requirements will determine which isolation level is more appropriate.

Isolation level	Definition
Read uncommitted	The lowest isolation level; dirty reads are allowed. One transaction may see not-yet-committed changes made by other transactions.
Read committed	A transaction can access data created or modified – and then committed – by another transaction. If data is modified, Azure SQL keeps write locks (acquired on selected data) until the end of the transaction. Read locks are released as soon as the SELECT operation is performed.
Repeatable read	Azure SQL keeps read and write locks that are acquired on selected data until the end of the transaction. Range locks are not managed, so phantom reads can occur. A range lock protects all the data in the range to be modified, including modification done by INSERT or DELETE statements.
Serializable	Highest level, where transactions are completely isolated from one another. Azure SQL keeps read and write locks on selected data and will be released at the end of the transaction. Range locks are acquired when a SELECT operation uses a ranged WHERE clause, especially to avoid phantom reads.

In addition to these isolation levels, which are defined as ISO standards for all database management systems, Azure SQL also supports two additional transaction isolation levels that use row versioning.

Row versioning isolation level	Definition
Read Committed Snapshot (RCSI)	In Azure SQL Database, *this is the default isolation level for newly created databases*, and read committed isolation uses row versioning to provide *statement-level* read consistency. Read operations require only SCH-S (shared schema locks, which simply prevent table schema to be changed while the table is being read) and no page or row locks. *Azure SQL uses row versioning* to *provide each statement* with a transactionally consistent snapshot of the data as it existed at the start of the statement. Locks are not used to protect the data from updates by other transactions. *With this isolation level, writers and readers don't block each other.*
Snapshot	*The snapshot isolation level uses row versioning to provide transaction-level read consistency.* Read operations acquire no page or row locks; only SCH-S table locks are acquired. When reading rows modified by another transaction, they retrieve the version of the row that existed when the transaction started. You can only use Snapshot isolation against a database when the ALLOW_SNAPSHOT_ISOLATION database option is set ON, which is the default in Azure SQL.

Before moving further, let's clarify some of the terminology just used, especially around locks. A Shared Schema Lock (SCH-S) is used to make sure that no one can change the table definition while you are using it. In a highly concurrent system, it could happen that someone will try to DROP a table or ALTER it while you are running your SELECT. Azure SQL will protect your SELECT by placing a SCH-S lock so that those commands who would like to change the schema will have to wait until your SELECT is done.

A Range Lock is used to protect a running transaction from data that doesn't exist yet, but that, if allowed to be created, could interfere with the running transaction.

The Azure SQL engine manages concurrency between multiple users executing transactions against databases by requesting locks on data. Locks have different modes, such as shared or exclusive. Lock modes define the level of dependency the transaction has on the data. Locks cannot be granted for a transaction if they would conflict with the type of a lock already granted on that data to another transaction. If a transaction requests a lock type that conflicts with a lock that has already been granted on the same data, Azure SQL will pause the requesting transaction until the first lock is released. When a transaction modifies a piece of data, it holds the lock protecting the modification until the end of the transaction. How long a transaction holds the locks acquired to protect read operations depends on the transaction isolation level setting. All locks held by a transaction are released when the transaction completes (either commits or rolls back).

Applications do not typically request locks directly; rather, locks are managed internally by a part of the Azure SQL engine, called the lock manager. When processing a Transact-SQL statement, Azure SQL determines which resources are to be accessed. The query processor determines what types of locks are required to protect each resource based on the type of access and the transaction isolation level setting. The query processor then requests the appropriate locks from the lock manager, a subsystem that exists within the Azure SQL engine. The lock manager grants the locks if there are no conflicting locks held by other transactions.

Azure SQL has multi-granular locking that allows different types of resources to be locked by a transaction. To minimize the cost of locking (lock structures are held in memory), Azure SQL lock resources automatically work at a level appropriate to the task. Locking at a smaller granularity, such as rows, increases concurrency but has a higher overhead because more locks must be held if many rows are locked. Locking at a larger granularity, such as tables, is expensive in terms of concurrency because locking an entire table restricts access to any part of the table by other transactions. However, it has a lower overhead because fewer locks are being maintained. Azure SQL automatically selects the best lock granularity based on the amount of data that it needs to lock, trying to balance between resource costs and concurrency impact.

Azure SQL often must acquire locks at multiple levels of granularity to fully protect a resource. This group of locks at multiple levels of granularity is called a lock hierarchy. For example, to fully protect a read of an index, an instance of the Azure SQL may have to acquire Shared locks on rows and Intent Shared locks on the pages and table. Intent Locks are something used to indicate that, in the future, lock could be acquired on that resource. This information helps the lock manager to avoid future conflicts.

Note   As you have seen, transaction and lock management are pretty complex topics. You can get more insights on how locking works internally, and how different lock types and level can impact concurrency on underlying data can be found on "Transaction Locking and Row Versioning Guide" on the Azure docs at this link: `https://aka.ms/sstlarv`.

As developers, we can control how our applications are dealing with different isolation levels and concurrency through specific T-SQL statements and client driver APIs like Microsoft.Data.SqlClient or SQL Server JDBC Driver.

In a T-SQL script or procedure, you can use `SET TRANSACTION ISOLATION LEVEL isolation_level` to control locking and row versioning behavior of all the following statements issued over that connection:

```
SET TRANSACTION ISOLATION LEVEL REPEATABLE READ;
GO
BEGIN TRANSACTION;
GO
SELECT * FROM HumanResources.EmployeePayHistory;
GO
SELECT * FROM HumanResources.Department;
GO
COMMIT TRANSACTION;
GO
```

Various client driver APIs are providing slightly different behaviors and semantics regarding managing isolation levels when executing transactions. The first example here is related to Microsoft.Data.SqlClient driver, where you can specify isolation level when invoking *BeginTransaction()* method:

```
// Start a local transaction.
transaction = connection.BeginTransaction(
        IsolationLevel.ReadCommitted, "SampleTransaction");
```

In Microsoft SQL Server JDBC Driver instead, you specify isolation level through the *setTransactionIsolation()* method of the *Connection* class:

```
con.setTransactionIsolation(Connection.TRANSACTION_READ_COMMITTED);
```

In addition to drivers' APIs and connection-level isolation settings, *table hints* can also override default behaviors of Azure SQL engine for the duration of data manipulation language (DML) statements' execution and let you control things like lock type, granularity, and so on by specifying a locking method. For example, using a table hint of type *HOLDLOCK* (or its equivalent, *SERIALIZABLE*) makes shared locks more restrictive by holding them until a transaction is completed, instead of releasing the shared lock as soon as the required table or data page is no longer needed. *ROWLOCK* specifies that row locks are taken when page or table locks are ordinarily taken (as opposed to *TABLOCK* or *PAGLOCK*).

Table hints are specified in the FROM clause of the DML statement and affect only the table or view referenced in that clause; here's an example of how you can use them:

```
FROM t (ROWLOCK, XLOCK)
```

Note that not all the hints are compatible with different DML command types, and to get all details about this interesting topic, you can follow this link in official product documentation: https://aka.ms/uathaaqh.

Note   Slow or long-running queries can contribute to excessive resource consumption and be the consequence of blocked queries. The cause of the blocking can be poor application design, bad query plans, the lack of useful indexes, and so on. You can use the *sys.dm_tran_locks* dynamic management view to get information about the current locking activity in the database.

As we mentioned, the default isolation level for Azure SQL is Read Committed Snapshot Isolation (RCSI), and this provides the best trade-off between concurrency and data integrity, letting readers and writers don't block each other for most scenarios. As a best practice, you should limit the usage of other transaction isolation levels or statement-level table hints to very specific use cases where you need specific behaviors. In all other cases, default settings will work just fine. At the same time, rest assured that if you need to go into great detail and fine-tune even just a single statement, that can be done. This amazing flexibility is unique in the database cloud market!

Natively compiled procedure

Natively compiled Stored Procedures are T-SQL Stored Procedures compiled to machine code, rather than interpreted by the query execution engine as regular Stored Procedures. They work in conjunction with In-Memory OLTP tables in Azure SQL to provide very fast response times for frequently executed queries on performance-critical parts of an application. Performance benefits of using a natively compiled Stored Procedure increases with the number of rows and the amount of logic that is processed by the procedure, and works best when performing aggregations; nested loops joins on large number of row; multi-statement select, insert, update, and delete operations; or complex procedural logic, such as conditional statements and loops.

When we use traditional interpreted Transact-SQL statements to access In-Memory OLTP tables, query processing pipeline looks very similar to disk-based tables, with the exception of the fact that rows are not retrieved from classical buffer pools but from the in-memory engine:

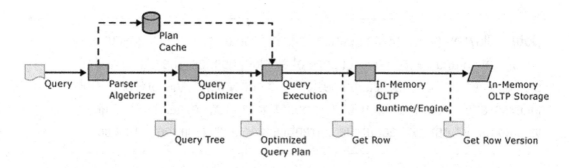

When using natively compiled Stored Procedures, the process is split into two parts. First parser, algebrizer and optimizer create optimized query execution plans for all the queries in the Stored Procedure, and then Stored Procedure gets compiled into a native code and stored in a .dll file:

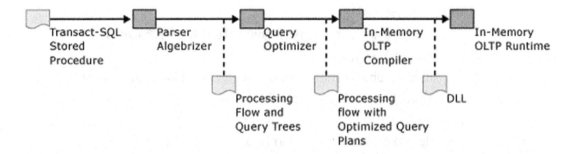

When the Stored Procedure is invoked, the In-Memory OLTP runtime locates the DLL entry point for the Stored Procedure, machine code in the DLL is executed, and the results are returned to the client:

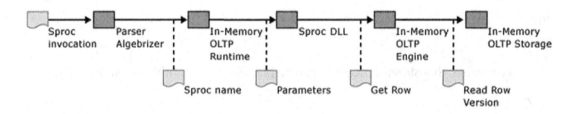

Syntax for creating a natively compiled Stored Procedure is quite straightforward, as shown in the following example (that tests how fast 100.000 GET + PUT operations can be done on a table acting as a key-value store cache):

```
create or alter procedure cache.[Test]
with native_compilation, schemabinding
as
begin atomic with (transaction isolation level = snapshot,
language = N'us_english')
    declare @i int = 0;
    while (@i < 100000)
    begin
        declare @r int = cast(rand() * 10000 as int)
        declare @v nvarchar(max) = (select top(1) [value] from dbo.
        [MemoryStore] where [key]=@r);
```

```
        if (@v is not null) begin
                declare @c int = cast(json_value(@v, '$.counter')
                as int) + 1;
                update dbo.[MemoryStore] set [value] = json_modify
                (@v, '$.counter', @c) where [key] = @r
        end else begin
                declare @value nvarchar(max) = '{"value": "' + cast
                (sysdatetime() as nvarchar(max)) + '", "counter": 1}'
                insert into dbo.[MemoryStore] values (@r, @value)
        end
        set @i += 1;
    end
end
go
```

Once created, this Stored Procedure can be invoked like any other by our application:

```
EXEC cache.[Test];
```

There are few restrictions on operators supported within a natively compiled Stored Procedure. For example, the syntax SELECT * FROM table is not supported, and you need to specify the complete column list. For more information on these details, you can look at product documentation at https://aka.ms/ncsp.

Note   As a best practice, you shouldn't consider using natively compiled Stored Procedures for query patterns like point lookups. If you need to process only a single row, in fact, using a natively compiled Stored Procedure may not provide a performance benefit compared to traditional interpreted Stored Procedures.

Optimizing database roundtrips

Reducing the number of roundtrips between your application tier and the database tier is likely the single most important optimization you can think about when designing or troubleshooting an application working with Azure SQL. Wherever your application logic permits, batching operations to Azure SQL Database and Azure

SQL Managed Instance significantly improves the performance and scalability of your applications. Batching calls to a remote service is a well-known strategy for increasing performance and scalability. There are fixed processing costs to any interactions with a remote service, such as serialization, network transfer, and deserialization. Packaging many separate transactions into a single batch minimizes these costs.

The multitenant characteristics of Azure SQL mean that the efficiency of the data access layer correlates to the overall scalability of the database. In response to usage in excess of predefined quotas, Azure SQL can reduce throughput or respond with throttling exceptions. Efficiencies, such as batching, enable you to do more work before reaching these limits.

There are several batching techniques we can adopt to make our applications more efficient, and these apply to most programming languages and frameworks. Let's start expanding on these techniques by starting from various batching strategies you should consider.

Leveraging transactions

It seems strange to begin a review of batching by discussing transactions. But the use of client-side transactions has a subtle server-side batching effect that improves performance. And transactions can be added with only a few lines of code, so they provide a fast way to improve performance of sequential operations.

Moving from individual calls executed as implicit transactions to wrapping several calls in a single transaction effectively delays writes to the transaction log until the transaction is committed, reducing the impact of latency between Azure SQL engine and transaction log storage.

Depending on specific table structures and number of operations to wrap in a transaction, this technique can provide up to 10x performance improvement for data modification tasks.

Table-valued parameters

Table-valued parameters support user-defined table types as parameters in Transact-SQL statements, Stored Procedures, and functions. This client-side batching technique allows you to send multiple rows of data within the table-valued parameter. To use table-valued parameters, first define a table type. The following Transact-SQL statement creates a table type named MyTableType:

```
CREATE TYPE MyTableType AS TABLE (
    mytext NVARCHAR(MAX),
    num INT
);
```

In your application code, you can create an in-memory data structure with the exact same shape of the table type and pass this data structure as a parameter in a text query or Stored Procedure call. The following example shows this technique in a .NET Core application:

```
using (SqlConnection connection = new SqlConnection(connString))
{
    connection.Open();

    DataTable table = new DataTable();
    // Add columns and rows. The following is a simple example.
    table.Columns.Add("mytext", typeof(string));
    table.Columns.Add("num", typeof(int));
    for (var i = 0; i < 10; i++)
    {
        table.Rows.Add(DateTime.Now.ToString(),
        DateTime.Now.Millisecond);
    }

    SqlCommand cmd = new SqlCommand(
        "INSERT INTO MyTable(mytext, num) SELECT mytext, num FROM
         @TestTvp", connection);
```

```
    cmd.Parameters.Add(
        new SqlParameter()
        {
            ParameterName = "@TestTvp",
            SqlDbType = SqlDbType.Structured,
            TypeName = "MyTableType",
            Value = table,
        });

    cmd.ExecuteNonQuery();
}
```

To improve the previous example further, use a Stored Procedure instead of a text-based command. The following Transact-SQL command creates a Stored Procedure that takes the SimpleTestTableType table-valued parameter:

```
CREATE PROCEDURE [dbo].[sp_InsertRows]
@TestTvp as MyTableType READONLY
AS
BEGIN
INSERT INTO MyTable(mytext, num)
SELECT mytext, num FROM @TestTvp
END
GO
```

Then we can just change few lines of previous example to invoke the Stored Procedure:

```
SqlCommand cmd = new SqlCommand("sp_InsertRows", connection);
cmd.CommandType = CommandType.StoredProcedure;
```

In most cases, table-valued parameters have equivalent or better performance than other batching techniques. Table-valued parameters are often preferable, because they are more flexible than other options. With table-valued parameters, you can use logic in the Stored Procedure to determine which rows are updates and which are inserts. The table type can also be modified to contain an "Operation" column that indicates whether the specified row should be inserted, updated, or deleted.

For more complex application scenarios where using table-valued parameters can provide great benefits on both overall performance and also simplifying your implementation, you can refer to this link to product documentation: https://aka.ms/piubbs.

Bulk copy

Azure SQL offers specific support for bulk loading large sets of records into a table from an application. This support spans from the TDS wire protocol up to various APIs available in many client drivers (e.g., SqlClient, JDBC, or ODBC).

As an example, .NET applications can use the SqlBulkCopy class to perform bulk insert operations. SqlBulkCopy is similar in function to the command-line tool, Bcp.exe, or the Transact-SQL statement, BULK INSERT. The following code example shows how to bulk copy the rows in the source DataTable, represented by the table variable, to the destination table, MyTable:

```
using (SqlConnection connection = new SqlConnection(connString))
{
    connection.Open();

    using (SqlBulkCopy bulkCopy = new SqlBulkCopy(connection))
    {
        bulkCopy.DestinationTableName = "MyTable";
        bulkCopy.ColumnMappings.Add("mytext", "mytext");
        bulkCopy.ColumnMappings.Add("num", "num");
        bulkCopy.WriteToServer(table);
    }
}
```

You may be wondering now what you should use table-valued parameters and when it would be better to use the bulk copy API. Using table-valued parameters is comparable to other ways of using set-based variables; however, using table-valued parameters frequently can be faster for large datasets. Compared to bulk operations that have a greater startup cost than table-valued parameters, table-valued parameters perform well for inserting up to a few 1000 rows. If you're batching 10000 rows or more instead, bulk copy will definitely be the most efficient way of loading data into Azure SQL.

Multiple-row parameterized INSERT statements

One alternative for small batches is to construct a large parameterized INSERT statement that inserts multiple rows. T-SQL language provides direct support to this use case through the following syntax:

```
INSERT INTO [MyTable] ( mytext, num ) VALUES (@p1, @p2), (@p3, @p4), (@p5, @p6), (@p7, @p8), (@p9, @p10)
```

From your language of choice then, you can use specific drivers' APIs to leverage these capabilities. As an example, you can take a look at this Python code fragment:

```
params = [ ('A', 1), ('B', 2) ]
cursor.fast_executemany = True
cursor.executemany("insert into t(name, id) values (?, ?)", params)
```

Basically, by setting *fast_executemany* cursor property to True, pyodbc driver will pack multiple parameter tuples into a single batch, drastically reducing the number of roundtrips between your application code and the back-end database.

Higher-level frameworks like EntityFramework Core or SQLAlchemy are leveraging underlying client drivers' capability and provide equivalent batching options. It's always a recommended practice to check if these capabilities are available for your own combination of programming language and framework.

Recommendations and best practices

It's important to understand the trade-offs between batching/buffering and resiliency. If a database operation fails, the risk of losing an unprocessed batch of business-critical data might outweigh the performance benefit of batching, so implementing proper retry logic techniques introduced in previous chapters is even more important when adopting batching.

If you choose a single batching technique, table-valued parameters offer the best performance and flexibility. For the fastest insert performance, follow these general guidelines, but test your scenario:

- For < 100 rows, use a single-parameterized INSERT command.

- For < 1000 rows, use table-valued parameters.

- For >= 1000–2000 rows, use SqlBulkCopy in .NET or equivalent bulk copy techniques in other languages (e.g., SQLServerBulkCopy in Java).

For update and delete operations, use table-valued parameters with Stored Procedure logic that determines the correct operation on each row in the table parameter. Use the largest batch sizes that make sense for your application and business requirements.

Test the largest batch size to verify that Azure SQL does not reject it. Create configuration settings that control batching, such as the batch size or the buffering time window. These settings provide flexibility: you can change the batching behavior in production without redeploying the cloud service.

Avoid parallel execution of batches that operate on a single table in one database. If you do choose to divide a single batch across multiple worker threads, run tests to determine the ideal number of threads. This number depends on several factors, including log generation rate limits for each service tiers and compute sizes, locking effects on data and index pages on target tables, and so on. The net effect is that more threads can effectively decrease performance rather than increase it, so it's important to test your own workload and potentially adjust the number of threads.

If you want to know more

Managing data consistency is a tough task. Doing it concurrently and at scale, it's even more challenging. As mentioned in the introduction of this chapter, it's not by chance that almost all the most used databases provide support for transactions. Managing everything in the application code would be tremendously difficult and inefficient. And today the discussion between scalability and consistency is almost gone. Thanks to the new cloud-born architecture, like the one used to build Azure SQL DB Hyperscale, you can have both. The technology behind Azure SQL Hyperscale database is amazing. If you want to know more, here's a list that will give you a kickstart:

- Unit of Work – https://martinfowler.com/eaaCatalog/unitOfWork.html

- Spanner: Becoming a SQL System – Google Research – https://static.googleusercontent.com/media/research.google.com/en//pubs/archive/46103.pdf

- Socrates: The New SQL Server in the Cloud – `www.microsoft.com/research/publication/socrates-the-new-sql-server-in-the-cloud/`

- Is SQL Beating NoSQL? – `https://dzone.com/articles/is-sql-beating-nosql`

- 6 Data Management Patterns for Microservices – `http://progressivecoder.com/6-data-management-patterns-for-microservices/`

- Transaction Locking and Row Versioning Guide – `https://docs.microsoft.com/sql/relational-databases/sql-server-transaction-locking-and-row-versioning-guide`

- How to use batching to improve Azure SQL Database and Azure SQL Managed Instance application performance – `https://docs.microsoft.com/azure/azure-sql/performance-improve-use-batching`

CHAPTER 8

Multi-model Capabilities

Azure SQL is not a traditional relational database platform. Every modern database must enable you to use various data formats for different scenarios. Although traditional normalized relational format is battle-tested and proven as optimal technology for a wide range of different scenarios, in some cases, you might find that some other formats might be the better fit for the problem that you are solving.

One common example is denormalization. Traditionally, you are representing domain objects as a set of tables in the so-called *normal form* described in the previous chapters. This is a well-known database design technique where every complex domain structure, such as list or array, is placed in a separate table. The normalized model is optimal for highly concurrent workloads where many threads simultaneously update and read different parts of the domain object without affecting the threads that are updating other parts. However, if you have a workload where one thread accesses a single object at a time, a highly normalized database might force you to join a lot of tables to reconstruct the domain object from its physical parts. In this case, you might consider serializing the object as a single unit instead of decomposing it.

Azure SQL enables you to use both relational and non-relational structures in the same physical data model.

The ability to work with relational, structured, or several types of semi-structured formats categorizes Azure SQL as a Multi-Model database. If you visit `https://db-engines.com/en/ranking` site that scores popularity of databases, you might notice that all highly ranked relational databases are also classified as multi-model databases, because supporting various data formats is a must-have requirement for all modern database systems.

© Davide Mauri, Silvano Coriani, Anna Hoffman, Sanjay Mishra, Jovan Popovic 2021
D. Mauri et al., *Practical Azure SQL Database for Modern Developers*,
https://doi.org/10.1007/978-1-4842-6370-9_8

Leveraging multi-model capabilities in database design

Before we deep dive into multi-model capabilities of Azure SQL, let us see when you should use them in your applications. Some software engineers like NoSQL concepts because they make a database easier to use and don't require (apparently) a lot of design upfront, and as such, you can start to use it right away without putting too much effort, and it also doesn't require complex joins between tables. Others prefer relational model because it is battle-tested and guarantees that you may model any domain regardless of complexity. As a mature software engineer, you should not use dogmatic architectural decisions based on some arbitrary preference. The choice between relational and non-relational models or their combination should be based on the domain model of your application.

If you are using something like Domain-Driven Development (DDD), you are probably identifying Aggregates in your domain. Aggregate objects in DDD are the core entities in your domain model that represent the main access point for data and reference other entities and values. As an example, *Customer* might be the primary entity that you will use in your sales management module. This entity has some value objects and the reference to the other entities like *Order* or *Invoice*. If you know that client code will access customer orders and invoices through *Customer* object, then *Customer* is an aggregate that binds other entities that belong to him and represents the main access point for any external component that references any of the entities.

Attention!   Do not confuse Aggregates in DDD with aggregate functions (SUM, AVG, MAX) in SQL terminology.

The dogmatic NoSQL approach would be to serialize the entire *Customer* aggregate and all related entities (*Orders, Invoices*) as one big collection that contains everything that you need in your application layer. This is a perfect choice for the applications that can fetch all necessary data using a single data access operation. Dogmatic relational approach would be to break every entity into a separate highly normalized table so different services in your application can access only a minimal set of information that they need. This is a perfect choice for highly concurrent applications where different threads at the same time access and modify different parts of entities or aggregates.

The drawback of dogmatic decisions is that in both cases people assume the access patterns instead of analyzing usage patterns in the business domain. The proper approach is to analyze data access patterns that will be used and choose the best fit for the domain. Here are some examples of data access patterns that might influence your data design decisions:

- If you have big and complex forms where you need to preload both *Order* and *Invoice* entities after fetching *Customer* root aggregate and update information in *Customer*, *Invoice*, and *Order* entities once you save data on the form, it makes sense to store dependent entities as denormalized collections. This way you will read and persist all data with a single data access and avoid complex joins that gather data and transactions that span over multiple tables.

- If you know that different forms and services in your application might simultaneously update *Invoice* or *Order* entities that belong to the same *Customer* aggregate or you are frequently using lazy loading techniques, it makes sense to break entities into separate tables. This way, you can implement granular services that write and read only the objects that are needed. Breaking the entities to separate tables increases concurrency of your system, because different transactions can touch different parts of the entities without blocking each other. Otherwise, they would be synchronized and potentially blocked on each other.

The application access patterns are the key factors that can guide your decision to use normalized or denormalized models.

Classifying domain models

Behavior analysis of your services and identification of data access patterns will enable you to identify what is the optimal storage design for your domain models. Depending on data access patterns in your application, you can classify your data models as

- *Highly normalized relational model* where you have dependencies and relationships between the entities (like classes in UML diagrams). This model is a perfect choice for highly concurrent applications and services updating or loading different parts of entities.

- *Graph* models are special kinds of models where nodes are interconnected with edges forming logical graph structure. This structure is a perfect choice for services that frequently break or establish bounds between the entities and traverse through the relations finding best paths or "friend-of-a-friend" type of analytics.

- *Non-relational* data where information is self-contained into the isolated data entities with very weak or non-existing relationships between them. This structure is perfect for the services that read and save domain objects as a single unit.

Depending on the structure of your data entities, your models can be classified as

- *Structured* where all data entities have uniform or fixed schema. These types of entities can be easily visualized as rows and columns in Excel tables or serialized in CSV format.

- *Semi-structured* where data entities have some structure, but it is not always strict or uniform. Data entities have some common properties that are repeated across all entities, and some properties vary. Imagine a key-value collection with the different keys across entities or a hierarchically organized document with some missing values and sub-objects. These objects are typically serialized in JSON format.

- *Unstructured* data where patterns highly vary between data entities, and it is hard to find the common structure. The typical examples can be textual documents, images, or videos – there is a well-defined format that enables you to read information, but a combination of information in images makes them very different.

Azure SQL is the best fit for relational structured and also a good fit for relational semi-structured data. The querying capabilities of SQL language enable you to apply the same processing rules over a large set of structured and semi-structured data and also easily traverse through foreign key and edge relationships.

Structured information without relationships might be more efficiently stored as CSV or Excel files, especially if you need to store a large amount of data on Azure Data Lake or Azure Blob Storage. It doesn't mean that you are losing query capabilities because Azure SQL still enables you to easily load these files from external storage and query them as in-database rows. Semi-structured and self-contained documents that are not related to other entities might be more efficiently stored in specialized document databases such as Azure Cosmos DB. Azure Cosmos DB provides many functionalities specialized for querying and indexing self-contained documents that you might leverage if you don't need to cross-relate entities or implement some complex reports.

Why would you choose Azure SQL for non-relational models?

Azure SQL is a multi-model database that enables you to combine different relational and non-relational models to find the best fit for your scenario.

Unlike the traditional relational and NoSQL databases where you need to upfront decide what physical model you want to use, Azure SQL enables you to combine these relational and non-relational concepts and find the model that is the best fit for your needs.

One of the key advantages of multi-model support in Azure SQL is the fact that data models are not mutually exclusive. Azure SQL enables you to seamlessly combine multiple models and leverage the best from all of them. You can create a classical relational model with some columns containing JSON or Spatial data, declare some of the tables as graph nodes and connect them using edges, place JSON columns in memory-optimized tables to leverage the speed and non-locking behavior. Multi-model capabilities can leverage all advanced language and storage features that Azure SQL provides. You can use the same T-SQL language to query both structured and semi-structured data, which enables a variety of applications and libraries to use any data format that you store in Azure SQL database.

The main reason why you would select the multi-model capabilities of Azure SQL is the fact that they are seamlessly integrated in the core battle-tested features of relational databases. The combination of JSON, Graph features with advanced querying capabilities, possibility to use all collations to process strings in JSON documents, Columnstore, and memory-optimized objects that can provide extreme performance, in-database machine learning with Python/R would provide you advanced data processing experience that you might not get even in the fully specialized NoSQL database.

Azure SQL enables you to represent your models using the following non-relational concepts:

- *JSON* that enables you to integrate your databases with a broad range of web/mobile applications and log file formats or even to denormalize and simplify your relational schema. JSON functionality also simplifies a lot of the work needed to be done by a developer to communicate with Azure SQL. You may ask Azure SQL, in fact, to return the result as JSON documents instead of a table with columns and rows, if doing so can simplify your code.

- *Graph* capabilities that enable you to represent your data model as a set of nodes and edges. This structure is an ideal choice in the domains where the domain entities are organized in network structure and where you can take advantage of a specialized query language to query graph data.

- *Spatial* support that enables you to store geometrical and geographical information in databases, index them using specialized spatial indexes, and use advanced spatial queries to retrieve the data.

- *XML* support that enables you to store XML documents in the tables, index XML information using specialized XML indexes, query XML data using T-SQL or XQuery languages, and transform your relational data to or from XML format.

In the following sections, you will learn about the core multi-model capabilities that exist in Azure SQL Database.

JSON support

JSON (JavaScript Object Notation) is a popular data format initially used data exchange format used to transfer data between web clients and browsers, but it is also used to store semi-structured information such as settings and log information. This is the mainstream format for representing self-contained objects especially in the modern NoSQL database such as Azure Cosmos DB, MongoDB, and so on.

Azure SQL enables you to parse JSON text and extract information from JSON documents, store JSON text in the tables like any other type, and produce JSON text based on a set of rows.

The core JSON functionalities are shown in Figure 8-1.

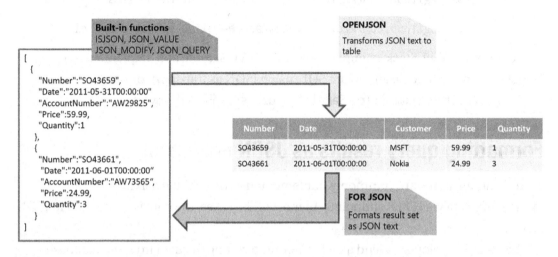

Figure 8-1. *JSON functionalities in Azure SQL*

Azure SQL enables you to work with JSON text that you are storing in tables or sending from your application by applying built-in functions JSON_VALUE, JSON_QUERY, ISJSON, and JSON_MODIFY. These functions enable you to parse JSON from text and extract and modify information in JSON documents.

If you want to transform your semi-structured data represented in JSON format and load JSON documents into tables, you can use OPENJSON function. The OPENJSON function takes an array of objects in JSON format and splits them into a set of rows. You can use this Table-Valued Function to transform JSON into tables and load data in a relational format.

Azure SQL also enables you to format the results of the SQL queries into JSON format. There is a FOR JSON clause that can specify that the results of the query should be returned in JSON format instead of a set of rows.

These functionalities will enable you to implement most of the functionalities that you might want to use in your applications that require some handling of JSON data. In addition to built-in JSON functions and operators, you can combine other features of Azure SQL like indexes, collations, and advanced query capabilities on JSON data. Thanks to JSON support, it is very easy to integrate Azure SQL in Full-Stack or Back-End solutions, as – from a developer perspective – you will just send and receive JSON from Azure SQL. Here's a list of Back-End API implemented in various languages, leveraging JSON and Azure SQL to simplify the development effort:

- `https://github.com/Azure-Samples/azure-sql-db-node-rest-api`

- `https://github.com/Azure-Samples/azure-sql-db-python-rest-api`

- `https://github.com/Azure-Samples/azure-sql-db-dotnet-rest-api`

And here's a Full-Stack example of the ToDoMVC sample app, implemented using NodeJS, Azure Functions, and Azure SQL, using JSON as transport format:
`https://github.com/Azure-Samples/azure-sql-db-todo-mvc`

Formatting query results as JSON document

Modern applications are commonly implemented as distributed services that are exchanging data via HTTP endpoints. In most of the cases, the data is exchanged in JSON format.

Back-end developers spend a lot of their time getting the data from the database and serializing the results as JSON text that will be returned to the caller (e.g., front-end code). You might find a large amount of back-end code in a REST API that is just a wrapper around SQL queries. Some model classes are used just to temporarily load a set of rows returned as a result of SQL queries into memory and then immediately serialize these memory objects as JSON text that will be returned to the caller. This is known as the DTO (Data Transfer Object) pattern where model classes just transfer data between the application layers. Many DTO-like model classes are not even used by back-end code and represent just a template that data access frameworks will use to load data and serialize it as JSON results. This might affect performance and especially memory consumption because data returned by a query is copied into model memory objects and then copied again into JSON text that will be returned as result. Besides resource consumption, this approach might increase the latency in your services, not to mention the fact that such code is just a very low added-value plumbing code. Every transformation is blocking, and the results returned by the query must be fully loaded into a collection of memory objects and then some serializer (like JSON.Net in .Net languages) serializes the entire collection as JSON text.

Azure SQL enables you to extremely simplify this process. FOR JSON query clause enables you to specify that the query results should be returned as JSON string and not as collection of rows. This way, you can directly stream the results of your query to the client instead of building the layers and wrapper that just pass parameters from client to the query and transform results as JSON results.

The following example shows a simple ASP.NET MVC action method that will be executed once a user sends HTTP GET request to the URL *http://<web -application-domain>/LogAnalytic/CountBySeverity*. The action gets the results of the query as JSON text and directly streams it into the HTTP response body:

```
public class LogAnalyticController {
  [HttpGet]
  public void CountBySeverity(){
    var QUERY = @"SELECT severity, total = COUNT(*)
          FROM WebSite.Logs
          GROUP BY severity
          FOR JSON PATH";
    connection.QueryInto(Response.Body, QUERY);
  }
}
```

This action method uses .NET, the micro-ORM Dapper and the `Dapper.Stream` extension that enables you to execute a SQL query on a connection to Azure SQL. The query has `FOR JSON` clause that instructs Azure SQL to return results in JSON format instead of tabular format. `QueryInto` method – from the `Dapper.Stream` extension – will stream the JSON result into the body of the HTTP response. This way, you need two C# lines of code to transform your query into a JSON web service. `FOR JSON` clause enables you to easily finish the journey from any SQL query to a fully functional REST API with a couple of lines of code.

Storing JSON documents

In some cases, you will have data structures that have high variety, and these structures could not be effectively represented as normalized schema. In this case, you might follow the NoSQL approach and serialize complex structures as JSON text.

JSON is, by definition, Unicode text format, so it is represented using `NVARCHAR` type in Azure SQL. You don't need to use some specialized types in your applications, special client-side drivers, or API to send or retrieve JSON data. Any string type in most of the programming languages can be used to read or write content in JSON columns. The following example shows a simple table that stores website log messages that has few fixed columns (`logDate` and `severity`) that are common to all log messages and `log` column that contains all variable information that could be found in logs:

```
create table WebSite.Logs (
    _id bigint identity,
    logDate datetime2,
    severity tinyint,
    log nvarchar(max)
);
```

This way, you can store semi-structured data or data with volatile structure without creating a custom subset of tables for every new variation. In this scenario, log messages are write once and read many times, so we don't need to worry about efficient updates of semi-structured values in JSON log columns.

If you decide to store data in a table, you need to understand how to parse the values from a JSON column and use them in queries, speed up queries using indexes, and ensure that JSON content is valid.

Querying JSON data

Azure SQL enables you to run standard SQL queries that use both classic scalar columns and the values extracted from JSON text. Azure SQL provides four simple functions that process JSON text:

- `JSON_VALUE(json, path_to_value)` function will return a scalar value from JSON document on the specified path.

- `JSON_QUERY(json, path_to_object)` function will return a complex object or array from JSON document on the specified path.

- `JSON_MODIFY(json, path_to_object, json_object)` will take the JSON document provided as the first argument and locate value or object on the path specified with the second parameter, and instead of this value, it will inject the value provided as third parameter. The first argument will not be modified, and the modified JSON text will be returned. If you provide `NULL` value as a third parameter, the value on the path will be deleted.

- `ISJSON(json_string)` returns value 1 if the string provided as argument is properly formatted JSON and 0 otherwise.

Using these simple functions, you can parse any JSON text in columns, parameters, or variables and extract the values in any query clause. The path in these functions represents the location of a value within the JSON document. The syntax used in paths is easy to understand because it is similar to most of the modern object-oriented languages that reference the fields within the object (e.g., `$.info[3].name.firstName`).

The following query creates report that uses both standard and JSON columns on the `WebSite.Logs` table shown in the previous section:

```
SELECT
    severity,
    ip = JSON_VALUE(log, '$.ip'),
    duration = AVG(CAST(JSON_VALUE(log,'$.duration') as int))
FROM
    WebSite.Logs
WHERE
    CAST(JSON_VALUE(log,'$.date') as datetime) > @datetime GROUP BY
    severity, JSON_VALUE(log, '$.ip')
HAVING
    AVG(CAST(JSON_VALUE(log,'$.duration') as int) ) > 100
ORDER BY
    AVG(CAST(JSON_VALUE(log,'$.duration') as int) )
```

Scalar values from the `severity` column are directly referenced, and scalar values from the JSON column are extracted using `JSON_VALUE` function. In this query, you can notice the true advantage of multi-model capabilities of Azure SQL. You are using one SQL language with few additional functions to process semi-structured data mixed with the scalar relational columns. If you are familiar with standard SQL language, learning JSON extension will be an easy task.

JSON paths

In the previous examples, you have seen that all JSON functions use a path that references properties within the JSON that is going to be parsed. JSON paths in Azure SQL can have the following elements:

- $ represents the current JSON document that is provided as a first argument of JSON function.

- Field references start with a dot and reference the sub-property within the context. As an example, `$.info.name.firstName` will find an "info" property and then find `name` property within that object and then `firstName` object within `name`.

- Array references that can be applied on arrays and reference elements by index. As an example, `$.children[2].name` will find a "children" array, take the element with index 2, and then find name property within that object. Indexes in the array references are zero-based.

With this syntax of JSON paths, you can reference any property within the JSON document using the same style that is used in object-oriented languages.

Collation awareness

Collations in Azure SQL are the rules that define how the query processor must compare and sort values. For example, in French language, the last accent in each word determines the sort order, so the following four words would be sorted this way:

1. cote

2. côte

3. coté

4. côté

JSON standards don't define how values should be compared and sorted in documents; however, you can leverage Azure SQL collations to apply some custom language rules while working with JSON data. If you specify a collation `French_100_CS_AS` on a `NVARCHAR` column that contains the JSON documents, Azure SQL will use French language rules to compare and sort results based on the values extracted from the JSON content from this column. Even if the collation is not specified on the column, we can always explicitly apply required collation in the query:

```
SELECT JSON_VALUE(log,'$.msg')
FROM WebSite.Logs
ORDER BY JSON_VALUE(log,'$.msg') COLLATE French_100_CS_AS
```

Collation awareness is one important feature especially for international applications. The fact that JSON functions can leverage this feature makes it a powerful addition to multi-model capabilities of Azure SQL.

Ensuring data integrity in JSON documents

Azure SQL will not check if you have placed a valid JSON document in the NVARCHAR column. If you are sure that you are always landing JSON documents in the table or if you have validation in application logic that ensures this, this is not an issue. Validation of JSON format requires some time and resources, so Azure SQL will not slow down the inserts and updates. If you want to ensure that your JSON documents are always valid, you can explicitly add CHECK CONSTRAINT that will do this validation:

```
ALTER TABLE Webite.Logs
ADD CONSTRAINT [Data should be formatted as JSON]
CHECK (ISJSON(log) = 1);
```

This way, you have full control over the storage process, and you choose when JSON data should be validated. In this example, a simple rule is used to make sure that values inserted in the log column are valid JSON documents. You can create custom rules that extract the values from a JSON document using JSON_VALUE function and compare the returned value in a separate CHECK CONSTRAINT.

Indexing JSON values

Indexes generally help to boost the performance of your queries. Azure SQL doesn't have specialized index for JSON documents, but you can effectively use the following standard indexes to improve performance of JSON queries:

- Clustered Columnstore indexes compress JSON documents and enable high-performance analytics on JSON values.

- B-Tree indexes enable you to quickly find the rows with some value in the JSON column.

A Clustered Columnstore index is a core analytical technology in Azure SQL that provide high compression of data and fast analytic capabilities. A Clustered Columnstore index might be a good solution if you have a large number of documents in the table because it can efficiently compress JSON documents, decreasing IO required to load documents and improving performance of analytic reports that you might run on your documents. The following code can add Clustered Columnstore index on a table containing JSON documents:

```
CREATE CLUSTERED COLUMNSTORE INDEX cci ON WebSite.Logs;
```

Clustered Columnstore indexes on top of tables with JSON documents are a good choice if you need to do analytics on JSON documents. Columnstore indexes will apply so-called batch mode processing where they will leverage vector processing and SIMD instructions that can boost performance of your analytic queries over JSON data.

In the scenarios where you need to filter or sort documents using some specific property in JSON text, you can also leverage standard SQL language features such as computed columns and indexes. Computed columns can expose a value from JSON content with the JSON_VALUE function, and you can create standard B-tree index on this computed expression, as it is shown in the following code:

```
alter table WebSite.Logs
add [$severity] AS JSON_VALUE(log, '$.severity');
go

create index ix_severity on WebSite.Logs ([$severity]);
```

The computed column $severity is just a named expression that exposes value from JSON content stored in column log. It doesn't use additional space unless you want to explicitly pre-compute the extracted value by adding a PERSISTED keyword. Whenever you filter or sort rows using the JSON_VALUE(log, '$.severity') expression, Azure SQL will know that there is an index on the matching and use it to speed up your query.

Importing JSON documents

Modern services send data formatted as JSON, and in many cases, you will need to store these JSON values in Azure SQL tables. Azure SQL provides the OPENJSON Table-Value Function that accepts a textual parameter containing JSON text, parses it, and returns the values from the JSON document in tabular format. If you want to import an array of objects by providing them as a parameter to a procedure, you can use something like the following code to insert an incoming JSON message into a table:

```
CREATE OR ALTER PROCEDURE InsertDeviceLog (@msg nvarchar(max))
AS
INSERT INTO WebApi.Logs(logDate, severity, log)
SELECT *
FROM OPENJSON(@msg)
    WITH (
        logDate datetime2 '$.properties.DeviceTime',
        severity tinyint '$.properties.severity',
        log nvarchar(max) '$.info' AS JSON
    );
GO
```

The first argument of OPENJSON function is a text containing the JSON array that should be parsed. This function expects to get an array of JSON objects where every object will be converted into a new row in the result. If the array that should be converted is placed somewhere within the document, you can provide a second parameter that represents a JSON path where OPENJSON function should find the array of objects that should be transformed to the resultset. Every object in the referenced array will become one object in the resultset that will be returned.

The WITH clause is used to define the output schema and to map the properties from the objects in the JSON array to the output columns. This section will contain one entry per each output column with the following information:

- Name of the output column. If an optional JSON path is not provided, this name is also the key of the JSON property that should be returned as a result value in this column.

- SQL type of the output column. OPENJSON will use the semantic of CONVERT T-SQL function to convert the textual value in parsed JSON text to SQL value.

- Optional JSON path that will be used to reference the property in the JSON object that contains the value that should be returned. If this path is not specified, the name of the column will be used to reference the property. As an example, if the column name is severity and the JSON path is not specified, then OPENJSON will try to find a value on the $.severity path.

- Optional AS JSON clause. By default, OPENJSON will use JSON_VALUE function to get the value from the object that is currently converted. Therefore, it cannot return sub-objects or sub-arrays. If there is a JSON object or array on that path, it will not be returned unless you specify the AS JSON clause.

The result of the OPENJSON function will be a resultset that can be inserted into the table.

Graph structures

Graphs are complex structures with objects (nodes) that are connected with relationships (edges). Scenarios where you would use graphs might be:

- Social networks where you have people connected with relationships like friends, family, partners, or co-workers

- Transportation maps where you have towns and places connected with roads, rivers, and flight lines

- Bill-Of-Materials solutions where you have parts connected to other parts that are themselves connected to other parts and so on

The graph structures might be represented as tables and foreign keys relationships in some scenarios. The key reason why you would choose graph model instead of relational model is when you are working on a project where relationships are dominant and there are a small number of entities connected to each other in many different, direct, and indirect ways. In fact, the key difference in that domain is the transitive nature of the relationship. The term transitive is hereby used for its mathematical meaning: if a is connected to b and if b is connected to c, then a is connected to c. In these cases, you would not be interested only in a single-hop relationship (like fetching order lines for an order via foreign key relationship), but in all the hops needed to move from one node to another. To do that efficiently, you would like to leverage graph-specific semantics for query processing. Examples might be abilities to find the transitive closure (is a connected to z?), to find a shortest path between two objects or recursively traverse across all relationships starting with a specified object.

In Azure SQL, nodes and edges are represented using special tables. You may be wondering why using relational tables has been the chosen implementation to represent graph elements and if that is a good idea at all.

First, it is very common to have some information tied to nodes and edges, and tables are a perfect structure to hold that information. A second benefit of using tables is that the Azure SQL query optimizer can be leveraged to improve overall query performance. The third benefit of this choice is that, as they are just tables, columnstore and indexes can be used to improve performance even further.

As an example, let's look at the simple structure that models Airports and the Flight lines that represent connection between them. This domain might be modeled using the following structure:

```
CREATE TABLE Airport (
    AirportID int PRIMARY KEY,
    Name NVARCHAR(100),
    CityID int FOREIGN KEY REFERENCES Application.Cities(CityID)
) AS NODE
GO
CREATE TABLE Flightline (
    Name NVARCHAR(10)
) AS EDGE;
```

Airport is a node of the graph, but it behaves as a regular table. We can add any column, index, or constraint to describe information in this node. This is another example of how Azure SQL multi-model capabilities enable you to combine advanced battle-tested database features in the new scenarios. Node table has a hidden column that represents a unique identifier of the node that would be explained later.

Flightline is an edge table that links two Airport tables. The columns in this table represent additional information that describe the relationship between two nodes. Edge table shown in this example is a generic edge, and there is no specification that it is designed to connect two Airports and not some other nodes. In order to explicitly specify that Flightline connects Airport, we need to introduce the following edge constraint:

```
ALTER TABLE Flightline
ADD CONSTRAINT [Connecting airports]
                CONNECTION (Airport TO Airport)
                ON DELETE CASCADE;
```

This constraint specifies that you cannot use Flightline edge to connect nodes other than Airport. This constraint also defines what would happen with the edge if the node is deleted.

Loading graph data

Node tables are classic tables that can be loaded or read like any other classic table. Every node table has a hidden column called $NODE_ID that you will use only in some special scenarios. An Edge table has hidden "foreign key relationship" columns that are under the hood used to connect edges with associated nodes using $NODE_ID values. This is important to know when you import data in the edges because you need to fetch the $NODE_ID value of related nodes to bind them. Let us assume that the Airport nodes are already loaded and that we are importing a set of edges from the blob storage using OPENROWSET function. In order to load data in the edge table, we need to join loaded records with nodes, find the $NODE_ID values, and insert them into the edge table together with imported airline name:

```
INSERT INTO Flightline ($from_id, $to_id, Name)
SELECT f.$NODE_ID, t.$NODE_ID, a.Name
FROM OPENROWSET(
        BULK 'data/flightlines.csv',
        DATA_SOURCE = 'MyAzureBlobStorage',
        FORMATFILE='data/flightlines.fmt',
        FORMATFILE_DATA_SOURCE = 'MyAzureBlobStorage') as a
    JOIN Airport f ON f.Name = a.FromAirport
    JOIN Airport t ON t.Name = a.ToAirport;
```

The Flightlines CSV file contains information about source and destination airport and the name of the flight line between them. We need to join this data with Airports by Name column and get the $NODE_ID values that should be imported.

Querying graph data

Once we load data, we can use Cypher expressions (`www.opencypher.org/`), one of the most common ways to query graph data. The following query will traverse all paths from source airport node via airline edge to another airport node:

```
SELECT
    src.Name, line.Name, dest.Name
FROM
    Airport src, Flightline line, Airport dest
WHERE
    MATCH(src-(line)->dest)
AND
    src.Name='Belgrade';
```

This query will return all destinations from Belgrade to all other towns. MATCH clause defines that a path from source airport (`src`) to destination airport (`dest`) should be established via flight line table (`line`).

The main advantage of graph processing support in Azure SQL is the ability to query across the edges of the nodes. As an example, SHORTEST_PATH predicate enables you to find the shortest paths between two nodes. You can leverage this function to find the shortest route between two towns, as it is shown in the following code:

```
WITH routes AS (
    SELECT
        src.Name,
        STRING_AGG(dest.name, '->')
            WITHIN GROUP (GRAPH PATH) AS path,
        COUNT(dest.name)
            WITHIN GROUP (GRAPH PATH) AS stops,
        LAST_VALUE(line.name)
            WITHIN GROUP (GRAPH PATH) AS lastFlight,
        LAST_VALUE(dest.name)
            WITHIN GROUP (GRAPH PATH) AS destination
    FROM
        Airport src,
            Flightline FOR PATH line,
            Airport FOR PATH dest
```

```
WHERE
      MATCH(SHORTEST_PATH(src(-(line)->dest)+))
AND
      src.Name='BEG'
)
SELECT TOP (10) path, stops, lastFlight, destination
FROM routes
WHERE destination IN ('JFK', 'SEA');
```

The SHORTEST_PATH clause within the MATCH clause will find the shortest path between starting and end location that are not directly connected. Aggregate STRING_AGG will concatenate all airport names on the path and display them with arrow -> separator. COUNT and LAST_VALUE will show the number of stops on itinerary and ending flight and town on the shortest route. Once the shortest path exploration is finished, we need to select destination towns in the final query.

Graph processing capabilities in Azure SQL enable you to reduce complexity of your models and queries that should analyze different paths and relationships between tables.

Spatial data

Representing spatial objects (places, roads, country borders) is something that doesn't ideally fit into a structured relational model in normal form. Although you can represent a road or a border as a set of small straight lines where every line is stored in a separate row with the ends connected to the lines that continue the road, this is not an efficient representation.

The queries that you would run against spatial objects usually have conditions like "is this place within the shape" or "how far is the place from the road." These are not the typical queries that you would describe using standard SQL language.

Azure SQL has specialized functionalities that conform to the Open Geospatial Consortium (OGC) standards that enable you to implement applications that work with spatial data:

- Specialized types that can be used to represent complex geometrical and geographical objects and shapes (Point, Line, Polygon). All shapes can be represented as geometry or geography models, which will be described more in detail soon.

- Functionalities specialized for spatial querying such as finding the distance between two points (ST_DISTANCE), determining whether an area contains a specified point (ST_CONTAINS), and so on.

- Specialized indexes that are optimized for spatial types of queries.

This set of capabilities enables you to create advanced queries that are specific for spatial domains.

Remember the airport and flight line model described in the previous section. Graph models that connect airports (nodes) using flight lines (edges) might be perfect to find the shortest route between two towns. However, imagine that you need to find all airlines that are crossing Nebraska or unnamed crossroads where two highways intersect. If there is no explicit relationship between highways and all crossroads or countries, it would be impossible to answer these questions.

In order to solve these problems, we would need to extend graph model with geographical data, as shown in the following script:

```
CREATE TABLE Airport (
    AirportID int PRIMARY KEY,
    Name NVARCHAR(100),
    Location GEOGRAPHY,
    CityID int FOREIGN KEY REFERENCES Application.City(CityID)
) AS NODE
GO
CREATE TABLE FlightLine (
    Name NVARCHAR(10),
    Route GEOGRAPHY
) AS EDGE;
```

Azure SQL has two main base types that can be used to represent geometrical and geographical figures:

- GEOMETRY type represents data in a Euclidean (flat) coordinate system.

- GEOGRAPHY type represents data in a round-earth coordinate system.

Geometry is perfect for representing relatively small objects like buildings or interiors; Geography is better suited to represent much bigger shapes, like river, city, or nation boundaries and in general anything that needs to work on close approximation of Earth surface to avoid errors.

Within these two types, as specified by Open Geospatial Consortium, you can create more specific types:

- `Point` used to represent 2D places like towns

- `LineString` and `CircularString` that can represent open or closed lines like roads or borders

- `Polygon` and `CurvePolygon` used to represent areas like countries

- `MultiPoint`, `MultiLine`, and `MultiPolygon` representing a set of disconnected geographical objects that logically belong together (an archipelago with a set of islands might be represented with `MultiPolygon`)

In Azure SQL, once you have created a Geometry or Geography column in a table, you can use any of these types to build the shape you need. You can even use more than one at the same time, using Collections or "Multi" types.

Querying spatial data

Spatial data types in Azure SQL have the built-in methods that enable you to easily query spatial data. Under assumption that all information about the flight lines and airports are populated, we can create easily find the routes crossing state of Nebraska:

```
DECLARE @nebraska GEOGRAPHY = (
    SELECT TOP (1) Border FROM Application.StateProvinces
    WHERE StateProvinceName = 'Nebraska'
);

SELECT *
FROM FlightLine
WHERE Route.STIntersects(@nebraska) = 1;
```

STIntersects method determines if two shapes intersect at some place. This method returns 1 if a geography instance intersects another geography instance and 0 otherwise.

STDistance method measures the distance between two objects and enables you to find the objects closer to some specific coordinate. The following query returns five airports closest to the current location of some object:

```
DECLARE @currentLocation GEOGRAPHY = 'POINT(-121.626 47.8315)';

SELECT TOP(5) *
FROM Airports
ORDER BY Location.STDistance(@currentLocation) ASC;
```

The spatial queries are enabling you to easily perform specific analysis to resolve problems where you would need to spend a lot of time dealing with the specific mathematical transformations, without having you to write them yourself or to use another more specialized solution to perform the calculation, so that you don't have to move the data around, thus making your solution much more efficient.

Spatial indexes

In theory, STIntersects method might be implemented as a self-contained function with complex mathematical calculations that are trying to determine relationships between the figures. However, due to complexity of calculations, running that kind of function on many objects would be both time- and CPU-consuming. For efficient processing, Azure SQL uses a special type of Spatial indexes.

Spatial indexes internally create grid (shown in Figure 8-2) where cells may or may not overlap with the parts of figures that should be indexed.

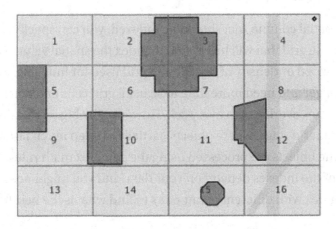

Figure 8-2. *Indexing spatial objects in 4x4 grid*

Azure SQL creates a grid, and for every spatial object that should be indexed, it records whether it fully or partially overlaps or doesn't overlap at all with the cells in the grid. This process is known as *tessellation*. With this technique, a STOverlaps method that needs to determine if two objects overlap will not immediately need to apply complex mathematical calculations to determine if there is some intersection between the objects. If an index is available, it will first use the index to check if there is at least one cell in the grid that belongs to both spatial objects or if the cell that belongs to one object also partially overlaps with another object. If this is true, then they overlap, and this is the faster way to determine if there is some interception. If there are no cells that at least partially overlap with both objects, then these objects do not overlap. If there are some cells that partially overlap with both objects, these objects might or might not overlap. Only in this case will Azure SQL apply complex spatial calculation, but not on the entire area of objects, just on smaller cells where they might potentially overlap. Although this might be CPU-consuming operation, it is performed on a small cell and probably the small part of objects that is within this cell. Therefore, this action would be few orders of magnitude faster than the naïve approach that would compare all parts of the objects.

Spatial indexes are created using the special CREATE SPATIAL INDEX syntax:

```
CREATE SPATIAL INDEX SI_Flightline_Routes
    ON Flightline(Route)
    USING GEOGRAPHY_GRID
    WITH (
    GRIDS = ( MEDIUM, LOW, MEDIUM, HIGH ),
     CELLS_PER_OBJECT = 64 );
```

Besides the spatial column that should be indexed, you can specify the characteristics of the grid that will be created to index the spatial values such as area that should be covered or density of tessellation grid used for indexing. More granular indexes will be bigger and need more time to scan all grid cells and determine whether the parts of the routes overlap with every cell. However, the bigger density of grids makes the worst-case scenario stage, where objects partially overlap much faster because smaller parts of the objects are processed using the complex math rules. This right size and parameters of the indexes depend on your data, and you might need to experiment and rebuild the index with different parameters to find what is the best fit for your data.

If you are unsure at the beginning, you can avoid the bounding box specification, and Azure SQL will try to guess the best bounding box and tessellation for you. Of course, the automatically defined values may not be the perfect ones in your scenario, so it is good to know that you can manually specify them if needed.

Geometry vs. Geography

As mentioned before, Azure SQL has two classes of spatial data types that are used in different scenarios:

- *Geometry data types* are used to represent planar mathematical shapes in classic 2D coordinate system.

- *Geography data types* are used to represent spherical objects and shapes projected into 2D plane.

The difference between geometry and geography types is one of the most important things that you need to understand to develop spatial applications.

Geography types are used to represent the objects placed in a classic 2D coordinate system, and you can imagine them as the objects that you could draw on the plain piece of paper. Distances and sizes of the objects are measured the same way you would measure distance of the objects drawn on a paper or a board. If you take a map and want to find the shortest flight trajectory between Belgrade, Serbia, Europe, and Seattle, Washington, US, you would probably use the straight horizontal line going via France and the US east coast. This is geometrically the shortest line between them. However, due to the rounded shape of the earth, the shortest trajectory (called *geodesic)* is going via Iceland, Greenland, and Canada. Geography data model is considering Earth's actual shape and is able to find the real-world shortest distance and path.

Mapping the Earth surface to a 2D plane is the most difficult spatial problem. Famous mathematician Carl Gauss proved in his Theorema Egregium (Latin for "Remarkable Theorem") that spherical surfaces cannot be mapped to 2D planes without distortion. You might notice on some maps that the territories closer to the poles such as Greenland, Antarctica, north of Canada, and Russia might look stretched or sometime bigger than actual. This happens due to the fact that dense coordinates closer to poles must be "stretched" to project them in 2D coordinates. To make things even harder, the Earth surface is not spherical nor even ellipsoid. Irregular shape of Earth and proximity to poles force people to use different strategies of mapping to 2D plane. There are

217

mapping rules that preserve correct distance shortest paths, shape, and vice versa, but in every strategy, something will be distorted. That's why every geography object has an associated *Spatial Reference Identifier (SRID)* that describes what spatial transformation strategy is used to translate the object from the earth globe into the 2D plane. *SRID* describes what coordinates are used (latitude/longitude, easting/northing), unit of measure, where is coordinate root, and so on. Azure SQL will derive information from SRID to compare positions of the objects.

In the following example, you can see how to transform coordinates to the Geography line by specifying that the World Geodetic System 1984 (WGS84) with SRID 4326 is used for transformation:

```
DECLARE @g GEOGRAPHY;
SET @g = GEOGRAPHY::STGeomFromText('LINESTRING(-122.360 47.656, -122.343
47.656)', 4326);
SELECT @g.STSrid;
```

Some countries need to use multiple SRID in their territory, especially if their north and south borders are far like in Chile. In these scenarios, you would need to align SRID before comparing positions of the geography objects. Specifying different SRID would result in the different positions or shapes. Measuring the differences between spatial objects with coordinates determined using different SRID would lead to wrong results. Therefore, in Azure SQL spatial operations cannot be performed between spatial objects with different SRIDs.

WGS84 is the most commonly used standard and is the one also used on the GPS system in our phone or car. If you are unsure of which SRID to use, very good chances are that WGS84 will work perfectly for you.

The good news for you is that all these complex transformations are built in into Azure SQL. The only thing you need to do is to leverage functionalities and learn the basic principles that will help you to understand how to use Spatial features.

XML data

XML data type is the older brother of JSON. This feature was introduced in SQL Server Database engine between 2000 and 2005, while XML was the mainstream format for data exchange between different applications.

XML support in Azure SQL is similar to the JSON support described in the previous sections. If you need to parse XML data or format results of the queries as XML, you can use the following functionalities:

- `OPENXML` table value function that can parse an XML document

- `FOR XML` clause that can format results of the query as XML document

- XML type with methods for processing values in XML documents

If you have understood the `OPENJSON` function and `FOR JSON` clause explained in the section about JSON support, then you probably understand the purpose of `OPENXML` function and `FOR XML` clause. The difference between these XML functionalities and matching JSON functionalities are trivial, so they will not be explained in more detail.

The key difference between JSON and XML support in Azure SQL is native XML type. Unlike JSON support where JSON text is stored in native `NVARCHAR` type, XML has a dedicated SQL type. XML is standardized type in many languages (e.g., `System.Xml.Document` in .NET framework), so it makes sense to have parity in SQL type. The key difference is that in JSON cases you are using string-like functions to parse JSON, while XML content is represented as an object where you can use various methods to extract data.

Querying XML data

XML type has the following member methods that you can use to extract value from and manipulate XML:

- `value(path, type)` that returns a node or attribute from XML object and automatically converts it into a SQL type. You need to specify a standard XPath expression that targets a single value in the XML document.

- `query(path)` – This method returns an object from the XML document on a specified XPath expression.

- `nodes(path)` is very similar to OPENXML/OPENJSON functions, and it is used to transform an array of XML elements on the specified path to a set of rows that can be used in a FROM clause.

- `exists(path)` is a method that checks if there's an existing element on the specified path.

- `modify(path, type)` method enables you to insert, delete, or replace values of some nodes in XML document.

XML querying capabilities will be explained using the following example:

```
DECLARE @i INT = 47;
DECLARE @x xml;
SET @x='<Family id="1804">
    <row id="17"><name>Robin</name></row>
    <row id="47"><name>Lana</name></row>
    <row id="81"><name>Merriam</name></row>
</Family>';

SELECT
  family_id = @x.value('(/Family/@id)[1]', 'int'),
  family_81_name = @x.value('(//row[@id=81]/name)[1]', 'varchar(20)'),
  family_name = @x.query('//row[@id=sql:variable("@i")]/name')

SELECT
  family_member = xrow.value('name[1]', 'varchar(20)'),
  family_member_id = xrow.value('@id[1]', 'varchar(20)'),
  family_member_xml = xrow.query('.')
FROM
  @x.nodes('/Family/row') AS Members(xrow)
WHERE
  xrow.value('@id[1]', 'int') < 50
AND
  xrow.exist('.[@id > 5]') = 1
```

The first query uses the value member function of @x variable to extract the values of family identifier and name of the family member with id 81 and the name of the member with identifier value equal to the variable @i.

The second query takes all /family/row nodes from XML document as a rowset under the condition that the id attribute of each row is less than 50 and greater than 5. Every node that satisfies this condition is returned as column named xrow. Method value() is used to extract the value that will be compared with 50 with SQL operator, while exist() method is used to directly push down predicate to XML variable. Finally, the methods value() and query() are used to get the name, identifier, and XML content from each returned row.

Another interesting feature is the ability to bind the values of SQL variables or columns in the XPath expressions. In the preceding example, you could see that the third expression in the first SELECT clause uses SQL variable @i from the outer script. This might be a flexible way to specify how to find the data.

Another functionality that might be handy is the ability to directly update XML documents without need to parse it, transform it into relational format, and then reconstruct XML again using FOR XML clause. Azure SQL provides modify() method where you can specify expression that will insert, delete, or replace value in the XML document:

```
SET @x.modify('insert <row id="109"><name>Danica</name></row>
            into (/Family)[1]') ;
SELECT @x;
```

Although XML functionalities in Azure SQL are not core scenarios that you will frequently use, given that XML is not a mainstream format anymore, you can still use them to resolve various problems that require querying and transforming XML data.

XPath and XQuery languages

Azure SQL supports XML standards that enable you to implement complex processing and querying over XML documents. XML support in Azure SQL is based on the following languages:

- XPath (XML Path Language) is a query language for selecting nodes from an XML document.

- XQuery (XML Query) is a query and functional programming language that queries and transforms collections of XML data.

XPath is an expression-based syntax used in value(), nodes(), and query() methods to specify the element within the XML document that should be located:

- Hierarchical expressions – Use XPath to specify the path from the root of XML document to desired element within the document. As an example, XPath /Family/row/name is used to reference the elements <name> that are placed under the <row> element, which is placed under the <Family> element that is the root of XML document. There can be multiple elements that match the same XPath expression, so you should use indexing operator [ ] to specify the elements that match expression should be referenced.

- Node and attribute references – XPath enables you to reference either node or their attributes. Any name that doesn't start with @ will be treated as a name of XML node, while the names starting with @ (e.g., @id in the preceding example) will be treated as an attribute.

- Recursive expressions – In some cases, you don't want to or cannot reference the entire path from the root, or you need to find elements that are positioned in the different locations of the document. Recursive operator // enables you to specify a "detached path" where XML functions will try to find any path that matches the expression right of the recursive operator. As an example, //row/name will find any <name> element within the <row> element that is placed anywhere in the XML document.

- Predicates enable you to specify some condition that elements must meet to be matched with XPath expression. As an example, //row[@id=17]/name specifies that the XML methods should find any <name> element within the <row> element that has id attribute with value 17. The predicates are the easy way to filter out some nodes that don't satisfy some condition.

XPath can be a very powerful language that you can use to declaratively specify criteria for selecting the information from XML documents.

You can also use other XPath features like namespaces that enable you to define the scopes of names and match only the names within the same namespace; seven-direction axis that enables you to reference parents, siblings, and descendants; or build-in functions that can help you transform the results within the expressions.

XPath is complemented with XQuery language that is also supported in Azure SQL. XQuery is a standardized language for querying and processing collections of elements in XML documents. XQuery defines a SQL-like syntax called *FLWOR* (pronounced "flower") that represents FOR, LET, WHERE, ORDER BY, and RETURN operators that you can use to transform XML nodes. These operators enable you to select, transform, and return new objects based on existing data. XQuery enables you to use the values from the nodes that are processed using the curly braces ({...}) template. An example of *FLWOR* operations in XML query() method selecting nodes from XML variable and transforming content into new XML structure is shown in the following listing:

```
SELECT xrow.query(
'let $r := self::node()
  return <person id="{$r/@id}">{$r/name/text()}</person>')
FROM @x.nodes('/Family/row') AS Members(xrow);
-------------------------------------------------------
<person id="17">Robin</person>
<person id="47">Lana</person>
<person id="81">Merriam</person>
```

The XML nodes() method emits three XML rows from the variable @x used in the previous example, and then the query method processes them using an XQuery expression. In the body of the XQuery expression, the current node is assigned to the variable $r, and the return statement creates a new XML node where id attribute and content of the name node are injected in template. As a result, this XQuery expression will return transformed XML shown below the query. As you can see, XQuery has a lot of power that can be used to implement complex processing of XML elements.

XML indexes

Due to the very specific nature of XML queries, standard B-tree indexes might not provide sufficient query performance boosts. Azure SQL provides several specialized types of indexes that enable efficient processing of XPath/XQuery expressions. The following types of indexes are available in Azure SQL:

- The *primary XML index* is a pre-computed structure that contains the shredded values and nodes from the XML column. Azure SQL uses the values from primary index instead of invoking expensive parsing of XML type with value(), nodes(), or query() methods. This is very similar to automatic index on JSON documents that Azure Cosmos DB uses.

- A *secondary XML index* improves the performance of the queries that search or filter XML documents using exists() method or returns multiple values from XML document using value() method.

- *Selective XML indexes* index only specified paths in XML column. This is very similar to multiple B-tree indexes on the predefined XML expressions.

Selective XML indexes are the recommended approach for indexing based on the learnings from the multiple XML scenarios in SQL Server. The SQL Server team found that automatic indexing of all possible fields leads to large size of XML indexes, and on the other side, most of the indexed paths are not used. Therefore, selective XML indexes became the best choice and trade-off between usability, performance, and size.

In the following example, you can see how to create a selective XML Index on a simple table:

```
CREATE TABLE XmlDocs (
  id INT IDENTITY PRIMARY KEY,
  doc XML
);
GO

CREATE SELECTIVE XML INDEX sxi_docs
ON XmlDocs(doc)
FOR (
    path_price = '/row/info/price' AS SQL INT,
    path_name = '/row/info/name' AS SQL NVARCHAR(100)
)
```

In selective indexes, you can choose the paths that should be included in the index and specify their types. The queries that use value() function on doc column with XPath queries as defined in the index specifications would be able to leverage the sxi_doc index, gaining a huge performance boost, even while the index is very small.

Key-value pairs

Azure SQL doesn't have a specialized structure that holds key-value pairs. The reason is simple: key-value maps can be implemented using the simple two-column table.

Azure SQL enables you to customize your two-column table and index the key column using various indexes. With memory-optimized tables, which will be discussed in detail in the next chapter, you can index the key column using B-tree or Hash indexes. In the following example, you can find a memory-optimized, lock-free, natively compiled, key-value table with a HASH index that enables faster access to the keys:

```
CREATE TABLE [Cache] (
    [key] BIGINT IDENTITY,
    value NVARCHAR(MAX),
    INDEX IX_Hash_Key HASH ([key]) WITH (BUCKET_COUNT = 100000)
) WITH (MEMORY_OPTIMIZED = ON, DURABILITY = SCHEMA_ONLY);
```

This structure enables fast retrieval of the keys using hash indexes, which is optimal for elementary get/put operations. Memory-optimized tables have optimistic lock-free data access, and SCHEMA_ONLY durability ensures faster updates because data is not persisted to disk. In addition, if the values are formatted as JSON format, we can use native JSON functions to filter and process data right in the database, as you learned at the beginning of this chapter.

One of the scenarios for key-value structures in Azure SQL is centralized caching. There is a well-known case study in SQL Server 2016 that showed how the customer replaced a distributed cache mechanism that was able to achieve 150K requests/sec on 19 distributed SQL Server nodes, with a memory-optimized table in a single server that increased performance to 1.2 million requests/sec. The targeted scenario was implementation of ASP.NET Session cache. Azure SQL uses the same technology as SQL Server, and the same technology can be used for caching in Azure cloud.

In many real-world projects, caching using a specialized engine is usually the preferred choice, but that means that you need to master another technology, and you need to figure out how to best integrate it with your solution. Usually this effort is a good choice as caching solutions are much cheaper than a full-blown Azure SQL database, but if you are already using Azure SQL in the first place, knowing that you have this ability right in the database can provide you an additional option that you may want to evaluate to simplify the overall architecture.

How to handle unstructured text?

The most difficult to handle but not so uncommon case is unstructured textual data. In some cases, you will have textual data that cannot be nicely organized in JSON or XML format, but you would need to implement some searches on that text. One common example is HTML code that is placed in the database. Ideally, HTML should be the same as XML if it conforms to XHTML specification, but in many cases, HTML might have some variation that breaks strict XML structure.

Azure SQL enables you to use LIKE clauses to determine if the text column matches some pattern. The following query finds all stock items where SearchDetails and Tags columns contain the text entered in some search text box in user interface:

```
SELECT si.StockItemID, si.StockItemName, si.Tags
FROM Warehouse.StockItems AS si
WHERE si.SearchDetails LIKE N'%' + @SearchText + N'%'
OR si.Tags LIKE N'%' + @SearchText + N'%'
```

LIKE predicate uses the percent sign (%) to match zero or more of any character and the underscore (_) matches any one character. These special characters in the pattern expression on the right side of LIKE operator enable you to define various patterns such as text beginning or ending with some text sequence. LIKE operator is a very handy tool that is commonly used for text searches on small datasets. Azure SQL can optimize and use indexes even when using the LIKE operator, especially if you are using LIKE to search all text that *starts with* some prefix. In such cases, an index and the LIKE operator can provide very good performance. If you need instead to do a more complex search, for example, looking for specific words *contained* somewhere in your text, especially if you are working with bigger text sets, you might want to consider some text indexing solution described in the next section to improve performance even more.

Indexing unstructured text

If you need to search huge amounts of unstructured textual data, you would need to use some kind of specific indexing. Azure has a generic Azure Cognitive Search index service that enables you to index various data sources. But again, using an external service would add a bit more complexity to your solution. While Azure Cognitive Search provides a great set of specialized features, if you don't need all of those, you may be happy to know that Azure SQL uses a similar localized text search index called Full-Text Search (FTS) index. An FTS index is a structure that indexes unstructured text fields in specified tables. An example of FTS index created on three text fields in StockItems table is shown in the following listing:

```
CREATE FULLTEXT CATALOG [Main] AS DEFAULT;
GO

CREATE FULLTEXT INDEX
ON Warehouse.StockItems (SearchDetails, CustomFields, Tags)
KEY INDEX PK_Warehouse_StockItems
WITH CHANGE_TRACKING AUTO;
GO
```

An FTS index contains a set of text fragments (tokens) divided using a set of word breakers. The tokens in the FTS index have the keys of the origin rows where the text is found. FTS enables you to provide some simple description of text pattern and return the keys of the rows that match the criterion.

Querying unstructured text

Once you set up your FTS index, you can use the following functionalities to search rows using text match:

- CONTAINS and FREETEXT that check whether the values in some columns match the predicate defined in the text predicate

- Table-value functions CONTAINSTABLE and FREETEXTTABLE that return identifiers of the rows where text matches some criterion

The following example shows how to find all keys from Warehouse.StockItems table where the SearchDetails column contains text that matches search criterion that is defined in @SearchCriterion variable:

```
DECLARE @SearchCondition NVARCHAR(200) = 'blue car';

SELECT StockItemID = ft.[KEY], ft.[RANK]
FROM FREETEXTTABLE(Warehouse.StockItems, SearchDetails, @SearchCondition)
AS ft
```

⊞ Results 🗗 Messages

	StockItemID	RANK
1	58	83
2	59	83
3	60	142
4	61	83
5	62	83
6	63	83
7	67	83
8	68	83
9	69	142
10	70	83

The KEY column is an identifier of a row in StockItems table that is used in the FTS index and represents the record that is returned by FREETEXTTABLE or CONTAINSTABLE functions. RANK column describes how well the row matched the selection criteria. This resultset can be joined with the original table using the KEY column to get more results. The following example shows how to find all stock items with the keys returned by FTS function:

```
DECLARE @SearchCondition NVARCHAR(200) = 'blue AND car';

SELECT
  si.StockItemID,
  si.StockItemName,
  ft.[RANK]
FROM
  Warehouse.StockItems AS si
INNER JOIN
 CONTAINSTABLE(Warehouse.StockItems, SearchDetails, @SearchCondition) AS ft
ON si.StockItemID = ft.[KEY]
ORDER BY
  ft.[RANK];
```

	StockItemID	StockItemName	RANK
1	60	RC toy sedan car with remote control (Blue) 1/5...	64
2	69	Ride on toy sedan car (Blue) 1/12 scale	64

Table-value functions CONTAINSTABLE and FREETEXTTABLE match text based on exact or fuzzy match. One difference between these functions is that CONTAINSTABLE does more exact matching, while FREETEXTTABLE uses fuzzy matching using thesaurus, synonyms, and inflectional forms. If the word "children" is provided as a search criterion, FREETEXTTABLE will also match rows containing "child", but CONTAINSTABLE will not. In CONTAINSTABLE, you need to explicitly specify the expression FORMSOF(INFLEC TIONAL,children) to instruct Azure SQL to include inflectional forms of this word.

Another difference is that CONTAINSTABLE enables you to specify operators like AND, OR, or NEAR to define how you want to search text. In the previous examples, you might see that we have provided set of words "blue car" to FREETEXTTABLE, and this function will return all rows that have any of these words like in most web search engines. In the CONTAINSTABLE example, we need to explicitly specify operators like AND, OR, or NEAR to specify what should be searched, for example, "blue AND car" or "blue OR car".

Instead of functions FREETEXTTABLE and CONTAINSTABLE, you can use equivalent predicates FREETEXT and CONTAINS. These predicates can be used in WHERE clause of the query, and they are functionally equivalent with explicit JOIN with FREETEXTTABLE and CONTAINSTABLE, with the exception that you won't have the RANK column available:

```
DECLARE @SearchCondition NVARCHAR(200) =
          'FORMSOF(INFLECTIONAL,children) OR car';
SELECT
  si.StockItemID,
  si.StockItemName,
  si.SearchDetails
FROM
  Warehouse.StockItems AS si
WHERE
  CONTAINS(SearchDetails, @SearchCondition);
```

If there is some stock item containing the word `'cars'`, it will not be returned in the result because `CONTAINS` uses exact match using the word `'car'`. However, if we use `FREETEXT` with `'children cars'` search expression, this predicate will use inflectional forms of both words.

Full-text search is a very powerful tool that can help you to implement very complex searches with a simple expression.

How to leverage unstructured indexes on semi-structured data?

Full-text search is not limited only to unstructured text. You can use FTS indexes to improve performance of some JSON search queries where you need to filter documents that have key-value pairs defined by the client. After all, an FTS index is very similar to a *Generalized Inverted Index (GIN)* that is used in many databases exactly to index JSON data.

Let's imagine that we need to implement functionality that searches a large set of JSON documents using arbitrary key-value combinations. Adding a B-Tree index on every possible key would be inefficient, and a `CLUSTERED COLUMNSTORE` index on JSON data is designed for analytical use cases and thus is not a good solution for filtering.

If we know that value is a single word, we can leverage the fact that JSON is stored as text and that key and value are near to each other. In that case, FTS that filters all JSON texts that have required key and value near to each other might provide correct results. The query that finds all JSON document with pairs

```
{"Color":"Silver","MakeFlag":true,"SafetyStockLevel":100}
```

is shown in the following listing:

```
SELECT si.StockItemID, si.StockItemName, si.Tags
FROM Warehouse.StockItems AS si
WHERE CONTAINS(CustomFields, 'NEAR((Color,Silver),1)
                    AND NEAR((MakeFlag,true),1)
                    AND NEAR((SafetyStockLevel,100),1)')
```

The NEAR operator in the CONTAINS predicate is a good choice for JSON scenarios where key of json property is near value. This kind of predicate will quickly find all text cells that have words "Color" and "Silver" close together, which is actually the case in JSON structure. In addition, CONTAINS clause enables us to specify complex predicates with AND, OR, and other relational predicates. However, FTS will not guarantee that "Color" is key and that "Silver" is value in the text, because it doesn't understand the semantic of text parts in JSON structure. If you have some JSON document containing text "color silver", it will be returned by CONTAINS predicate, although this is not key-value pair.

In order to remove false-positive results, we can apply standard JSON predicates that double-check condition and guarantee the correctness of results:

```
SELECT ProductID, Name
FROM ProductCatalog
WHERE CONTAINS(Data, 'NEAR((Color,Silver),1)
AND NEAR((MakeFlag,true),1)
AND NEAR((SafetyStockLevel,100),1)')
AND JSON_VALUE(Data,'$.Color') = 'Silver'
AND JSON_VALUE(Data,'$.MakeFlag') = 'true'
AND JSON_VALUE(Data,'$.SafetyStockLevel') = '100'
```

This query leverages the best of FTS and JSON features to return the required result:

- CONTAINS will quickly filter out most of the entries that don't satisfy the condition and might significantly reduce the number of candidate rows that might contain the needed data. Without this part, we would end up with full table scan and applying the JSON functions on every row.

- JSON_VALUE will perform an exact check on the smaller candidate set returned by FTS. These predicates guarantee that correct results will be returned, and we are sure that we don't need to apply them on every document.

This example again shows how Azure SQL features nicely fit together and enable you to implement various scenarios.

Multi-model in Azure SQL: why and when

Azure SQL is a modern multi-model database platform that enables you to use different data formats and combine them in order to design the best data model that will match the requirements of your domain. Depending on your scenario, you can represent relations as classic foreign key relationships or graph nodes/edges. Semi-structured data can be stored in JSON, Spatial, or XML columns.

You just learned how you can use all these features. It's now time to discuss why and when.

One of the biggest advantages of Azure SQL is interoperability between core database features and multi-model capabilities. You can easily combine Columnstore with graphs or JSON data to get high-performance analytics capabilities on graph/JSON data, built-in language processing rules to customize application for any market, use all features that T-SQL language provides to create any query or powerful report, and integrate it with a variety of tools that understand T-SQL.

With Azure SQL, you are getting the core functionalities that other NoSQL databases provide, plus a lot of standard relational database functionalities that can be easily integrated with NoSQL features. This is the most important reason why you should choose the multi-model capabilities of Azure SQL.

So, should you choose Azure SQL with its multi-model capabilities or some specialized NoSQL Database engine that has more advanced features in these areas? That's a very interesting – and not easy – question to answer.

Azure SQL is not a NoSQL database. If you have a classic NoSQL scenario that requires advanced graph or document support and you don't expect to have to deal with other data that would otherwise be better stored into a table, then you should surely evaluate full-fledged graph or document databases such as Azure Cosmos DB, MongoDB, Neo4j, and so on. These database engines are fully oriented on NoSQL scenarios and have implemented richer and more advanced NoSQL features. They address a very specific area and they are extremely good at it.

The most important question that you need to ask yourself is what kind of additional NoSQL functionalities would your application need. Both Azure SQL and NoSQL database engines provide similar levels of fundamental graph and document processing functionalities (e.g., inserting, modifying, indexing, and searching). If you need more than these basic features, Azure SQL gives you an ability to leverage advanced querying using T-SQL, Columnstore technology for analytic, built-in machine learning capabilities with R/Python support, collations, replication mechanisms, and other functionalities that are proven as necessary in most of the real-world application. If you believe that these functionalities might be important for your application, then Azure SQL is the right choice for you.

If you want to know more

Lots of concepts and technologies have been discussed in this chapter. As usual, if you want to know more, you can find more food for your brain here:

- Multi-model capabilities of Azure SQL Database & SQL Managed Instance – `https://docs.microsoft.com/azure/azure-sql/multi-model-features`

- Dapper.Stream – `https://github.com/JocaPC/Dapper.Stream/`

- JSON Data in SQL Server – `https://docs.microsoft.com/sql/relational-databases/json/json-data-sql-server`

- Getting started with JSON features in Azure SQL – `https://docs.microsoft.com/azure/azure-sql/database/json-features`

- Graph processing with SQL Server and Azure SQL – `https://docs.microsoft.com/sql/relational-databases/graphs/sql-graph-overview`

- Spatial Data – `https://docs.microsoft.com/sql/relational-databases/spatial/spatial-data-sql-server`

- Spatial Indexes Overview – `https://docs.microsoft.com/sql/relational-databases/spatial/spatial-indexes-overview`

- World Geodetic System (WGS84) – `https://gisgeography.com/wgs84-world-geodetic-system/`

- Full-Text Search – `https://docs.microsoft.com/sql/relational-databases/search/full-text-search`

CHAPTER 9

More Than Tables

In the previous chapter, we learned about the Hobits (HoBT, Heap or B-Tree) – classic tables and indexes that are the most common objects in relational databases. In this chapter, you will learn about some special types of tables and indexes that can help you to build better designs for certain scenarios. Objects that will be explained in this chapter are:

- Columnstore structures that can improve performance of your reporting and analytic workloads

- Memory-optimized tables that can improve your OLTP workloads with CRUD-like actions

- Temporal tables that can preserve the entire history of the changes you made and enable you to perform historical and time travel analysis of data

Columnstore format

Rowstore format is the default storage format for tables in Azure SQL, and it is proven as an optimal structure for most general-purpose workloads. In rowstore format, the cell values belonging to a single row are physically placed close together in fixed-size 8KB structure called *pages*.[1] This is a good solution if you should execute the queries that select or update the entire row or a set of rows. If you run the queries like `SELECT * FROM <table> WHERE <condition>`, where the `<condition>` predicate will select a single row or a small set of rows, the rowstore format is an excellent choice. Once the database engine locates the 8KB pages where the row(s) is placed, most of the data will be on that page and loaded with a single data page access.

---

[1]There are some exceptions such as Large Objects (LOB) types that are placed outside of 8KB page.

© Davide Mauri, Silvano Coriani, Anna Hoffman, Sanjay Mishra, Jovan Popovic 2021
D. Mauri et al., *Practical Azure SQL Database for Modern Developers*,
https://doi.org/10.1007/978-1-4842-6370-9_9

However, this is not the best solution in analytical and reporting queries that scan many rows like the one shown in the following listing:

```
SELECT State, AVG(Price)
FROM Sales.Products
GROUP BY State
```

In this type of analytical and reporting query, we need to access just two columns from all rows to calculate the result. Even in the presence of a Clustered Index, which would help to keep related data physically close to each other, a lot of resources will be put in loading data from unneeded columns: as obvious, this will have a negative impact on query performances.

It's important to highlight that since a database is usually a very concurrent system, the fact that Azure SQL loads into memory data that it doesn't need at all may not necessarily be a bad thing, as this will help other queries to have that data already in memory, and thus they will have better performance. As memory is a very limited resource, compared to disk space, it's important to understand what are the typical workload patterns for your system, so that every recommendation or best practice can be put into your system perspective. Especially with databases that cannot be optimized only for reads or for writes, finding the best balance is the key goal for developers and DBAs.

Columnstore format is used in many analytical systems to improve performance in these scenarios. In Columnstore format, the cells are physically grouped together in column *segments*. Column segment is a physically close set of all values from a single column. The table is physically represented as a set of column segments instead of a set of rows. The difference between rowstore and Columnstore formats is shown in Figure 9-1.

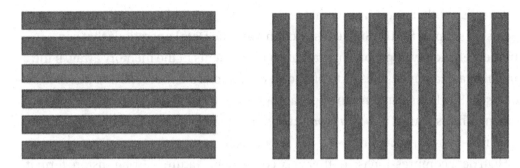

Figure 9-1. *Rowstore format is optimal when a query needs to access all values from single or few rows (on left), while columnstore is optimal when the query accesses all values from single or few columns (on right)*

In the rowstore format shown on the left side, a reporting query would need to go through all rows in the table, read every page, and take two out of ten columns in each row to calculate the result. This means that a query that uses two out of ten columns will roughly use only 20% of memory pages that need to read. If you have a table where you are using just the smaller columns for analysis, but you have big NVARCHAR columns in the row that will be discarded by the query, as they are not used in the specific query, the efficiency is even worse because NVARCHAR columns will occupy more space as their memory pages that must be fetched and discarded.

This might be a problem in memory caching architectures where underlying hardware takes the pages from the lower-level caches (or storage) to the higher-level memory caches because most of the data movement is in vain. Although that might look like a micro-optimization, you can see huge performance issues if you try to run these kind of queries on hundreds of thousands of rows already. Years of analysis and real-world experience show that the rowstore technology is not suitable for high-performance analytics and reporting.

Let's now focus on the Columnstore representation of the rows on the right side of Figure 9-1. All values per column are physically grouped together. This means that the reporting query would easily pick up two columns that are necessary to compute the result and read only these values. Other values in the different columns are not used at all, and maybe they are even not in memory. Since the full-scan queries need to read all values from all or the majority of rows, the efficiency of memory read is close to 100%. All values within the same column are physically placed close to each other, and all of them will be read and used by the query. This significantly boosts performance of analytical queries. It's actually quite common to see performance improvements of 10 or 100 times the original times based on rowstore.

There is another optimization that can be leveraged in this case. All modern processors support SIMD (Single Instruction Multiple Data) operations that can extremely efficiently apply one operation on all elements in the memory array. If the storage organization enables us to provide a continuous array of cells that needs to be processed, SIMD instruction can apply a single operation on all values in the column segment. This is known as *batch mode execution*, and it is much more efficient than classic row-by-row processing.

High data compression is another very convenient feature of Columnstore format. Columnstore structures might leverage the fact that the cell values that are stored together in column segments are similar. This characteristic enables Columnstore to apply various compression algorithms on the cells, such as:

- NULL-Values elimination – If there is a large percentage of missing values in the cells, Columnstore will just avoid storing these rows.

- Duplicate elimination – If a column has many identical values, Columnstore can record only one value and just mark the range of rows where this value occurs. This technique is also known as Run-Length Encoding.

- Dictionary normalization – String and other discrete values are placed in internal key-value dictionaries per column segment. Keys are placed in column segments instead of actual values.

In addition to these strategies, entire segments can be compressed which can additionally save space. This is a common technique for the archival of data that is not commonly used but must stay in the database.

These are generic characteristics and advantages of columnstore format. In the following sections, you will learn about the specific implementation of Columnstore format in Azure SQL.

Columnstore in Azure SQL

Azure SQL doesn't use the classic Columnstore organization described in the previous section. In theory, we could create large column segments where each one would contain all values from a single table column and compress it. However, on any update we would need to decompress the entire column segment to insert, update, or delete a single value and then compress it again. To avoid this overhead, it might be better to split the unique column area into multiple column segments and perform the needed operations only on the segments that contain cells that need to be updated. In addition, most of the queries would not need to scan all rows, so most of the cells that would be decompressed would not be used. If we split a column into multiple column segments, maybe we can pick only the segments that are needed in query. The idea is very similar to a partitioning technique, but just applied within the column segment and in a totally transparent way for the user.

Azure SQL introduces some enhancements of the original Columnstore structure to address these issues. Two main modifications are:

- Column segments do not span over the entire table. Azure SQL will divide table rows in the groups up to 1 million rows. These *row groups* are organized in Columnstore format, and every column segment has up to one million rows' values.

- All new rows are inserted in a buffer row group organized using the rowstore format. Rowstore format is the perfect choice for row-oriented operation, so it makes sense to use it as an area for inserting new rows. These row groups are called *Deltastore*. Once these row groups reach one million records, they are transformed and compressed – transparently and in the background – into columnstore format.

Organization of Columnstore structure in Azure SQL is shown in Figure 9-2.

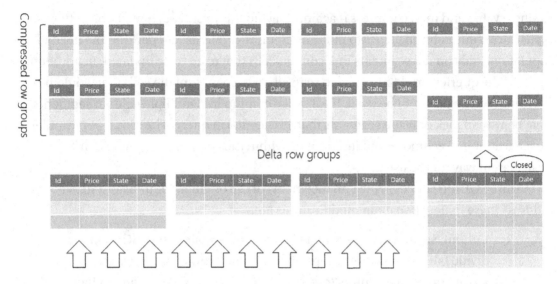

Figure 9-2. *Columnstore structures have a compressed area in Columnstore format and input area in rowstore format (Delta)*

In Azure SQL, the data rows in columnstore structure are divided into the row groups with up to one million rows. A million rows provide enough values to get good compression and still not too many rows to operate with row groups as independent units. Row groups can be placed in two areas:

- Compressed area containing many columnstore organized groups of rows where column segments in row groups are highly compressed. Ideally, all row groups would be compressed in this area.

- Deltastore area containing one or more rowstore organized groups of rows. This is the temporary buffer area with the rows that are waiting to be compressed and moved to the compressed area.

If you already have some Columnstore index in your database, you can find the row groups using the following system view:

```
SELECT * FROM sys.columnstore_rowgroups;
```

The columns in the compressed row groups are organized into the column segment that contains all values from the designated column in the row group. This segment is highly compressed, and all values are stored as one continuous physical location. Every column segment contains the statistics that describe min and max values in the segment.

This is an important information that the Azure SQL engine can use to optimize reports and analytics query performance on the Columnstore structure. We can easily find the existing column segments in Azure SQL Database using the following view:

```
SELECT * FROM sys.columnstore_segments;
```

The compressed area should contain more than 95% of data, and compressed data should not be changed. It's undesirable to modify data in the compressed area because Azure SQL would need to decompress all values in the segment to update just one and then compress everything again.[2]

There is another area in the Columnstore structure called Deltastore. Deltastore contains a smaller set of row groups organized in a classic rowstore format (or Hobit described in the previous chapter). The main purpose of this area is buffering the new inputs and changes before they get compressed. Splitting every new row into each column and re-distributing values into corresponding column segments would be an inefficient strategy to insert data. Therefore, all new rows are inserted in the rowstore delta area where they reside until the row group gets up to one million rows. Once the row group in the delta store is filled, it is *closed* for new changes, and a background process will start converting this row group into Columnstore format and moving it into the compressed area. The goal is to move as much as possible row groups from delta storage into compressed storage, and delta storage should contain less than 5% of rows.

In theory, we could have only one row group in the delta store. However, one row group might affect concurrency because one transaction that is inserting data might lock the row group and other requests that are trying to insert data would need to wait until the first one releases the lock. Therefore, the Columnstore structure creates new row groups to facilitate concurrent inserts.

Updating values in Columnstore

As already mentioned, updating compressed Columnstore data is not a desired action. Columnstore format is not read only, but updates have a bigger penalty compared to classical rowstore. Azure SQL has some enhancements that optimize updates of compressed data.

---

[2]Columnstore structure has additional optimization that just marks values as invalidated and prevents decompressing and compressing column segments just for one change.

One optimization is the Deltastore described in the previous section. Delta row groups buffer incoming rows until enough rows are available to successfully compress them. Deltastore is not always used though: Azure SQL decides if the incoming data should go into Deltastore or maybe it is better to directly compress it without buffering. Azure SQL uses the following rules:

- If you insert a smaller amount of (less than 102,400) rows, all rows will land into some Delta row group.

- If you insert more than 102,400 rows using single BULK INSERT or SELECT INTO statements, Azure SQL will stream these values directly into new compressed row groups.

Another problem that needs to be solved is how to efficiently delete rows from a columnstore. Unpacking 1,000,000 rows to delete one and then compress 999,999 is not a desirable technique. Azure SQL uses so-called *Delete indexes* and *Delete bitmaps* to "virtually" delete the rows. Whenever you need to delete a row from a compressed row group, Azure SQL will just "mark position" of this row as deleted. Whenever you read the rows from compressed column segments, Azure SQL will just ignore the rows marked as deleted at runtime. This way, the query that is reading data from the column segments is getting only existing rows and doesn't need to be aware that the deleted rows are transparently excluded once the row groups are decompressed.

There is only one operation left to be dealt with now: updating data. This is the most complex operation, as Azure SQL cannot just inject an updated value into an existing, highly compressed column segment without decompressing and compressing again everything else also. For this reason, every row update is represented as a combination of delete and insert operations. Old values of the row in the compressed row group are marked as deleted, and the new value is inserted in the delta store.

Marking deleted rows and representing updates as a pair of delete and insert operations are used only if the affected row is in a compressed area. If the row is in the Delta store, it will be updated or deleted as any other row in regular Hobits.

Querying Columnstore structure

Columnstore structures are the ideal option for reporting queries that use a smaller subset of columns and need to scan a large percent of the table. An example of the query that might get huge performance boost is shown in the following sample:

```
SELECT State, AVG(Price)
FROM Products
WHERE State IN ('Available', 'In Stock')
GROUP BY State
```

Let's imagine that the table in the example has six compressed row groups with five columns (five column segments per each row group).

The most important optimization that Columnstore format enables is the column segment elimination. Azure SQL can determine what column segments are not necessary for query processing even before the query processing starts using the following rules:

- Column segments that belong to the columns that are not used in the query are ignored.

- Column segments that don't have the values required in the query are ignored.

Using these rules, Azure SQL might discard most of the column segments as it is shown in Figure 9-3.

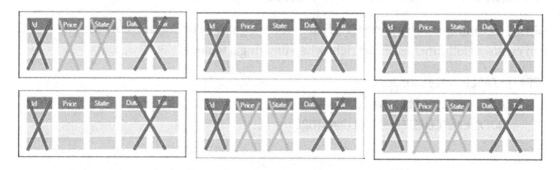

Figure 9-3. *Columnstore will discard column segments that are not needed for the query (red) and column segments that don't contain data required by query (orange)*

The columns Id, Date, and Tax are not used in the query, so Azure SQL will not even load them into the memory if they are still on disk. This way, we are reducing the required IO and memory footprint to 40% because three of five column segments are ignored.

Each column segment contains some statistics about the values in the segment (e.g., min-max values). Azure SQL knows what column segments contain the values Available and In Stock. Let's imagine that these values appear only in three row groups out of six row groups. Azure SQL will discard State column segments that don't contain the values used in the query and related Price column segment from the same row groups. This way, Azure SQL will discard another half of the data without even starting the query. These optimizations have a huge effect if most of the data is stored in compressed column segments and not in Deltastore.

Imagine that the dataset used in this example initially had 100GB. Under assumption that columnstore structure can have 10x compression and that column segment elimination can discard 80% of data before query starts, we are getting 2GB that should be processed instead of full table scan. This is a huge reduction of required IO and memory for the query that can boost performance up to 50x.

Another important optimization is batch query processing. Azure SQL will leverage underlying hardware SIMD instructions and apply a small number of operations on large vectors of data. The vectors of data are column segments containing the continuous range of values. This hardware acceleration in a batch mode processing significantly improves performance of the queries and is completely transparent to the query and thus to the application using it. The query will just run faster.

Clustered Columnstore indexes

Clustered Columnstore Indexes (CCI) are tables organized in Columnstore format. We can create a Columnstore index right when creating a table:

```
CREATE TABLE Sales.Orders (
    <column definitions>
    INDEX cci CLUSTERED COLUMNSTORE
)
```

Or even on existing tables:

```
CREATE CLUSTERED COLUMNSTORE INDEX cci ON Sales.Orders
```

We are using CCI to store highly compressed data with dominant read and massive (bulk load) insert workload patterns. This workload pattern is very common in data warehouses, and this is the reason why CCI is a very common structure in modern data warehousing scenarios. However, CCI is applicable in any scenario where you are going to append and analyze data, such as IoT scenarios.

CCI boosts performance of reporting and analytic queries using compression and batch mode execution, which are the primary benefits of Columnstore format.

One CCI-specific optimization is very helpful to improve bulk load performance: in the previous section, it was described that loading 102,400 rows will have special treatment and directly compress all incoming data. This direct compression might boost performance of your data load process because any data pages that must be saved to disk will be immediately compressed. Smaller inserts land in the delta store where they are buffered before they are compressed and moved to a compressed Columnstore area. If your workload produces many open row groups that don't meet criterion for closing, you can merge them using the following statement:

```
ALTER INDEX cci ON Sales.Orders REORGANIZE
```

CCI reorganize operation is a lightweight non-blocking operation that will merge and compress open delta row groups without major impact on your workload.

Nonclustered Columnstore indexes

Nonclustered Columnstore Indexes (NCCI) are indexes organized in Columnstore format that are created on top of Hobits. This makes Azure SQL pretty unique in the market, as it allows the co-existence of both Columnstore and Rowstore indexes on the same table. Figure 9-4 shows a classic rowstore table with seven columns and additional columnstore structure where we extracted the values from three columns and compressed them into columnar format.

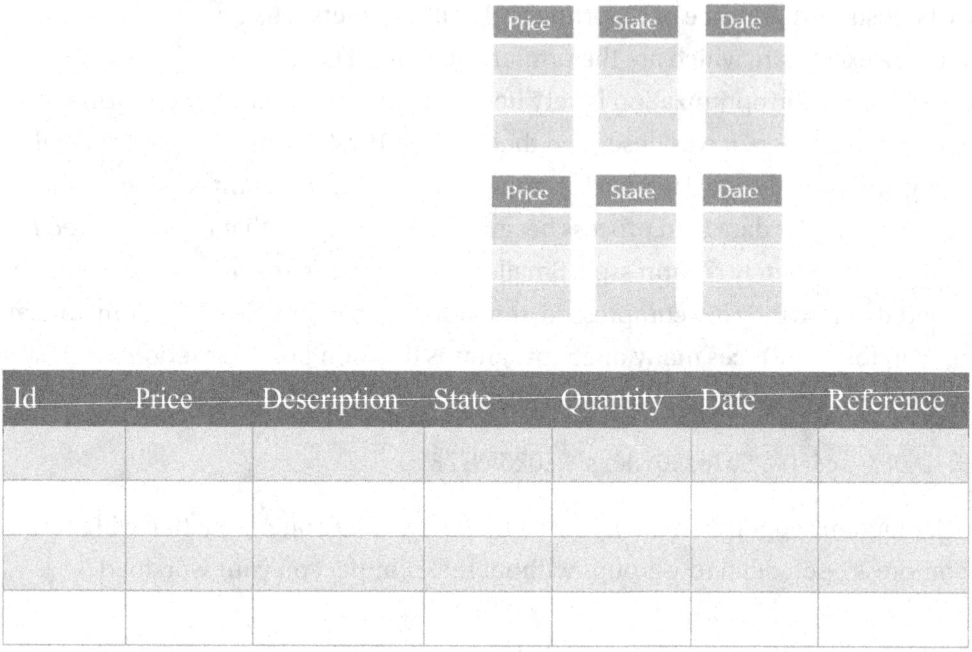

Figure 9-4. *Classic rowstore table with additional Columnstore index (NCCI) built on top of the tree columns from this table*

The main purpose of NCCI is to optimize analytical and reporting queries on the subset of columns in the existing rowstore tables without changing the original table structure.

NCCI can be created in a table using the following definitions:

```
CREATE TABLE dbo.Sales (
  <column definitions>
  INDEX ncci NONCLUSTERED COLUMNSTORE (Price, Quantity, SalesID)
)
```

With NCCI on top of classic tables, you are enabling Azure SQL to choose the optimal format for either transactional or analytical queries:

- If you run some query that selects a single row or small set of rows, Azure SQL will use the underlying rowstore table. Database will leverage index seek or range scan operations that are the perfect fit for this scenario.

- If you run some report that scans the entire table and aggregates data, Azure SQL will read information from NCCI index, leveraging column segment elimination and batch mode execution to quickly return process all table.

Any update, delete, or insert will immediately end up in the underlying rowstore table, and NCCI will be updated via Deltastore. This double update might slow down your transactional workload, but this should be acceptable if you need to make a trade-off between boosting reporting capabilities on a table and speed of transactional statements.

Memory-optimized tables

Azure SQL has memory-optimized tables that might extremely improve performance and the scalability of your OLTP workload. The main purpose of memory-optimized tables is to improve CRUD-like operations like selecting a few rows or updating or deleting existing rows.

Some people assume that keeping the rows always in memory is the key factor that improves performance. However, this is a naïve assumption that in many cases is far from the real reason.

Azure SQL always works with rows that are placed in memory. It has an excellent mechanism for caching data in memory (called Buffer Pool), picking the most important data that should be fetched from disk, and smartly evicting the rows that should not be needed in the near future to make space for more likely-to-be-used rows. If your database is smaller than memory, all rows will probably be in RAM, so you will already have an "in-memory database." So, the question is what kind of additional "memory optimization" do we get with the memory-optimized tables?

Let's first see how a regular table works and how disk and memory are used during query processing. The core query processing assumptions are based on the following premises:

- As mentioned before, all data stored in the database is memorized on disk using 8KB data structures called pages. A 10GB uncompressed database will have something like a million data pages at minimum.

- Every time a row is accessed, the related data page is loaded in memory. Azure SQL will try to keep as many data pages in memory as possible. This memory section is called the Buffer Pool.

- Buffer pool cannot cache all data if the database is bigger than the available memory, and thus the pages must be fetched from disk and persisted back to disk if they are changed. Every page is read or written as an atomic 8KB unit. Sometimes, databases can read bigger chunks of disk with a single IO operation (so-called read-ahead operations) to optimize IO performances.

- The most expensive operation in a query is transferring 8KB pages between memory and disk.

- Data transfer between memory and disk should be minimized. The database engine should do its best to prevent unnecessary IO interactions.

Azure SQL must orchestrate workload to minimize number of IO operations. Let's look at the two threads/queries updating the rows on two 8KB pages. We need to decide how to isolate this change from the other queries until the change is confirmed (committed). We have two approaches to handle concurrency:

- *Pessimistic* where we are blocking other threads that would like to access rows already modified by another thread, until the modifying thread decides to save or reject the changes.

- *Optimistic* where we let other threads access the original version of the modified rows. We need to make a copy of the rows that will then be a "private version" available only to the current thread, while others are accessing the original row.

Ideally, we should be optimists because a pessimistic approach blocks other threads, which mean less performances, concurrency, and scalability. But we need to be aware of pros and cons of both approaches.

A story about optimistic concurrency

Let's see how the database processes updates with optimistic concurrency. An example of two rows on the same 8KB page that are changed by two threads (or transactions) Tx_1 and Tx_2 and another thread Tx_3 with optimistic concurrency is shown in Figure 9-5. For every change, we need to create a new version of the row that will be a private copy for the thread that changed it. Copies will stay private until the transaction commits the changes and makes the updated version available to everyone. In the meantime, other transactions should keep using the original version of the row available in the original page.

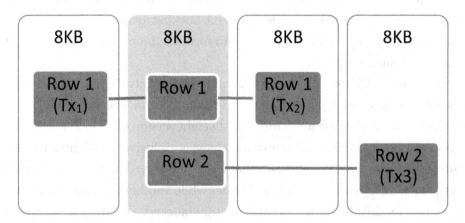

Figure 9-5. *Creating new versions of updated rows for every transaction that makes the changes*

Once Tx_1 commits the changes on row 1, the easiest thing that Azure SQL can do is to declare the old data page as invalid and use the new page. Because it would be hard to copy part of the page back to the original 8KB page. Tx_2, which was also working on a private copy of row 1, would not be able to commit its own row because it updated a version that is not valid anymore. Once Tx_2 tries to commit the change, it will be rolled back and would need to retry the operation with latest valid data. This might be expected because both transactions tried to update rows without locking it exclusively. If there is a collision, retry is the only solution. In addition to this, there is also another, maybe unexpected, side effect. Tx_3 would not be able to commit its own row changes, even if those were done on a row different than row 1, and thus didn't clash with the row 1 updated by Tx_1. Since the binary content is changed and maybe the page is split into two new pages, Azure SQL cannot easily get the binary content of the changed row from a new valid page. Therefore, this transaction will be rolled back too.

In addition, there is a performance impact of creating new pages with temporary rows. Azure SQL has a background process called "Checkpoint writer" that saves modified memory pages to underlying storage. If we get a lot of temporary pages, they would be saved on disk, and then after rollback, original content must be saved again. In this case, temporary generated pages would cause more damage and we might want to prevent this.

Should we be pessimists?

Since the 8KB page is the main unit of data transfer, transactions that update the rows might take a lock on the entire page and prevent others making changes that would very likely be rolled back and cause additional IO. Locking mechanisms are pessimistic approaches that help to prevent damage, due to *race conditions*, that concurrent queries might cause on a single page.

As you learned in Chapter 7, usually the database prevents the risk of having too many IO operations by using pessimistic concurrency control. Every transaction is taking locks or latches (latch is just a more lightweight version of lock) to ensure that one version of a potentially shared row or data page is exclusively dedicated to the thread that is modifying it. Other threads that want to change data on the same page are temporarily blocked by row locks or page latches while another thread is modifying it. Threads cannot modify the same rows and they are blocked. This way, we avoid a need to create new pages and cause additional IO, but we are decreasing concurrency and affecting performance.

Now, let's imagine that we can forget about disk IO and that we don't have 8KB pages that would need to be persisted even for the temporary changes. We could use high, optimistic concurrency that uses just inexpensive memory copy operations and easily generate new row versions. This is possible only if we can be sure that table data will be placed in memory without data transfer between buffer pool and disk storage and that there is no 8KB container that causes dependency between rows. Memory-optimized tables provide these guarantees.

Memory-optimized tables are the tables where we know that data will be in memory so we can apply optimistic concurrency and allow a large number of concurrent updates. This is the main advantage of memory-optimized technology and the key differentiator compared to classic Hobits.

Memory-optimized tables

Now when you understand what the main benefit of memory-optimized technology is, we can start using them. You can leverage memory-optimized features by marking the table as memory-optimized:

```
CREATE TABLE dbo.Cache
(
    [key] INT IDENTITY PRIMARY KEY NONCLUSTERED,
    data NVARCHAR(MAX)
)
WITH (MEMORY_OPTIMIZED=ON)
```

The only change that you need to do is to add a WITH clause with the property MEMORY_OPTIMIZED=ON. With this property, data rows are always kept in memory, data pages are not used anymore, and memory-optimized features such as optimistic concurrency are enabled on the table data.

There are three types of memory-optimized tables:

- Memory-optimized non-durable schema-only tables. These tables are very similar to temporary tables. The table schema will be preserved after restarts or potential system crashes. Azure SQL will re-create the table structure after restart, but it will not preserve the content. The main purpose of these tables is caching scenarios (like ASP.NET session state), being an intermediate store for complex data processing and fast loading of data (so-called staging tables).

- Memory-optimized durable tables where both schema and data are preserved even after process crash or failover. Azure SQL will ensure that a minimal set of information is sent to log and persisted so data will survive system crashes. These tables are logically equivalents of classic tables with memory-optimized enhancements and used to improve performance of the existing rowstore tables.

- Memory-optimized Columnstore tables are a combination of Columnstore structures and memory-optimized tables. The main scenario is a combination of analytic and transactional workloads (OLTP) on the same table. This combination is known as Hybrid Transactional-Analytical Processing (HTAP).

In the following example, you can see how to create a memory-optimized table that serves as a cache:

```
CREATE TABLE dbo.Cache
(
    [key] INT IDENTITY PRIMARY KEY NONCLUSTERED,
    data NVARCHAR(MAX)
)
WITH (MEMORY_OPTIMIZED=ON, DURABILITY=SCHEMA_ONLY)
```

If you are wondering why you may want to use Azure SQL Memory-Optimized tables to create a caching solution, since there are other specific solutions like Redis or Cosmos DB that are usually better suited for caching, you should keep in mind that one of the best advices in software development is keeping things simple. If you are already using Azure SQL in your project, the option to create a custom transactional caching mechanism right into the database without having to resort to another technology can simplify your solution a lot (and also decrease maintenance costs, as you don't have to learn and maintain another technology). In addition to that, Memory-Optimized table offers a deep integration with all other features of Azure SQL. For example, you can create a secured caching solution by using Row-Level Security with Memory-Optimized tables.

There are two WITH options that you can use to define would data be persisted even if database crashes:

- DURABILITY=SCHEMA_ONLY defined non-durable table where only table structure will be re-created if Azure SQL Database restarts.

- DURABILITY=SCHEMA_AND_DATA defines a durable table where both table structure and data will survive failover or crash.

Columnstore format of memory-optimized table must be specified with definition of clustered Columnstore index within memory-optimized table, as shown in the following example:

```
CREATE TABLE Accounts (
    AccountKey int NOT NULL PRIMARY KEY NONCLUSTERED,
    Description nvarchar (50),
    Type nvarchar(50),
    UnitSold int,
    INDEX cci CLUSTERED COLUMNSTORE
) WITH (MEMORY_OPTIMIZED = ON, DURABILITY = SCHEMA_AND_DATA)
```

Columnstore memory-optimized tables combine best from both worlds – extremely fast analytic and compression of data that can fit into memory and highly-concurrent and extremely fact ingestion and updates of data provided by memory-optimized tables. The only risk here is the amount of data that you can process. Classic Columnstore indexes analyze all data in memory; however, it lets you keep column segments on disk if they cannot fit into the memory. Memory-optimized Columnstore requires all data to reside in memory. Since Azure SQL reserves ~60% of available memory to memory-optimized data, you need to be sure that your data can fit. Since we are talking about large amounts of data in a Columnstore analytic scenario, if you are not sure that your data can fit into memory, use disk-based tables.

For these reasons, Memory-Optimized Clustered Columnstore Indexes cover a niche scenario. In fact, using classic rowstore tables with NCCI indexes for HTAP scenarios is the general approach on average, and Memory-Optimized Clustered Columnstore Indexes are used only on very performance-intensive workloads. For example, if you need to be able to handle up to 5 million of rows per second, like described in the article "Scaling up an IoT workload using an M-series Azure SQL database" referenced in the last section of this chapter, you will needed Memory-Optimized Clustered Columnstore Indexes for sure.

While we are talking about memory-optimized storage, we cannot separate this discussion from indexing. In-memory rows are objects scattered in memory space and need some structure that will bind them together. These structures are the indexes. Whenever you create memory-optimized, you need to have at least one index.

In the previous examples, you have seen NONCLUSTERED B-Tree indexes and CLUSTERED COLUMNSTORE indexes. There is another kind of index that is specific for memory-optimized tables, the NONCLUSTERED HASH index, shown in the following example:

```
CREATE TABLE [dbo].[Employees](
     [EmpID] [int] NOT NULL
         CONSTRAINT PK_Employees_EmpID PRIMARY KEY
         NONCLUSTERED HASH (EmpID) WITH (BUCKET_COUNT = 100000),
     [EmpName] [varchar](50) NOT NULL,
     [EmpAddress] [varchar](50) NOT NULL,
     [EmpDEPID] [int] NOT NULL,
     [EmpBirthDay] [datetime] NULL
) WITH (MEMORY_OPTIMIZED = ON, DURABILITY = SCHEMA_AND_DATA)
```

NONCLUSTERED HASH index is an in-memory hash table that uses column values as keys (EmpID in this case) and contains a list of pointers to the actual rows in the table. Every hash table consists of a fixed number of slots (hash buckets) with an array of pointers to the actual rows. Row pointers with the same hash values are linked into the list that represents its own hash bucket.

The bucket count must be specified at index creation time and impact the length of the pointer list in every bucket. The ratio of distinct key values and the number of hash buckets would represent the expected average bucket link list length. Longer lists imply more operations to find the row based on key.

The bucket count should be between one and two times the number of distinct values in the index key. In practice, it is hard to estimate the number of distinct values in a column; however, you will get good performance if the BUCKET_COUNT value is within ten times the actual number of values in the indexed column. Note that overestimating is generally better than underestimating. If you find a bad ratio after some time, you can always rebuild the index with new bucket count.

Accessing memory-optimized tables

Another advantage of memory-optimized tables is the fact that they can be accessed like any other classic table. You can use the same Transact-SQL queries to join memory-optimized tables, Columnstore table, and classic Hobits.

Interoperability between the different features such as Columnstore, memory-optimized tables, JSON, and graphs is one of the core value propositions of Azure SQL. Any feature that is specific or optimized for some scenario will have the same or similar access methods.

Memory-optimized tables use optimistic concurrency control that quickly creates a new version of row whenever some transaction updates it. This way, transactions that update data are getting their own private version of row without getting blocked by readers or blocking other writers.

Three rows are shown in Figure 9-6: r1 with three versions, r2 with two versions, and r3 with four versions. Every version is created by some transaction that updates the row. Note that there are no 8KB boundaries around the rows so there is no risk that updating one row might affect others.

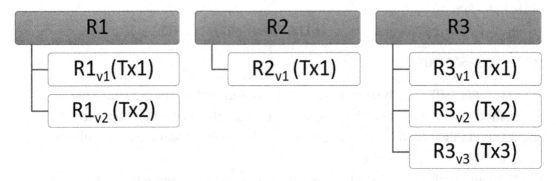

Figure 9-6. *New row version is created whenever some transaction updates the row*

This row versioning has some implications on some transaction isolation levels used in Azure SQL. Disk-based tables enable you to read the temporary uncommitted values of the rows if you are sure that this is what you want and bypass the locks. This is not possible in memory-optimized tables because there can be multiple uncommitted copies of the same row and Azure SQL doesn't know which of these versions you would like to use.

Also reading committed rows is not as easy as with regular tables. If you would like to read committed rows, your transaction would always need to check if the current row is really the latest or if there is some transaction that committed a new public version. This might be huge performance overhead that you surely want to avoid.

The solution is to use a committed version of a row at the time of beginning your transaction, which looks like a snapshot of table data. The transaction isolation level that works with snapshot of data at the beginning of a transaction is called SNAPSHOT isolation level.

If you need to use READ COMMITTED or READ UNCOMMITTED transaction isolation levels, you should explicitly put the snapshot isolation hint on the memory-optimized table to override it just for this table:

```
SET TRANSACTION ISOLATION LEVEL READ COMMITTED;
GO

BEGIN TRANSACTION;  -- Explicit transaction.

-- Employees is a memory-optimized table.
SELECT * FROM
          dbo.Employees  as o  WITH (SNAPSHOT)  -- Table hint.

COMMIT TRANSACTION;
```

WITH(SNAPSHOT) hint instructs Azure SQL to interpret the values in the table as a snapshot of the data state at the time of execution. This isolation level ignores the changes that might occur in the meantime. This hint will prevent the error with code 41368 in other isolation modes.

As an alternative to query hint, you can use the database option that will automatically elevate isolation level on memory-optimized tables to snapshot if needed:

```
ALTER DATABASE current
 SET MEMORY_OPTIMIZED_ELEVATE_TO_SNAPSHOT = ON;
```

If you properly set up transaction isolation level, there are no big limitations in DML statements that you can use to query memory-optimized tables.

Natively compiled code

Azure SQL interprets the batches of T-SQL code that you use to work with data. This means that the query batches (one or more T-SQL statements) are parsed, then every query in the batch is compiled into an Execution Plan, which is broken down into operators (e.g., scan, join, sort), and the operators are executed to fetch or update the rows. This strategy of query processing might be a big bottleneck while working with memory-optimized data. Although you have data available in memory and minimal locks, chains of operators will still use classic mechanisms to fetch row by row and process it.

Azure SQL enables you to use natively compiled modules to improve performance of your T-SQL code. You can imagine natively compiled modules in Azure SQL Database like customized C programs – yes, that's right, C programs! – that process your data. Transact-SQL code will be pre-compiled into native .dll – dynamically linked libraries – and then executed by the Azure SQL engine to operate on data. Imagine that you have an API that accesses memory rows as lists or iterators and that you want to create a C code that iterates through the rows and applies some processing (similar to LINQ queries in .NET technology). This would probably be the faster way to work with data, but it might be hard to write this.

As writing C modules to manipulate data is not an easy task, in order to remove complexity and still enable you to boost performance, Azure SQL Database allows you to declaratively write standard T-SQL code that accesses rows in memory-optimized tables. This T-SQL code will be translated into the equivalent C code that accesses table rows using internal API and compiled into native executable that will be executed in Azure SQL database process. This way, you are still expressing what you want to do using T-SQL code, and Azure SQL Database handles all complexity of accessing API via C language, unlocking extreme performances.

Azure SQL enables you to write SQL procedures, functions, and Triggers that will be compiled into native executables. Natively compiled code might be orders of magnitude faster than classic counterparts. The only limitation is that they can access only memory-optimized tables and use a subset of T-SQL language.

Natively compiled Stored Procedures are a commonly used approach to access and modify memory-optimized table data. A template that represents natively compiled Stored Procedure is shown in the following example:

```
CREATE PROCEDURE myProcedure(@p1 int NOT NULL, @p2 nvarchar(5))
WITH NATIVE_COMPILATION, SCHEMABINDING
AS BEGIN ATOMIC WITH
(TRANSACTION ISOLATION LEVEL = SNAPSHOT,
 LANGUAGE = N'us_english')
  /* Procedure code goes here */
END
```

Any T-SQL code that is placed in the body of this procedure will be parsed, and the equivalent C code will be generated and compiled into a small dynamically linked library (.dll) file.

Two main components of natively compiled procedures are

- WITH clause that defines procedure properties such as marking procedure as natively compiled and specifying schema binding. Schema binding means that the tables referenced by the Stored Procedure cannot be altered as long as the procedure exists. These are the only required options, but you can also specify others such as EXECUTE AS and so on.

- ATOMIC block representing a unit of work that will be either processed or canceled. In the atomic block, you need to specify options such as isolation level or language because these settings will be compiled into the dynamically linked library.

Azure SQL enables you to write natively compiled functions and Triggers. One example of a natively compiled function is shown in the following listing. This function gets a string formatted as JSON text, parses it, and returns the properties from the JSON object as table columns:

```
CREATE FUNCTION PeopleData(@json nvarchar(max))
RETURNS TABLE
WITH NATIVE_COMPILATION, SCHEMABINDING
AS RETURN (
 SELECT Title, HireDate, PrimarySalesTerritory,
        CommissionRate, OtherLanguages
 FROM OPENJSON(@json)
     WITH(Title nvarchar(50),
          HireDate datetime2,
          PrimarySalesTerritory nvarchar(50),
          CommissionRate float,
          OtherLanguages nvarchar(max) AS JSON)
)
```

We have seen in Chapter 8 that Azure SQL does not use native JSON type. JSON is stored as a NVARCHAR string that should be parsed at the query time. With a natively compiled function, we can explicitly define parsing rules that should be used and create a native built-in custom JSON parser.

A natively compiled function is called the same way as any other function. We can use standard CROSS APPLY operator to provide a value as a parameter of the function and join results with the main row:

```
select p.FullName, p.EmailAddress, j.Title, j.CommissionRate
from Application.People p
    cross apply PeopleData(p.CustomFields) j
```

Accessing memory-optimized tables using natively compiled code is the recommended way as it provides the best performance and scalability possible.

Temporal tables

Regular tables in a database contain the latest versions of data rows. Whenever some query updates the values, the old values are overwritten. This is usually the expected and desired behavior, but in some cases, you may like to also have the ability to access old values. Some examples might be

- Error correction – Someone accidentally changed or deleted a row in a table, and you need to correct or revert this change.

- Historical analysis – You need to analyze the changes that are made in the table over time.

- Auditing – You need to find out who changed the values, when, and what was changed.

Temporal tables are adding time dimension to your data so that they can keep information about all changed data and the time the change occurred. This is done completely automatically and transparently, thanks to a system managed *History Table*. A History Table is a shadow table with the column structure identical to the main table. Whenever some rows in the main table, shown in Figure 9-7, are changed (deleted or updated), the old versions are written in the history table, along with additional information that tracks the lifetime of those rows.

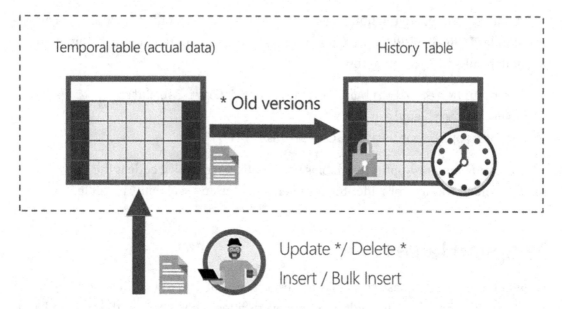

Figure 9-7. *Temporal table automatically sends the row that will be updated or deleted into a separate history table*

The queries that just insert or select data will work only with the main temporal table, where the current version of data is stored, and they would not affect the history table. Temporal tables modify behavior or the queries that update or delete data and silently send current row values to the history table before they are updated in the main table. This is completely transparent, and you can keep using the standard T-SQL queries to access data.

Moving old rows in the history table before they are changed is one of the most common scenarios for Triggers. Temporal tables provide native support for this behavior by automatically moving rows. The method used in temporal tables should be much faster than equivalent Triggers in most of the cases.

Querying temporal data

Automatic movement of old rows from the temporal to history table is important, but not the only benefit that you are getting from temporal tables. Even if you have all required row versions in the history table along with their validity range, querying historical data is still not easy. If you want to see how tables looked at some point in time in history, you would need to take some old row values from history but also some rows from the main table because they might be still valid at current time.

Azure SQL enables you to use a special syntax to select data at some point in time and handles complexity of temporal queries for you. In addition to standard SELECT queries that will read the current rows from the main table, Azure SQL is enabling you to use temporal operators (shown in Figure 9-8) that can be used to get the row versions at some point in time in the past, in some specific period, all versions of some row, and so on.

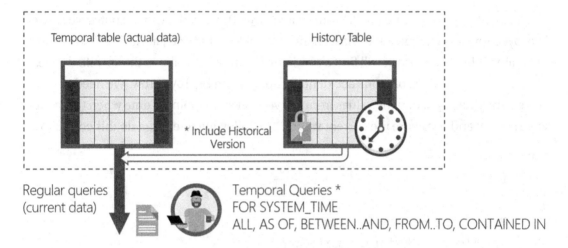

Figure 9-8. *Temporal table enables you to fetch historical data for temporal queries*

Azure SQL Database provides several operators that can be applied on a temporal table. The most common are

- `FOR SYSTEM_TIME AS OF <datetime>` – The query will read the content of the table at the specified datetime in the past.

- `FOR SYSTEM_TIME ALL` – The query will read all rows that existed at any point in time in the past.

More are available and you can find more details on those in the referenced resources at the end of this chapter. Depending on the temporal operator and the values provided to the operator, Azure SQL will decide if data must be read from the main table or from both tables and create the right plan that will fetch and merge resultsets from both tables.

As an example, the following query will get the Employee with the specified primary key value at the specified point of time:

```
SELECT *
FROM Employee FOR SYSTEM_TIME AS OF @asOf AS History
WHERE EmployeeID = @EmployeeID
```

Azure SQL will compare the datetime value of @asOf variable with the dates when the Employee row was changed. If the last change was before that date, it will fetch data from the main table. Otherwise, it will find a row in history that was valid in the specified time.

Let us imagine that someone accidentally updated an Employee row. We need to correct the error by taking the values from the version at the point in time when the values were correct and overwrite the current values. The following query can do this correction:

```
UPDATE
    E
SET
    Position = History.Position,
    Department = History.Department,
    Address = History.Address,
    AnnualSalary = History.AnnualSalary
FROM
    Employee AS E
JOIN
    Employee FOR SYSTEM_TIME AS OF @asOf AS History
    ON E.EmployeeID = History.EmployeeID
WHERE
    E.EmployeeID = @EmployeeID
```

We are updating a row in the Employee table with a specified Employee primary key value (@EmployeeID). We are joining the row with the version of the row with the same primary key value at the specified time (@asOf) using FOR SYSTEM_TIME AS OF clause. Then, we are just overwriting the values in the recent version with the values from the valid version. Note that the faulty values are not overwritten without trace. When the error is corrected, the wrong values are moved into the History table, and you can track when they were corrected and what were the errors. The History table is the source of truth where you can find information about any change that was made on the temporal table.

Configuring temporal tables

Temporal and history tables are independent tables. You can configure and optimize them separately by adding different indexes. The optimal configuration that you can use to improve temporal table performance is

- The table that contains current data should be implemented as a memory-optimized schema and data table, if possible.

- History table should be implemented with a Clustered Columnstore index.

If you are using the Business Critical service tier, a memory-optimized table will provide you the best performance in the workloads that insert, update, and delete data, which is the main scenario for tables with the current rows. You should not use memory-optimized tables if you think that all rows cannot fit into the memory, as having all rows in memory is a requirement for memory-optimized tables, as explained in earlier sections.

Columnstore format is the optimal solution for the history table because you can have many column cells with the same values. In many cases, you will update just a few columns leaving other cells unchanged. Temporal tables will physically copy the entire previous row to the history table, meaning that unchanged cells will have the same values in different row versions in history. Columnstore format has the most efficient compression if it can replace a set of cells with the same values with a single marker describing the range of rows where this value appears. In this scenario, the Clustered Columnstore index created on the history table could provide extreme compression and improved history analysis performance on the temporal table.

Under the assumption that you have a DepartmentHistory table for historical data, the following indexes may improve performance of the queries running on temporal history:

```
CREATE CLUSTERED COLUMNSTORE INDEX cci_DepartmentHistory
    ON DepartmentHistory;
CREATE NONCLUSTERED INDEX IX_DepartmentHistory_ID_PERIOD_COLUMNS
    ON DepartmentHistory (SysEndTime, SysStartTime, DeptID);
```

Clustered Columnstore indexes will provide high compression and improve analytic capabilities when the query scans large amounts of history data. Nonclustered indexes on range columns and primary key would be very helpful to boost the performance of those queries that are accessing values of some rows at a specified point in time in history (e.g., using FOR SYSTEM_TIME AS OF clause). Depending on the types of the historical queries that you are running, you might want to add the first, the second, or both indexes.

Another important optimization is database history retention. You can define how long historical data should be stored in the history table. Temporal tables enable you to define time-to-live period for the history records using the HISTORY_RETENTION_PERIOD setting:

```
ALTER TABLE dbo.WebsiteUserInfo
SET (SYSTEM_VERSIONING = ON (HISTORY_RETENTION_PERIOD = 9 MONTHS));
```

This setting implies that all records in the history tables that are entered more than 9 months ago will be automatically deleted from the history table to avoid an infinite growth. You can also globally enable or disable these rules using the following database property:

```
ALTER DATABASE current
    SET TEMPORAL_HISTORY_RETENTION ON
```

This database-level option enables you to switch on or off retention policy for all tables in the database.

If you want to know more

Columnstore tables and indexes, memory-optimized tables, and temporal tables described in this chapter enable you to get more value from your databases. General-purpose Hobits, described in the previous chapter, are a good solution for most of the scenarios; however, if you can recognize specific characteristics of your workload, the tables and indexes described in this chapter will enable you to boost performance of your applications by order of magnitude:

- Columnstore indexes: Overview – https://docs.microsoft.com/sql/relational-databases/indexes/columnstore-indexes-overview

- Columnstore indexes - Data loading guidance – https://docs.microsoft.com/sql/relational-databases/indexes/columnstore-indexes-data-loading-guidance

- Get started with Columnstore for real-time operational analytics – https://docs.microsoft.com/sql/relational-databases/indexes/get-started-with-columnstore-for-real-time-operational-analytics

- Niko Neugebauer Blog Columnstore Series – www.nikoport.com/columnstore/

- In-Memory OLTP and Memory-Optimization – https://docs.microsoft.com/sql/relational-databases/in-memory-oltp/in-memory-oltp-in-memory-optimization

- Memory-Optimized tempdb Metadata – https://docs.microsoft.com/sql/relational-databases/databases/tempdb-database#memory-optimized-tempdb-metadata

- Optimize JSON processing with in-memory OLTP – https://docs.microsoft.com/sql/relational-databases/json/optimize-json-processing-with-in-memory-oltp

- Temporal Tables – https://docs.microsoft.com/sql/relational-databases/tables/temporal-tables

- Querying data in a system-versioned temporal table – https://docs.microsoft.com/sql/relational-databases/tables/querying-data-in-a-system-versioned-temporal-table

- Scaling up an IoT workload using an M-series Azure SQL database – https://techcommunity.microsoft.com/t5/azure-sql-database/scaling-up-an-iot-workload-using-an-m-series-azure-sql-database/ba-p/1106271#

Monitoring and Debugging

Azure SQL and its underlying SQL Server query engine are well known in the industry for the low administrative barrier generally required for applications to get good performance and reliability on most conditions with different data sizes and shapes.

That said, it is important for application developers to understand the foundations and internals of how query processing works in Azure SQL and what tools and capabilities are available to monitor and troubleshoot performance on both development and production phases. Generally speaking, there are two major scenarios where these capabilities are important for us to master:

1. Understanding how the system is behaving under a given workload: this means looking at major performance and availability metrics during your load test or production periods to make sure the system is up and running and can cope with a given workload.

2. Investigate deeply into specific activities that may happen, or have happened, if results of the previous point are showing some critical behaviors.

The former is a continuous, long-term, monitoring scenario that is crucial to make sure your solution will "keep the lights on" and usually requires specific characteristics, like the ability to store and analyze vast amounts of data points and trigger some alerts when key metrics are crossing certain thresholds. On the Azure platform, there is a common backbone across all services to collect diagnostic information emitted by all components of a given solution, called Azure Monitor. All services can be configured to asynchronously emit logs and metrics to Azure Monitor, which can then redirect these to both near real-time (through visualizing metrics in Azure Portal or pushing data into

© Davide Mauri, Silvano Coriani, Anna Hoffman, Sanjay Mishra, Jovan Popovic 2021
D. Mauri et al., *Practical Azure SQL Database for Modern Developers*,
https://doi.org/10.1007/978-1-4842-6370-9_10

an Azure Event Hub instance for further processing and alerting) and more long-term analytical options (like Azure Blob Storage or Log Analytics), depending on your needs.

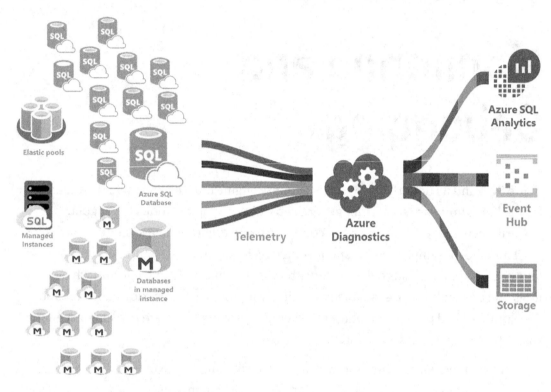

You can get more details on this specific scenario by looking at official documentation at this link: https://aka.ms/asdbmto.

The other major scenario is instead related to immediate diagnostic and troubleshooting investigations that you can execute, while a specific issue is happening, thanks to the extensive instrumentation capabilities exposed by the Azure SQL engine. Every single internal subsystem of the service, from connection and session management down to query processing and storage engine, is in fact emitting a rich and detailed set of diagnostic information that we, as developer, can take advantage of to understand how a single query is executed or how subsystems like memory management or resource governance are behaving.

As developers, we don't necessarily need to understand every single aspect of how the internals of the service are working, but it is quite important to know the basic tools and techniques available to make sure we can investigate how our queries and workloads are performing and how we can make our applications more efficient when working with Azure SQL.

Dynamic Management Views (DMVs)

Dynamic management views (and functions) are a way to execute T-SQL queries against an Azure SQL endpoint and return state information that can be used to monitor the health of an Azure SQL server or database instance, diagnose problems, and tune performance.

As mentioned, the SQL Server engine is highly instrumented and captures tons of information on how various subsystems are working, from the integration with the underlying operating system and hardware up to how queries are executed. All these details are maintained in memory structures within the database process space (we'll talk about how things evolved recently with Query Store later in this chapter) and are front-ended by a layer of system views and functions that can be queried by regular T-SQL commands, from a connection opened by a login that has SELECT permission on the selected DMV and VIEW SERVER STATE (for Azure SQL Managed Instance) or VIEW DATABASE STATE (for Azure SQL Database) permission. We can grant access to a given instance by executing this command:

```
GRANT VIEW DATABASE STATE TO database_user;
```

Azure SQL enables a subset of dynamic management views to diagnose performance problems, which might be caused by blocked or long-running queries, resource bottlenecks, poor query plans, and so on. In an instance of SQL Server and in Azure SQL Managed Instance, dynamic management views return server state information. In Azure SQL Database, they return information regarding your current logical database only.

While hundreds of these views and functions are available, there are really three main categories we should focus on:

- Database-related dynamic management views (prefixed by *sys.dm_db_**)

- Execution-related dynamic management views (prefixed by *sys.dm_exec_**)

- Transaction-related dynamic management views (prefixed by *sys.dm_tran_**)

Let's start from a few basic use cases that can be common while you're investigating what's going on with your database instance. First, you may want to understand what's current resource utilization on a given instance where you're running your application against. You can open your client tool of preference (e.g., Azure Data Studio or SQL Server Management Studio) pointing to your database and execute this query:

```
SELECT * FROM sys.dm_db_resource_stats ORDER BY end_time DESC;
```

The result you'll get back will be something similar to this:

	end_time	avg_cpu_percent	avg_data_io_percent	avg_log_write_percent	avg_memory_usage_percent	xtp_storage_percent	max_worker_percent	max_session_percent
1	2020-10-29 18:41:31.473	47.72	2.36	9.52	8.32	0.00	1.00	0.01
2	2020-10-29 18:41:16.460	48.19	0.00	12.24	6.25	0.00	0.50	0.01
3	2020-10-29 18:41:01.460	39.36	0.00	10.68	3.36	0.00	1.00	0.01
4	2020-10-29 18:40:46.450	0.00	0.00	0.00	0.77	0.00	0.00	0.00
5	2020-10-29 18:40:31.403	18.88	0.00	0.00	0.77	0.00	1.50	0.01
6	2020-10-29 18:40:16.353	83.00	0.00	0.02	0.77	0.00	1.50	0.01
7	2020-10-29 18:40:01.347	37.09	0.00	0.00	0.76	0.00	1.00	0.01
8	2020-10-29 18:39:46.323	0.00	0.00	0.00	0.16	0.00	0.00	0.00
9	2020-10-29 18:39:31.277	35.21	0.00	0.00	0.16	0.00	1.00	0.02
10	2020-10-29 18:39:16.233	68.28	0.00	0.00	0.16	0.00	1.00	0.02
11	2020-10-29 18:39:01.223	72.44	0.00	0.00	0.16	0.00	1.00	0.02
12	2020-10-29 18:38:46.213	13.18	0.00	0.00	0.16	0.00	1.00	0.02
13	2020-10-29 18:38:31.173	0.00	0.00	0.00	0.07	0.00	0.00	0.00
14	2020-10-29 18:38:16.137	0.65	0.00	0.00	0.07	0.00	0.50	0.00

Basically, this view is returning key metrics around resource consumption for your database instance for the last hour, with a granularity of 15 seconds. If any of these metrics is getting closer to 100%, you usually have the choice of scaling up your database service or compute tier or, more likely, drilling deeper into resource utilization to understand if there are ways to make your workload more efficient.

Let's say, as an example, that you're maxing out on CPU utilization: a good next step would be to look at what are the top CPU-consuming queries to understand if there are ways to improve them in any way.

For demonstration purposes, we will clear up the procedure cache of our test instance to not be distracted by potentially 100s of other queries that may have ran in the past and will use this script to execute a simple query:

```
--!!! Test purposes only, don't do it in production!!!--
ALTER DATABASE SCOPED CONFIGURATION CLEAR PROCEDURE_CACHE;

-- Execute a simple query
SELECT * FROM [Sales].[Orders] WHERE CustomerID=832
```

On the same connection, or on a different one, we can now run the following diagnostic query targeting few *sys.dm_exec_*DMVs:

```
--- Returning TOP 25 CPU consuming queries for this database
SELECT TOP 25
    qs.query_hash,
    qs.execution_count,
    REPLACE(REPLACE(LEFT(st.[text], 512), CHAR(10),''), CHAR(13),'') AS
    query_text,
    qs.total_worker_time,
    qs.min_worker_time,
    qs.total_worker_time/qs.execution_count AS avg_worker_time,
    qs.max_worker_time,
    qs.min_elapsed_time,
    qs.total_elapsed_time/qs.execution_count AS avg_elapsed_time,
    qs.max_elapsed_time,
    qs.min_logical_reads,
    qs.total_logical_reads/qs.execution_count AS avg_logical_reads,
    qs.max_logical_reads,
    qs.min_logical_writes,
    qs.total_logical_writes/qs.execution_count AS avg_logical_writes,
    qs.max_logical_writes,
    CASE WHEN CONVERT(nvarchar(max), qp.query_plan) LIKE
    N'%<MissingIndexes>%' THEN 1 ELSE 0 END AS missing_index,
    qs.creation_time,
    qp.query_plan,
    qs.*
FROM
    sys.dm_exec_query_stats AS qs
CROSS APPLY
    sys.dm_exec_sql_text(plan_handle) AS st
CROSS APPLY
    sys.dm_exec_query_plan(plan_handle) AS qp
WHERE
    st.[dbid]=db_id() and st.[text] NOT LIKE '%sys%'
```

```
ORDER BY
    qs.total_worker_time DESC
OPTION (RECOMPILE);
```

What this query returns is a row for the 25 queries that are consuming more CPU time, in our case just one, with a number of attributes as you can see from the following picture:

In details, we're getting a binary value indicating all queries with the same "shape" (where there may only be a change in a parameter value or such), an indication of how many times that query has been executed followed by the query text itself. From there, a long list of very important metrics indicating total, min, average, and max usage of critical resources like CPU (worker) time, data page reads and writes, and much more. By changing the order by column, we can look at what queries are executed more often (by execution_count) or what queries are reading or writing more data pages and so on.

This example here is just scratching the surface of what we can do with DMVs, but there is much more. We can investigate and identify performance bottlenecks due to poorly designed table or index structures, monitoring database and object sizes or locking and blocking issues between concurrent users and so on. For more details on what is possible, we recommend you to take a look at Azure SQL official documentation here: https://aka.ms/asdbmwd.

Execution plans

In our previous example, one of the columns retrieved through those DMVs was an XML fragment returning the query execution plan:

creation_time	query_plan	
2020-06-28 13:46:13.540	<ShowPlanXML xmlns="http://schemas.microsoft.com/sqlserver/2004/07/showplan" Version...	

By clicking that column within SQL Server Management Studio, a new window gets opened showing something like this:

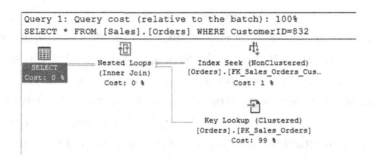

```
Query 1: Query cost (relative to the batch): 100%
SELECT * FROM [Sales].[Orders] WHERE CustomerID=832
```

This is the graphical representation of the query execution plan used to resolve that particular query and shows all detailed steps that Azure SQL engine took to be able to produce the result returned to the client. Azure SQL has a pool of memory that is used to store both execution plans and data buffers. When any Transact-SQL statement is executed, the Database Engine first looks through the plan cache to verify that an existing execution plan for the same Transact-SQL statement exists. The Transact-SQL statement qualifies as existing if it literally matches a previously executed Transact-SQL statement with a cached plan, character per character. Azure SQL reuses any existing plan it finds, saving the overhead of recompiling the Transact-SQL statement. If no execution plan exists, Azure SQL generates a new execution plan for the query, trying to find the one with the lowest cost in terms of resource utilization, within a reasonable time interval.

Understanding how this execution plan is created and executed is critical to make sure that the workload generated by our application is optimized for our data model and indexing strategy or instead requires some optimizations.

Note   Many modern databases use the more technical term DAG – Directed Acyclic Graph – instead of the user-friendlier term Execution Plan. If you already have experience with Apache Spark, for example, a DAG and an Execution Plan are basically the same thing.

As a rule of thumb, execution plans visualized via Management Studio steps should be interpreted *from right to left and from top to bottom* to determine the order in which they have been executed. In our preceding example, the first step is a Seek operator using a nonclustered index created on the CustomerID column of the Orders table to find one or more rows with a value of 832. As the index that the query engine is using does not likely contain all the columns in the select list (where we mistakenly used an asterisk instead of the full column list), the next step in the execution plan is to loop on all rows retrieved by the first operator and for each of them to execute a Lookup operator that will use the clustered index key retrieved by the Seek operator to read all the other columns from clustered index (PK_Sales_Orders) created on the Orders table.

By overlying the mouse on a given operator, we can get a lot of insights on that step, like the execution mode (Row or Batch) or the underlying storage type of that object (RowStore vs. ColumnStore) and a detailed description of CPU and IO costs associated with that.

For example, we can see that the Key Lookup operator is accounting for the 99% of the cost of the entire query, and it is executed 127 times (like the number of rows filtered by the first Seek operator).

As developers, we can start thinking of what is needed to improve the efficiency of our query by only selecting the columns that we really need and maybe adding these columns as included to the nonclustered index used by the first operator. This would basically eliminate completely this expensive operator driving down overall query processing costs. Let's give it a try! By precisely doing the steps we just described, the new query plan does not contain indeed the Key Lookup operator anymore and, looking at overall subtree cost, it apparently went down to 1/100th of the original:

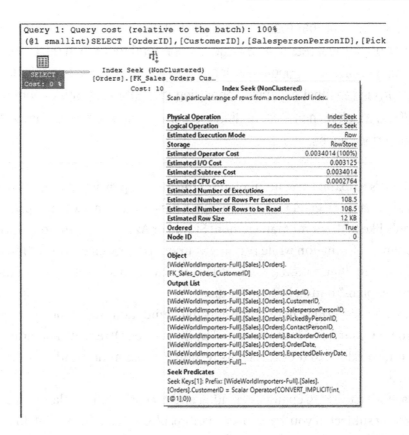

```
Query 1: Query cost (relative to the batch): 100%
(@1 smallint) SELECT [OrderID],[CustomerID],[SalespersonPersonID],[Pick
```

Looking at the metrics we're extracting through DMVs, we can notice that the execution time is less than half of the original query, and logical page read has reduced from 369 down to 5, indicating less IO operations required to read from storage and also less space utilized in the buffer pools:

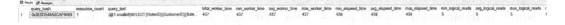

A logical page is nothing more than the page concept we discussed in previous chapters. Every time Azure SQL needs to read some data that is needed to process the query or to return the result to the end user, it will use one I/O operation to read an entire page, 8KB. A physical read is a read operation done on a page that was not already in memory – and therefore quite expensive. A logical read is a read operation done on a page that was already in the buffer pool, the in-memory cache. If a page is not already in the buffer pool, it will be read from the disk and added to the pool. For that reason, the logical reads are always greater or equal to the number of physical reads. As a page may be read more than once, the number of logical page reads is a good indicator of how much I/O your query is doing overall. As I/O is the most expensive operation in a database, you generally want to reduce I/O as much as possible, finding the perfect balance for you between read and write performances.

Using DMVs to extract execution plans of the most expensive queries hitting our Azure SQL database is a great way to investigate the performance of our application. In client tools like SQL Server Management Studio or Azure Data Studio, you can also obtain the same information while running your queries by selecting the "Include Actual Execution Plan" toolbar button (or use Ctrl+M shortcut) in Management Studio or clicking the "Explain" button in Data Studio.

What we have described here represents the foundational approach you can take to understand how your queries are executed by the Azure SQL engine and how you can optimize your workload to reduce useless resource consumption and improve overall performance.

The way the Azure SQL engine is creating and executing query plans is a complex and fascinating subject; if you want to learn more, please read the official documentation here: `https://aka.ms/qpag`.

Query store

We previously mentioned that all internal data structures representing the state of our Azure SQL databases and sourcing Dynamic Management Views and Functions are kept in database process memory, so when an instance is restarted or there's a planned or unplanned failover, all diagnostic information gets lost. Following the introduction of the Query Store feature, back in SQL Server 2016, now Azure SQL can persist most of this diagnostic information across restarts by default, as Query Store has been enabled on the entire cloud database fleet. This feature, in fact, provides you with insight on query plan choice and performance and simplifies performance troubleshooting by helping you quickly find performance differences caused by query plan changes. Query Store automatically captures a history of queries, plans, and runtime statistics and retains these for your review. It separates data by time windows so you can see database usage patterns and understand when query plan changes happened on the server. Query Store works effectively like a flight data recorder, constantly collecting compile and runtime information related to queries and plans. Query-related data is persisted in the internal tables and presented to users through a set of views.

It basically contains three main buckets:

- **Plan store**, containing execution plan details

- **Runtime stats store**, where execution statistics are persisted

- **Wait stats store**, with historical data around wait statistics

As we discussed previously, once created, query execution plans for any specific query in Azure SQL can change over time due statistics changes, schema changes, index changes, and so on. The procedure cache stores the latest execution plan, and plans can also get evicted from cache under memory pressure. If a newly created execution plan, for whatever reason, turns out to be suboptimal, it is usually quite challenging to understand what caused that change. By keeping multiple versions of an execution plan per a given query, Query Store can help figuring out what happened, and it is also possible to enforce a policy to direct the Query Processor to use a specific execution plan. This is referred to as plan forcing, where a mechanism like the USE PLAN query hint is applied without requiring any change to query syntax in your app.

Query Store collects plans for DML Statements such as SELECT, INSERT, UPDATE, DELETE, MERGE, and BULK INSERT.

Another great source of information during performance troubleshooting sessions is the availability of statistics related to wait states of the system, basically a collection of the underlying reasons why Azure SQL is taking a given amount of time to respond to user queries. Before the Query Store, wait statistics were usually available at the database instance level, and it was not trivial to correlate them to a specific query.

Let's look at how Query Store collects its data: query text and the initial plan are sent to the Query Store when a query gets compiled for the first time, and it is updated in case the query gets recompiled. In case a new plan is created, this is added as a new entry for the query, and previous ones are kept along with their runtime execution stats. Runtime statistics are sent to the Query Store for each query execution and are aggregated at plan level within the currently active time interval.

During the compile and check for recompile phases, Azure SQL detects if there is a plan in Query Store that should be applied for the currently running query and if there's a forced plan different than the one in cache, query gets recompiled (this is effectively the same way as if USE PLAN hint was applied to that query). This happens completely transparently to the user application. The following diagram describes the interactions between query processor and Query Store:

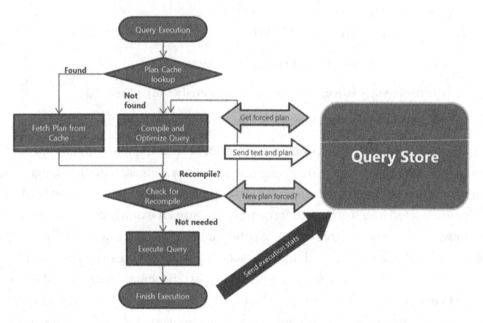

As mentioned, Query Store is enabled by default in Azure SQL and cannot be switched off. Default configuration is optimized for continuous data collection, but you can still control some of the configuration knobs like max store size (default 100MB) or the interval length used to aggregate statistics for query executions (default 60 minutes). If you don't have specific needs, like during short troubleshooting sessions where you want to speed up the process, we recommend leaving settings to default values for most use cases.

Query Store internal information gets surfaced through a series of views that can be used in your diagnostic queries to understand the behaviors of Azure SQL with your specific workload. The following diagram shows Query Store views and their logical relationships, with compile-time information presented as blue entities:

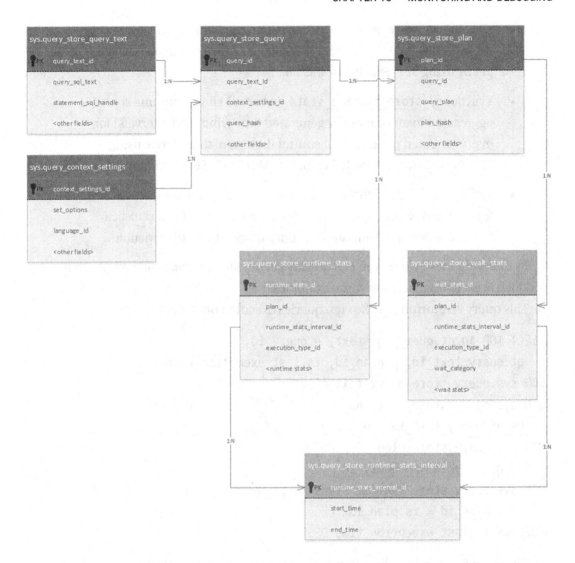

View names are straightforward, but let's go through some of the main ones and see how they can be useful to monitor and troubleshoot our workloads:

- `sys.query_store_query_text` is reporting unique query texts executed against the database, where every statement in the batch generates a separate query text entry.

- `sys.query_context_settings` presents unique combinations of plan-affecting settings under which queries are executed.

- `sys.query_store_query` shows query entries that are tracked and forced separately in Query Store.

- `sys.query_store_plan` returns an estimated plan for the query with the compile-time statistics. Stored plan is equivalent to one that you get by using `SET SHOWPLAN_XML ON`.

- `sys.query_store_runtime_stats_interval` shows runtime statistics aggregated in automatically generated time windows (intervals) for every executed plan. We can control the size of the interval using `INTERVAL_LENGTH_MINUTES` in `ALTER DATABASE SET` statement.

- `sys.query_store_runtime_stats` reports aggregated runtime statistics for executed plans. Captured metrics are in the form of four statistical functions: Average, Minimum, Maximum, and Standard Deviation.

By querying these views, you can quickly get detailed information on how your workload is executing; here are some examples.

This query is returning the last ten queries executed on the database:

```
SELECT TOP 10 qt.query_sql_text, q.query_id,
    qt.query_text_id, p.plan_id, rs.last_execution_time
FROM sys.query_store_query_text AS qt
JOIN sys.query_store_query AS q
    ON qt.query_text_id = q.query_text_id
JOIN sys.query_store_plan AS p
    ON q.query_id = p.query_id
JOIN sys.query_store_runtime_stats AS rs
    ON p.plan_id = rs.plan_id
ORDER BY rs.last_execution_time DESC;
```

These are the queries taking more time to execute within the last hour:

```
SELECT TOP 10 rs.avg_duration, qt.query_sql_text, q.query_id,
    qt.query_text_id, p.plan_id, GETUTCDATE() AS CurrentUTCTime,
    rs.last_execution_time
FROM sys.query_store_query_text AS qt
JOIN sys.query_store_query AS q
    ON qt.query_text_id = q.query_text_id
JOIN sys.query_store_plan AS p
    ON q.query_id = p.query_id
JOIN sys.query_store_runtime_stats AS rs
```

```
    ON p.plan_id = rs.plan_id
WHERE rs.last_execution_time > DATEADD(hour, -1, GETUTCDATE())
ORDER BY rs.avg_duration DESC;
```

These are the queries executing more I/O reads in the last 24 hours:

```
SELECT TOP 10 rs.avg_physical_io_reads, qt.query_sql_text,
    q.query_id, qt.query_text_id, p.plan_id, rs.runtime_stats_id,
    rsi.start_time, rsi.end_time, rs.avg_rowcount, rs.count_executions
FROM sys.query_store_query_text AS qt
JOIN sys.query_store_query AS q
    ON qt.query_text_id = q.query_text_id
JOIN sys.query_store_plan AS p
    ON q.query_id = p.query_id
JOIN sys.query_store_runtime_stats AS rs
    ON p.plan_id = rs.plan_id
JOIN sys.query_store_runtime_stats_interval AS rsi
    ON rsi.runtime_stats_interval_id = rs.runtime_stats_interval_id
WHERE rsi.start_time >= DATEADD(hour, -24, GETUTCDATE())
ORDER BY rs.avg_physical_io_reads DESC;
```

You're probably starting to get what possibilities this feature is opening in terms of monitoring and troubleshooting, right? Let's now look at some more complex scenarios where using the Query Store feature can help during our performance investigations.

Query Store at work

Let's say your application's performance has degraded over the last week, and you want to understand if this can be related to some changes in the database.

With Query Store, you can compare query executions based on different time windows like the recent period (last 4 hours) with what was happening last week when everything was fine in terms of performance:

```
--- "Recent" workload - last 4 hours
DECLARE @recent_start_time datetimeoffset;
DECLARE @recent_end_time datetimeoffset;
SET @recent_start_time = DATEADD(hour, -4, SYSUTCDATETIME());
SET @recent_end_time = SYSUTCDATETIME();
```

```
--- "History" workload - last week
DECLARE @history_start_time datetimeoffset;
DECLARE @history_end_time datetimeoffset;
SET @history_start_time = DATEADD(day, -14, SYSUTCDATETIME());
SET @history_end_time = DATEADD(day, -7, SYSUTCDATETIME());

WITH
hist AS
(
    SELECT
        p.query_id query_id,
        ROUND(ROUND(CONVERT(FLOAT, SUM(rs.avg_duration * rs.count_
        executions)) * 0.001, 2), 2) AS total_duration,
        SUM(rs.count_executions) AS count_executions,
        COUNT(distinct p.plan_id) AS num_plans
     FROM sys.query_store_runtime_stats AS rs
        JOIN sys.query_store_plan AS p ON p.plan_id = rs.plan_id
    WHERE (rs.first_execution_time >= @history_start_time
            AND rs.last_execution_time < @history_end_time)
        OR (rs.first_execution_time <= @history_start_time
            AND rs.last_execution_time > @history_start_time)
        OR (rs.first_execution_time <= @history_end_time
            AND rs.last_execution_time > @history_end_time)
    GROUP BY p.query_id
),
recent AS
(
    SELECT
        p.query_id query_id,
        ROUND(ROUND(CONVERT(FLOAT, SUM(rs.avg_duration * rs.count_
        executions)) * 0.001, 2), 2) AS total_duration,
        SUM(rs.count_executions) AS count_executions,
        COUNT(distinct p.plan_id) AS num_plans
    FROM sys.query_store_runtime_stats AS rs
        JOIN sys.query_store_plan AS p ON p.plan_id = rs.plan_id
    WHERE  (rs.first_execution_time >= @recent_start_time
```

```
                AND rs.last_execution_time < @recent_end_time)
        OR (rs.first_execution_time <= @recent_start_time
                AND rs.last_execution_time > @recent_start_time)
        OR (rs.first_execution_time <= @recent_end_time
                AND rs.last_execution_time > @recent_end_time)
    GROUP BY p.query_id
)
SELECT
    results.query_id AS query_id,
    results.query_text AS query_text,
    results.additional_duration_workload AS additional_duration_workload,
    results.total_duration_recent AS total_duration_recent,
    results.total_duration_hist AS total_duration_hist,
    ISNULL(results.count_executions_recent, 0) AS count_executions_recent,
    ISNULL(results.count_executions_hist, 0) AS count_executions_hist
FROM
(
    SELECT
        hist.query_id AS query_id,
        qt.query_sql_text AS query_text,
        ROUND(CONVERT(float, recent.total_duration/
                    recent.count_executions-hist.total_duration/hist.count_
                    executions)
                *(recent.count_executions), 2) AS additional_duration_
                workload,
        ROUND(recent.total_duration, 2) AS total_duration_recent,
        ROUND(hist.total_duration, 2) AS total_duration_hist,
        recent.count_executions AS count_executions_recent,
        hist.count_executions AS count_executions_hist
    FROM hist
        JOIN recent
            ON hist.query_id = recent.query_id
        JOIN sys.query_store_query AS q
            ON q.query_id = hist.query_id
        JOIN sys.query_store_query_text AS qt
            ON q.query_text_id = qt.query_text_id
```

```
) AS results
WHERE additional_duration_workload > 0
ORDER BY additional_duration_workload DESC
OPTION (MERGE JOIN);
```

This query is basically calculating what queries have introduced additional duration compared to the previous execution period and is returning information like recent and historical execution counts and total duration.

For queries that are showing regressions, you should check if those had different query plans recently compared to when they were executing faster. What you can do to fix the problem is trying to force a specific execution plan for that query with this procedure:

```
EXEC sp_query_store_force_plan @query_id = 48, @plan_id = 49;
```

If you want to revert back this forcing and let Azure SQL calculate the execution plan again, you can unforce the plan by calling:

```
EXEC sp_query_store_unforce_plan @query_id = 48, @plan_id = 49;
```

It's important to notice that, for this kind of optimization, you won't need to change your application code in any way.

If you prefer to run these investigations by using a visual tool instead of running T-SQL queries, SQL Server Management Studio offers a series of UI pages to interact with Query Store information. You can expand the Query Store node in your database to get what scenarios are supported:

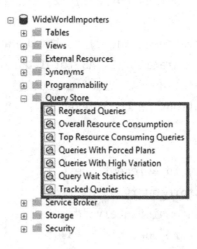

If you click *Regressed Queries,* for example, you'll get by default the list of top 25 queries that have regressed in performance during the last hour, and you can slice and dice data on multiple dimensions like CPU time or IO and memory to find what you need. From the same UI, you can also look at available query plans for a given query and force the most optimal one by clicking the *Force Plan* button. It is that easy!

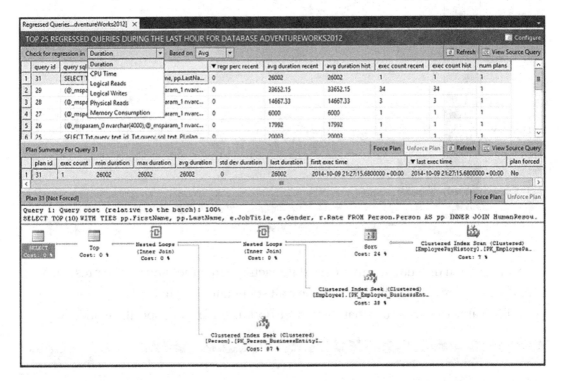

Another interesting scenario for investigating overall performance of your application is looking at *Query Wait Statistics* for a given database.

Clicking that option in the database tree will pop up a new window where most important wait state categories are shown in a chart ordered by total wait time, as you can see in this picture:

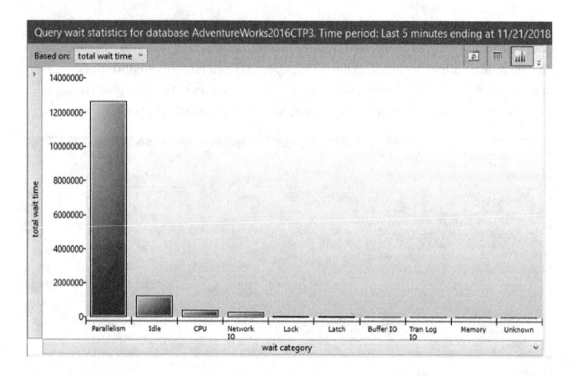

You can then drill down into the most impacting categories and will be presented with the top queries contributing to those wait states and their related query plans, so you will be able to force those that were more optimized for your specific workload:

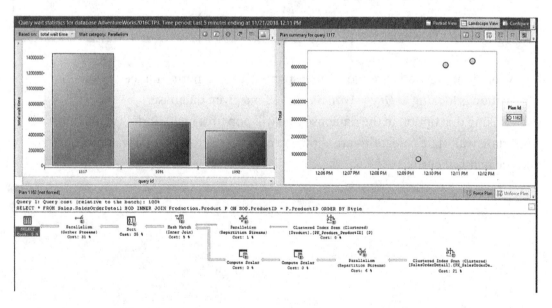

Other similar scenarios are related to *Top Resource Consuming Queries* or *Queries With The Highest Variation*, where you can follow similar paths.

Last but not least, Azure SQL also provides Query Performance Insight, part of the Azure Portal experience, which is based on Query Store data to provide intelligent query analysis tools for single and pooled databases. It helps identify the top resource-consuming and long-running queries in your workload. This helps you find the queries to optimize to improve overall workload performance and efficiently use the resource that you are paying for. While SQL Server Management Studio and Azure Data Studio can be used to get detailed resource consumption for all your queries, Query Performance Insight gives you a quick and efficient way, right from the Azure portal, to determine their impact on overall resource usage for your database.

You can still drill down to individual query level to get details on things like resource consumption or how many times queries have been executed in a given time windows, but you can also interact with performance recommendations provided by Database Advisor, a feature in Azure SQL that learns about your database usage and provides customized recommendations that enable to maximize performance. These recommendations are spanning between query plan forcing, index creation and deletion, and such. By clicking the *Automate* button in the following page, you can also automate the execution of these recommendations and let Azure SQL keep your databases always in the best state:

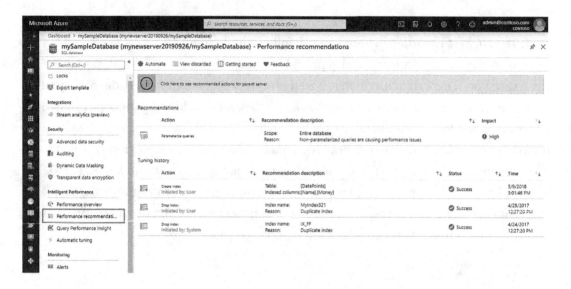

To get more details on these interesting capabilities of Azure SQL, we recommend you to take a look at the official documentation here: `https://aka.ms/daipr`.

Raising and catching exceptions in SQL

Error handling in Transact-SQL is similar exception handling in traditional programming languages. You can wrap a group of Transact-SQL statements in a TRY block, and if an error occurs, control is passed to the following CATCH block where other statements will be executed. Each error in Azure SQL is associated with a given *severity level*, and TRY... CATCH construct catches all execution errors that have a severity higher than 10 that do not close the database connection. If no errors happened in the TRY block, control passes to the statement immediately after the associated END CATCH statement. Within the CATCH block, you can use several system functions to get details about the error that caused the CATCH block to be executed: these function names are pretty self-explanatory (ERROR_NUMBER(), ERROR_SEVERITY(), ERROR_STATE(), ERROR_PROCEDURE(), ERROR_LINE(), ERROR_MESSAGE()). They return NULL if they are called outside the scope of the CATCH block.

The following example shows a script that contains error-handling functions:

```
BEGIN TRANSACTION;

BEGIN TRY
    -- Generate a constraint violation error.
    DELETE FROM Production.Product
    WHERE ProductID = 980;
END TRY
BEGIN CATCH
    SELECT
        ERROR_NUMBER() AS ErrorNumber
        ,ERROR_SEVERITY() AS ErrorSeverity
        ,ERROR_STATE() AS ErrorState
        ,ERROR_PROCEDURE() AS ErrorProcedure
        ,ERROR_LINE() AS ErrorLine
        ,ERROR_MESSAGE() AS ErrorMessage;

    IF @@TRANCOUNT > 0
        ROLLBACK TRANSACTION;
END CATCH;

IF @@TRANCOUNT > 0
    COMMIT TRANSACTION;
GO
```

When we trap errors within a CATCH block, these are not returned to the calling application. If instead we want to capture error details with the CATCH block, but also report back all or part of these details to the calling application, we could call RAISERROR or THROW to bubble up the exception to the caller or simply return a resultset through a SELECT statement.

We can create complex error management logics by nesting multiple TRY...CATCH constructs. When an error happens within a CATCH block, it is treated like any other error, so if the block contains a nested TRY...CATCH construct, any error in the nested TRY block will pass control to the nested CATCH block. If there is no nested TRY...CATCH construct, the error is passed back to the caller.

If our code is calling other Stored Procedures or Triggers, errors raised by those external modules can be trapped in their own code (if they contain TRY blocks) or can be trapped by TRY...CATCH constructs in the calling code. User-defined functions, though, cannot contain TRY...CATCH constructs.

There are some exceptions that we need to keep in mind when dealing with errors in our T-SQL code:

- If errors have a severity equal or lower than 10, then these won't be trapped by our TRY...CATCH block (as they are not considered errors, but just warnings).

- Some errors with severity equal or higher than 20 will cause Azure SQL to stop processing other tasks on that session, so TRY...CATCH won't equally trap these errors.

- Compile errors, such as syntax errors, that prevent a batch from running won't be trapped by our TRY...CATCH block, as such errors will happen at compile time and not at runtime.

- Statement-level recompilation or object name resolution errors (e.g., trying to use a view that has been dropped) will not equally be trapped.

When errors happening in a TRY block are invalidating the state of the current transaction, then the transaction is classified as an uncommittable transaction. An uncommittable transaction can only perform read operations or a ROLLBACK TRANSACTION. We can call the XACT_STATE function to verify if the current transaction has been classified as uncommittable. If the function returns –1, that is the case. At the end of the batch, Azure SQL rolls back uncommittable transactions and will send an error message to application.

Here's a more complex example using TRY...CATCH with XACT_STATE:

```
-- Check to see whether this stored procedure exists.
IF OBJECT_ID (N'usp_GetErrorInfo', N'P') IS NOT NULL
    DROP PROCEDURE usp_GetErrorInfo;
GO
```

```
-- Create procedure to retrieve error information.
CREATE PROCEDURE usp_GetErrorInfo
AS
    SELECT
         ERROR_NUMBER() AS ErrorNumber
        ,ERROR_SEVERITY() AS ErrorSeverity
        ,ERROR_STATE() AS ErrorState
        ,ERROR_LINE () AS ErrorLine
        ,ERROR_PROCEDURE() AS ErrorProcedure
        ,ERROR_MESSAGE() AS ErrorMessage;
GO

-- SET XACT_ABORT ON will cause the transaction to be uncommittable
-- when the constraint violation occurs, as it automatically rollback the
transaction
SET XACT_ABORT ON;

BEGIN TRY
    BEGIN TRANSACTION;
        -- A FOREIGN KEY constraint exists on this table. This
        -- statement will generate a constraint violation error.
        DELETE FROM Production.Product
            WHERE ProductID = 980;

    -- If the DELETE statement succeeds, commit the transaction.
    COMMIT TRANSACTION;
END TRY
BEGIN CATCH
    -- Execute error retrieval routine.
    EXECUTE usp_GetErrorInfo;

    -- Test XACT_STATE:
        -- If 1, the transaction is committable.
        -- If -1, the transaction is uncommittable and should
        --      be rolled back.
        -- XACT_STATE = 0 means that there is no transaction and
        --      a commit or rollback operation would generate an error.
```

```
-- Test whether the transaction is uncommittable.
IF (XACT_STATE()) = -1
BEGIN
    PRINT
        N'The transaction is in an uncommittable state.' +
        'Rolling back transaction.'
    ROLLBACK TRANSACTION;
END;

-- Test whether the transaction is committable.
IF (XACT_STATE()) = 1
BEGIN
    PRINT
        N'The transaction is committable.' +
        'Committing transaction.'
    COMMIT TRANSACTION;
END;
END CATCH;
GO
```

As you have seen, Azure SQL provides very complete and powerful exception handling features which are needed in any modern application, as managing exceptions is absolutely important to provide a great user experience.

Keep it simple!

Keep in mind that besides T-SQL, .NET or Python (or any of your preferred languages) code also has great exception support, and the best user experience is usually obtained when they work together as a team.

With this in mind and with the idea of keeping our solution as simple as possible, a very common pattern where your programming language of choice and T-SQL work very well together is the one that uses XACT_ABORT ON.

With XACT_ABORT ON, anything that is in a transaction must be correctly (exactly) executed, or Azure SQL will abort the transaction and terminate the current code execution.

If you plan to handle failure logic in the application, this command can really help you to have lean and clean code:

```
SET XACT_ABORT ON
BEGIN TRAN
INSERT INTO Orders VALUES (2,1,getdate());
UPDATE Inventory SET QuantityInStock=QuantityInStock-1
  WHERE ProductID=1
COMMIT TRAN
```

Thanks to the XACT_ABORT being set to on, in the preceding code, or both the INSERT and UPDATE will run without any errors so that the COMMIT will be executed, or if there is any error during execution of INSERT or UPDATE, the entire transaction will be automatically rolled back (even if there is no ROLLBACK TRAN in the code). Execution of the code will also be interrupted, and the raised error will be returned to the caller (the application code in our sample).

As you can see, you have the full spectrum of options when deciding how to deal with exceptions and errors. You can decide that it is better to handle it inside Azure SQL or you can bubble it up to the application. In both cases, you are in control so that you can implement the best option for your solution.

Integration with application insights

As application developers creating cloud-based solutions, it is quite critical to understand that to troubleshoot and debug our apps' issues, in most cases we cannot just connect to a specific server as we would have done in a traditional on-premises context. This is especially true for applications leveraging Platform as a Service components and services where you do not even have the notion of a physical or virtual server to connect. That is why it is so important to consider proper *instrumentation* within our codebase to emit all the diagnostic information required to remotely drill down into our application behaviors. Building all this infrastructure ourselves can be a challenging task; that's why several native and third-party solutions that solely focus on solving the instrumentation challenge became quite successful over the last years.

Application Insights, a feature of Azure Monitor, is an extensible Application Performance Management (APM) service for developers and DevOps professionals who can use it to monitor their live applications deployed on the Azure platform. It will help detect performance anomalies and includes powerful analytics tools to help you diagnose issues and to understand what users do with your app. It is designed to help you continuously improve performance and usability. It works for apps on a wide variety of platforms including .NET, Node.js, Java, and Python hosted on-premises, hybrid, or any public cloud. It integrates with your DevOps process and has connection points to a variety of development tools and services.

You can install a small instrumentation package (available as an SDK) in your application or enable Application Insights using the Application Insights Agent when supported like in Azure Virtual Machines. The instrumentation monitors your app and directs the telemetry data to an Azure Application Insights Resource using a unique GUID that we refer to as an Instrumentation Key. You can instrument not only a web service application or a VM but also any background components and the JavaScript in the web pages themselves. The application and its components can run anywhere – it does not necessarily have to be hosted in Azure.

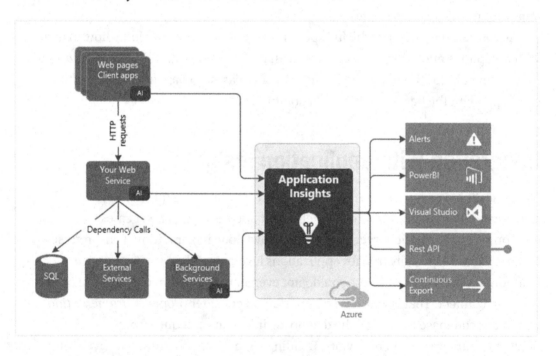

Application Insights will let you understand all sorts of insights related to how the components of your application are performing, things like *request rates*, *response times*, and *failure rates*. It also captures dependencies and interactions with Azure services like Azure SQL, plus a bunch of other bonuses. You can then create live dashboards on top of collected data to be used as part of regular production-level monitoring, but also drill down into specific issues or exceptions happening or export diagnostic data to other services.

From your application, once you have obtained your Instrumentation Key from the portal for your Application Insights instance, you just have to add to your project the proper SDK version depending on your programming language and framework and add a few configuration information. Let us see an example using Java Spring Boot; we need to start by adding a Maven dependency for the SDK:

```
<dependency>
  <groupId>com.microsoft.azure</groupId>
  <artifactId>applicationinsights-spring-boot-starter</artifactId>
  <version>2.5.1</version>
</dependency>
```

The next step is configuring the application properties passing the Instrumentation Key:

```
# Specify the instrumentation key of your Application Insights resource.
azure.application-insights.instrumentation-key=974d297f-aaaa-aaaa-bbbb-
4abcdabcd050
# Specify the name of your spring boot application. This can be any logical
name you would like to give to your app.
spring.application.name=SpringBootInAzureDemo
```

Then we can use proper classes like TelemetryClient to keep tracking metrics like Azure SQL call response times, as shown in this simple example:

```
@RestController
@RequestMapping("/")

public class Controller {

  @Autowired
  UserRepo userRepo;

  @Autowired
  TelemetryClient telemetryClient;
```

```
@GetMapping("/greetings")
public String greetings() {
  // send event
  telemetryClient.trackEvent("URI /greeting is triggered");

  return "Hello World!";
}

@GetMapping("/users")
public List<User> users() {
  try {
    List<User> users;

    // measure DB query benchmark
    long startTime = System.nanoTime();
    users = userRepo.findAll();
    long endTime = System.nanoTime();

    MetricTelemetry benchmark = new MetricTelemetry();
    benchmark.setName("DB query");
    benchmark.setValue(endTime - startTime);
    telemetryClient.trackMetric(benchmark);

    return users;
  } catch (Exception e) {
    // send exception information
    telemetryClient.trackEvent("Error");
    telemetryClient.trackTrace("Exception: " + e.getMessage());

    throw new ResponseStatusException(HttpStatus.INTERNAL_SERVER_ERROR,
    e.getMessage());
  }
}

}
```

You can then start seeing these metrics exposed in your Application Insight instance through various monitoring pages and custom dashboards you can create. The following picture is showing the Application Map, where you can see your application and how it interacts with other services like SQL reporting number of calls and response times:

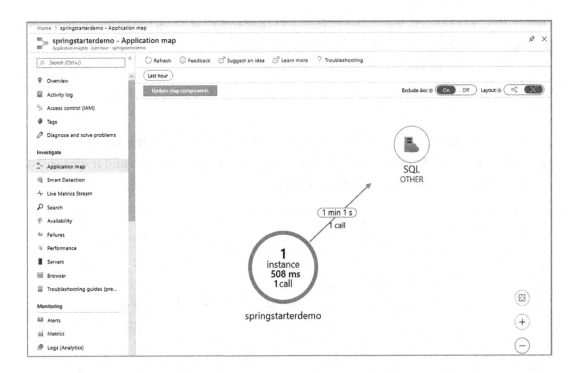

For .NET/.NET Core, we also have deeper integration between Application Insights SDK and Azure SQL client libraries like `Microsoft.Data.SqlClient`. You can automatically track dependencies between your application and other services by initializing this class that you'll find in the `Microsoft.ApplicationInsights.` `DependencyCollector` Nuget package:

```
DependencyTrackingTelemetryModule depModule = new
DependencyTrackingTelemetryModule();
    depModule.Initialize(TelemetryConfiguration.Active);
```

Then, you can configure your ASP.NET applications to track database interactions down to the SQL commands executed by just enabling telemetry at the service level:

```
services.ConfigureTelemetryModule<DependencyTrackingTelemetryModule>((modu
le, o) => { module. EnableSqlCommandTextInstrumentation = true; });
```

You also have to explicitly opt in to SQL command collection in the *applicationInsights.config* config file:

```
<Add Type="Microsoft.ApplicationInsights.DependencyCollector.
DependencyTrackingTelemetryModule, Microsoft.AI.DependencyCollector">
<EnableSqlCommandTextInstrumentation>true</
EnableSqlCommandTextInstrumentation>
</Add>
```

As a result of this configuration, you will be able to investigate performance of external services called by your application code and see database calls and response times prefixed by "SQL:" as in this screenshot:

Drilling down into individual samples, you will be able to see the end-to-end transaction flow for that request and see the contribution of the Azure SQL database call including the text of the T-SQL query:

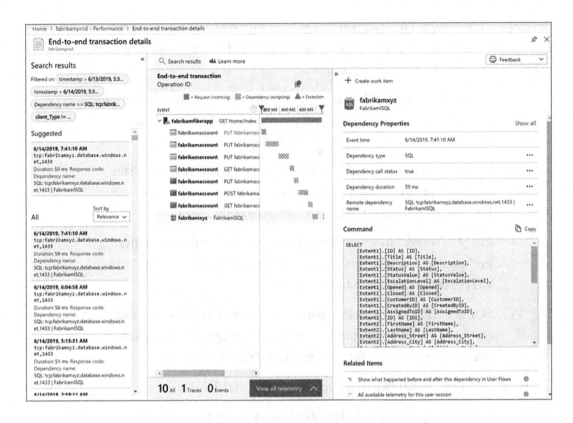

This is a very complete and useful tool that will assist you on both development and production phases for monitoring, debugging, and troubleshooting purposes.

You can get all details of what we discussed here and much more on the official Application Insights documentation here: `https://aka.ms/amaio`.

If you want to know more

Monitoring an application is a critical step and, just like debugging, many times overlooked. Their value became apparent when you have some issues to solve, and at that time, the more data you have, the better. Generally, the more your system is *transparent*, the better, as you can see through its layers down to where the problem is. Azure SQL is by far one of the most transparent databases available. DMVs provide an impressive amount of details up to the single execution thread if needed. This is a great value, as it is your insurance that if something doesn't go as expected, you or the customer support service (CSS) from Microsoft can have all the information needed to find and fix the problem. This is an incredible value that Azure SQL provides to developers natively and with a great integration with end-to-end instrumentation tools like Application Insights. A dream for a developer! And if you want to know more, as usual, here's a list of interesting resources:

- Query Store for SQL Server 2019: Identify and Fix Poorly Performing Queries – `www.amazon.com/Query-Store-SQL-Server-2019/dp/1484250036`

- Expert Performance Indexing in SQL Server 2019: Toward Faster Results and Lower Maintenance – `www.amazon.com/Expert-Performance-Indexing-Server-2019/dp/1484254635`

- Pro SQL Server 2019 Wait Statistics: A Practical Guide to Analyzing Performance in SQL Server – `www.amazon.com/Pro-Server-2019-Wait-Statistics/dp/1484249151`

- SQL Server 2017 Query Performance Tuning: Troubleshoot and Optimize Query Performance – `www.amazon.com/Server-2017-Query-Performance-Tuning-ebook/dp/B07H49LN75`

Here are some resources to dig deep into Azure SQL DMVs:

- Glenn Berry's DMVs – `https://glennsqlperformance.com/resources/`

- sp_WhoIsActive – `http://whoisactive.com/`

- sp_Blitz – `www.brentozar.com/blitz/`

- Tiger toolbox – `https://github.com/Microsoft/tigertoolbox`

DevOps with Azure SQL

DevOps is a discipline that brings together people, processes, and products to enable continuous delivery of value to end users. It does so by helping to bridge the gap between development, operations, and management. From a developer standpoint, probably the most important aspect of the DevOps discipline is the focus on having a healthy CI/CD pipeline. *Continuous Integration* (CI) and *Continuous Deployment* (CD) are two processes that help to support development agility while assuring product quality and stability.

CI/CD: Definitions and concepts

Continuous Integration means that you continuously push and merge the changes you have done to the codebase of the solution you're working on, so that they can be integrated with changes made by other developers in your team, tested, and verified. Automation tools to build and test the solution are part of this process to make it seamless and as automated as possible. The goal is to have a codebase that is healthy and tested and that could be released in production almost anytime.

Continuous Deployment is a process that deals instead with the deployment of new code into production, helping to make a very delicate and critical process more automated, repeatable, and less error-prone. The goal here is the same as the previous one but approached from a different perspective: the deployment process. Even if you have perfectly working code in your repository, deploying it in production is a non-trivial task. Continuous Deployment helps to make sure an organization is able to deploy in production the latest available, tested, working code at any time.

As you may have already figured out, DevOps and CI/CD, along with Agile principles, are a cornerstone for modern development. In fact, for a modern developer, adopting the DevOps discipline right from the start is without a doubt a best practice and, nowadays, a consolidated behavior.

© Davide Mauri, Silvano Coriani, Anna Hoffman, Sanjay Mishra, Jovan Popovic 2021
D. Mauri et al., *Practical Azure SQL Database for Modern Developers*,
https://doi.org/10.1007/978-1-4842-6370-9_11

CI/CD and Azure SQL

Applying the DevOps discipline to a database is for sure more challenging, as the database is only partially code: the biggest part of a database is, in fact, data. What does it mean to test a database? And how do you deal with data? How to continuously deploy and evolve the database without damaging existing data integrity and performances? There aren't any clear and globally accepted answers here. The DevOps discipline is relatively young (first formal mention was in 2009!), and its application to the data space is even younger, so there is still a lot to learn before being able to define a globally accepted set of best practices. What is clear, is that it needs to be done. Luckily for us, there are several tools that can help in the process. In this chapter, we'll discuss two of these tools: GitHub Actions and Azure DevOps and how they can be used in the context of Azure SQL. They both have a graphical UI but also support code-based (via YAML) configuration and definition for maximum flexibility. Once we know what the two tools can do for us and how they allow the creation of a CI/CD pipeline, we will go more in details of specific principles and solutions to deal with the added database and data complexity.

We'll assume that you are already familiar with the concept of Source Code Control Management and *git*. If not, you can start learning this fundamental development skill using the free git eBook *Pro Git* at `https://aka.ms/gitbookv2`.

GitHub Actions

GitHub is the most popular and highly-used code repository. It provides a wide range of features for free, and one called *GitHub Actions* has been recently released, and it has been specifically designed to help in DevOps. More specifically, it allows you to implement a CI/CD pipeline right from your repository. GitHub Actions allow the creation of a custom software development life cycle via the usage of a series of small tasks, called *actions*. Actions can be combined and orchestrated via a custom defined workflow to cover all the aspects of building, testing, and deploying your solution.

Aside from native actions, provided by GitHub, there is a Marketplace where actions built by the GitHub community can be published and used by anyone to support the most diverse needs. Microsoft released a free Azure SQL–specific action that allows a developer to deploy updates to a target Azure SQL database as part of the automation workflow.

GitHub Actions Marketplace

The GitHub actions marketplace is available at this link: https://aka.ms/ghmas.

Thanks to the Azure SQL deploy action, you can create a workflow that, after someone has pushed its code to the repository, will deploy the script to a target Azure SQL database, run any test you may have configured using your preferred testing framework, and notify you about the results.

Azure DevOps

Azure DevOps is a full-featured suite of products that can support a team in all DevOps aspects. It includes a git-compatible code repository, a pipeline to build and release the generated solution, a set of test tools to automate tests, an artifact store to locally and manage packages, and an agile planning and issue tracking system to make sure that work can be properly tracked, assigned, and monitored.

If you're working on a new project and the team is small, Azure DevOps can be a great choice as the first five users are free.

After you have pushed your code into the Azure DevOps source code repository, you can instruct the build pipeline to deploy the Azure SQL code into a specified Azure SQL database as part of your deployment.

A pipeline can use different *Tasks* to define the steps that will be executed when the code is pushed into the repository. The *Azure SQL Database deployment* task is the one that can be used to deploy a provided T-SQL script to a target Azure SQL database.

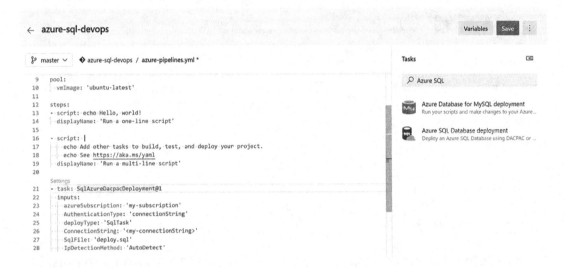

Database migrations

Now that you know where you can create your CI/CD pipeline, it's time to start to figure out how a database can be part of that pipeline too. The main challenge is that you have to deal with the fact that when you want to deploy the changes in an existing database, you may need to preserve the existing data already stored in the database. If that database is a production database, usually the "may" becomes a "must." All challenges start from this pivotal aspect of the database and are true for any database, relational or not. Extending the schema by adding a new column is easy and doesn't come with any particular complexity usually. The challenges arise when you need to change the schema used by existing data. And this challenge is always true no matter if you are using a schema-on-read or schema-on-write approach. With a schema-on-write, you need to make changes to the database so that all existing data will be updated to adapt to the new schema. With a schema-on-read, for example, if you are storing data into JSON documents, you may be able to reduce drastically the complexity of the operations needed to be done on the database, but you'll be moving that complexity into the application logic, which would need to be able to deal with different versions of the schema.

There is no such thing as a Schemaless solution. Martin Fowler cleared out this concept once and for all in his Schemaless Data Structures presentation, available to everyone for free online: `www.martinfowler.com/articles/schemaless/`. He introduced the concept of Implicit Schemas, which is the correct way to name what is known as Schemaless. Schemaless remains as a colloquial term, as it is so widespread, but to allow something to be manipulated, a schema must exist. And unless there are specific reasons to avoid that, an explicit schema is preferable.

Practically speaking, the challenge of dealing with database changes into a CI/CD pipeline is that usually you have a source database that has the evolved schema that your updated application is using, and you have the target database that has an existing schema that needs to be updated to become the new one. The problem is how can you create the T-SQL scripts that will bring the target database from the existing schema to the new one? And, aside from how, who will do that? And if the target database is not empty, what will be the performance implication of executing that update operation? Also, how can we be sure that data will be correctly preserved if something goes wrong? Yes, you always have transactions that can be rolled back, and in the worst case, you have a database backup available in Azure SQL for you, so at least on that side you are covered. But restoring a database may involve minutes or hours, and staying offline for that much time may not be an option you have.

To solve this challenge, it's better to split it into two parts, and let's do the same also with the CI/CD pipeline. It is very helpful to create two pipelines to target two different use cases.

Synthetic environment

The first pipeline will be used to make sure all changes applied to the database will be tested in a *synthetic environment*: an environment where the database is created from scratch every time, and the data contained in such database is a well-known set of data that represent the data we expect we'll have to manage, plus all the data that may create unexpected and undesired condition that we have learned over time we must deal with. For example, you may not expect to have a negative number as a result of a Stored Procedure that calculates updated products costs, but this happens if the input data, read from several different tables, has certain specific values. Along with the regular, correct data you expect to have in your database, you should make sure that the dataset that generates such a condition is present in this synthetic environment database, so you can correctly verify that such a situation is correctly handled over time.

These values, the correct ones plus the issue-related ones, will grow over time, as you should add new data to this set as soon as you receive feedback and issues from testers or users. By doing so, you will have a valuable reference dataset that will grow over time and that will be extremely helpful to keep your solution free of regression bugs and issues.

The following steps will be part of this pipeline:

- Create a new database.

- Deploy the schema and objects.

- Load the reference dataset.

- Run the tests.

Integration environment

If all the tests in the synthetic environment are executed successfully and without errors, you can then start the execution of a more complex pipeline. Now that you know your changes produce the desired results, you need to make sure that you can safely deploy them against a production database. The main goal here is to make sure that the scripts that will be used to update the existing schema and data to the new one are correct and run with the desired time.

This means that a copy of the production database is needed. For security reasons, you might not have access to it as it may contain sensitive data. You have two options to solve this new challenge. You can ask to have a production copy of the database with *obfuscated data*, so that any personal identifiable information or high-security data is stripped away, or if you work in a highly secured environment, you just need an empty production database that can be filled with mocked data. There are several tools that can generate mock, but realistic data. There are also libraries for Python, Node, and .NET in case you really need to create something very custom:

- Faker is available both for .NET and Python (and PHP, Perl, and Ruby if you really want to use some exotic languages).

- Mimesis is a Python Library.

- MockNeat for Java.

- Faker.js for Node.

- Bogus is a Faker.js port to .NET.

Once you have this reference database, you need to decide how you will update the existing database so that it will have the new schema, objects, and – if needed – data. This is a quite broad topic, so we'll discuss it in depth in the next section. Despite how you will choose to generate and apply the changes to the target database, your CI/CD pipeline for this integration environment will look like the following:

- Restore the reference database.

- Generate the T-SQL code needed to migrate the reference database to the target schema and update the existing objects while preserving existing data.

- Run the generated script.

- Run tests to verify results.

Database migration tools

Generating the scripts to migrate a database from an existing schema to another can involve different steps and technologies depending on which development philosophy you decided to adopt. Code first or Database first?

Code First

Code first means that you decided to drive database creation, change, and evolution directly via application code. No T-SQL script to execute manually, and no separate tools like SQL Server Management Studio or Azure Data Studio to be used.

An example of this approach is Django, a widely used Python framework to build web applications: the definition of data models happens completely in Python. Here is a code sample taken directly from Django official documentation:

```python
class Member(models.Model):
    """A model of a rock band member."""
    name = models.CharField("Member's name", max_length=200)
    instrument = models.CharField(choices=(
            ('g', "Guitar"),
            ('b', "Bass"),
            ('d', "Drums"),
        ),
        max_length=1
    )
    band = models.ForeignKey("Band")
```

To create the database, you have a *migrate* command that takes care of executing all the needed steps to bring an existing database in sync with what the model defines. For Django, the command is:

```python
python manage.py makemigrations
python manage.py migrate
```

and it will apply all the migrations. Keep in mind that this approach assumes that *no changes have been done manually and externally to the database.* For example, if someone manually added a column to a database that is target of the migration, without using the provided tool, the migration could fail as it does not check the current status of the object; it just assumes that the database is exactly in the same state, from a schema perspective, it was the last time a migration was applied.

Django is a full-featured web framework: if you need just an Object-Relational Mapper (ORM) to use in any Python application, SQLAlchemy also supports migrations via the Alembic package.

.NET Core also supports Code First and migrations, via Entity Framework, the native tool that comes with .NET Core.

Once you have created your .NET model

```
namespace AzureSQLForDevelopers
{
    public class BloggingContext : DbContext
    {
        public DbSet<Blog> Blogs { get; set; }
        public DbSet<Post> Posts { get; set; }

        [...]
    }

    public class Blog
    {
        public int BlogId { get; set; }
        public string Url { get; set; }
        public int Rating { get; set; }
        public List<Post> Posts { get; set; }
    }
}
```

you must generate and apply the migration steps, just like you did for Django:

```
dotnet ef migrations add FirstMigration
dotnet ef database update
```

What if you need or want to manually intervene in the migration process to make sure it can fit your needs? Automation is great, but often, some manual intervention is needed to take care of some situation that is more complex than what the automation tool can handle alone.

Luckily, all the most common Code First solutions provide a way to customize the migration steps. Depending on the language and framework you are using, there will be different strategies to apply the customization you need to have, but if, for example, you need to initialize the database with some data that must be present in the database to make your application work correctly or even make more complex changes, you are covered.

ORM and database migration tools are available almost for any platforms as a stand-alone object or embedded in frameworks; no matter what language or platform you want to use to code, if you like the idea of developing the database using a Code First approach, you can be quite sure that you'll find a tool that will help you with that.

Executing the migration as part of the CI/CD pipeline is pretty simple as you only have to execute the same tool you used to generate and apply the migrations in the pipeline tool.

In this case, you don't need any specialized Azure SQL Actions or Tasks in the CI/CD pipeline as you don't need to execute any T-SQL script. You just need to be able to invoke the migration tool, which usually is a command-line application, and for that, you just use the native support to run an arbitrary command (just keep in mind that you may need to install the chosen tool in the CI/CD environment) in both GitHub Actions or Azure DevOps.

Database First

Database First means that you want to model and evolve your database independently of the applications that are using it. The term is usually tied with ORM usage. Within the ORM context, it means that you'll have some tool that will create some of the classes you'll be using in your application starting from the existing database tables and objects. As you can see, this is completely opposite of the Code First approach, where you have the code taking care of creating the database and the related objects.

If we take the idea of "Database First" out of the ORM context and use it in a more generic and broad sense, it just means that you want to work on the database manually, using its own tools and languages to create and evolve it. In Azure SQL case, this means that you want to write and use T-SQL and that you'll be taking care of connecting the application and the database together, maybe using an ORM, maybe using a Micro-ORM, or maybe just doing it completely manually.

This option gives you as much as freedom you want. Once you have made all the changes to your development database, you have to create the script so that they can be applied to a target database to evolve it to the desired schema too. Again, you have a lot of freedom here: you can choose to have tools that generate the scripts automatically for you or you can provide the script by yourself.

DACPAC

If you prefer to have a tool that takes the development database you have worked on and compare it to a target database, calculate the differences, generate the needed scripts to migrate the target database to the new schema (without losing any data), and finally apply those scripts for you, you're lucky as such tool exists, is free, and is the same tool you have already used to restore a database in Azure SQL: SqlPackage.

With SqlPackage, you can extract the schema of an existing database into a .dacpac file and then use it against a target database to have SqlPackage generate the script with all the commands needed to sync the schema of the target database with the schema defined in the .dacpac. The following code will extract into blogs-v1.dacpac the schema and all the objects, but not the data, existing in the database named blogs hosted in Azure:

```
sqlpackage.exe
    /a:Extract
    /ssn:"<azure-sql-address>"
    /su:"<user>"
    /su:"<password>"
    /sdn:"blogs"
    /tf:"blogs-v1.dacpac"
```

Once you have the .dacpac file, you can use it to update a target database right away via the Publish action:

```
sqlpackage.exe
    /a:Publish
    /sf:"blogs-v1.dacpac"
    /tsn:"<azure-sql-address>"
    /tu:"<user>"
    /tp:"<password>"
    /tdn:"blogs-prod"
```

or to create the script that you can later use to update the database via the homonymous action:

```
sqlpackage.exe
    /a:Scripts
    /sf:"blogs-v1.dacpac"
    /tsn:"<azure-sql-address>"
    /tu:"<user>"
    /tp:"<password>"
    /tdn:"blogs-prod"
    /op:"blogs-db-v1.sql"
```

The ability to generate the script is useful if you want to customize it to add some initialization data, as it was happening for the Code First scenario, or just want to save the script into your code repository so that you know exactly what would be executed in the CI/CD pipeline. In this case, you may want to use the Azure SQL Action or Task in GitHub or DevOps to execute that script.

Another option could be to execute the SqlPackage directly in the CI/CD pipeline, using the specialized Azure SQL Action or Task, to apply the changes without even generating the script. This approach could be more risky, as you don't have full control of what's happening, and thus is not the recommended approach on average, but it is surely the most flexible as it will automatically figure out what are the needed changes to bring the target database to the desired state.

Comparison tools

Aside from SqlPackage, there are several third-party tools that can help you to find the difference between two existing databases so that you can generate the script to synchronize a target database with another reference one. The most common and well known are

- SQL Server Data Tools (Visual Studio workload extension)
- Redgate SQL Compare (commercial)
- ApexSQL SQL Compare (commercial)

DbUp

DbUp (https://dbup.github.io/) is an open source .NET library that helps in deploying scripts in a database, making sure that the same script is not deployed twice. This little tool is incredibly useful if you want to have total control on which scripts are deployed to the database, and you are keeping a list of scripts that must be executed in order, so that the changes that you wrote will be applied in the correct sequence, thus updating the database to the latest evolution. This approach is the one that gives you the highest level of control and works very well if you prefer to write the migration scripts by yourself. In a complex and critical system, this is quite always the case.

Using it is amazingly simple. You just need to add the NuGet package to your project (a recommendation is to create a dedicated project just for this) and then use the DeployChanges object and point it to the folder where you have the script you want to deploy, for example, a sql folder in your project structure:

```
var connectionString = "<connection-string>"
var upgrader = DeployChanges.To
        .SqlDatabase(connectionString)
        .JournalToSqlTable("dbo", "$__schema_journal")
        .WithScriptsFromFileSystem("./sql")
        .LogToConsole()
        .Build();

var result = upgrader.PerformUpgrade();
```

The preceding code, when executed, will do these:

- Connect to the target database.

- Create, if doesn't exist already, a table named $__schema_journal that will track the deployed scripts.

- Read all the T-SQL script available in the sql folder.

- Send the log to console.

- Run the scripts, saving which script has been executed in the journal table.

If you compile and run this application against an empty database, you'll see something like the following:

```
> dotnet run
Beginning database upgrade
Checking whether journal table exists..
Journal table does not exist
Executing Database Server script '001.sql'
Checking whether journal table exists..
Creating the [dbo].[$__schema_journal] table
The [dbo].[$__schema_journal] table has been created
Executing Database Server script '002.sql'
Executing Database Server script '003.sql'
Upgrade successful
Success!
```

If you try to run the same application again, without adding any new script to the sql folder, nothing will happen as all scripts have been executed already:

```
> dotnet run
Beginning database upgrade
Checking whether journal table exists..
Fetching list of already executed scripts.
No new scripts need to be executed - completing.
Success!
```

As this is a regular .NET application, deploying it into a CI/CD pipeline doesn't require any special Task or Action, aside those already used to have the .NET framework available in the pipeline.

Database testing

How do you properly test a database? That's another huge topic for which, frankly, there isn't yet a very good answer. Testing a database is a complex challenge as test results will completely depend on the data stored in the database. In addition to that, there aren't widely adopted testing frameworks focusing on this specific issue.

There is one community-supported unit testing framework that supports Azure SQL: *tSQLt*. With tSQLt, you can define tests by just using T-SQL code. It supports assertions for expected results, both scalar and tabular, and it also can create some mock objects to help you isolate dependencies.

But as a developer, my favorite method of testing a database is creating a test class using a common testing framework (like *NUnit* or *XUnit* for .NET, *pytest* for Python or *Mocha* for Node) and using the flexibility of these tools to get a nice testing experience.

It is widely known that a test must be self-contained, independent, and idempotent. The aforementioned testing frameworks all allow the execution of custom code before and after running the test, so that test data and environment can be prepared and then cleaned up.

I know that a pure Unit Test should not have any external dependency, and to test the database, we are actually introducing a dependency on the database itself. Still, I find the solution of using existing unit testing framework a good compromise that gives the needed flexibility in exchange for a small deviation from the perfect approach. Given that there aren't universally accepted unit test frameworks for databases, we have to do the best with what we have.

Here's an example of a database unit test using .NET and NUnit:

```
[Test]
public void CheckExpectedTotal()
{
  using(var conn = new SqlConnection(ConnectionString))
  {
    var result = conn.QuerySingle(
      "ConfirmOrder",
        new { OrderId = 38923 },
        commandType: CommandType.StoredProcedure);
    Assert.AreEqual("ConfirmedTotal", 10000);
  }
}
```

Ideally for each test you want to create, you'll generate one or more sets of data that will cover the possible scenario in which the query or the Stored Procedure you want to test will be used.

Usually to check that a query returns the expected result, you can use a small data sample, maybe even created with completely mocked values, so that you don't have to deal with Personal Identifiable Information and all the security issues that go with it. In the most complex scenarios, before running the test, you may need to restore a reference dataset or even an entire database, so that you'll have a well-known starting point for running the tests and thus having deterministic results.

Once you have created your tests, so that you have a solid pipeline to deploy and test the changes against a small but representative dataset, you can then instruct your pipeline to deploy your code on a bigger database, maybe containing a representative subset of production data, opportunely obfuscated, to run integration and performance tests. At this stage, you'll focus on query performances. Several frameworks allow you to also specify that a test must be executed within a defined amount of time in order to consider a successful execution.

At this point, usually your team will execute integration and performance tests, where the database and all the code that needs to interact with it will be tested as a whole. If you are creating an API solution, you may be already using tools like Locust. io or *K6* to perform a stress test and verify that the changes you have just completed are behaving as expected also from a performance, scalability, and resource consumption point of view.

Putting everything together

Creating a full, end-to-end, CI/CD pipeline can be a bit complex the first time. That's why in the code accompanying this book, you can find an end-to-end sample that shows how to create a simple C# REST API, backed by an Azure SQL Database, and deployed on Azure using Azure Web App. The CI/CD pipeline is created using GitHub and DbUp, and the testing framework used is NUnit.

If you want to know more

DevOps is a really broad topic, and in this chapter, we just scratched the surface. As mentioned at the beginning, DevOps is also a relatively young discipline that is evolving very rapidly, so staying updated with the freshest information is really important: there is no doubt on the fact that DevOps is a must for a modern developer and thus it is mandatory to have some familiarity with it and its tools. Here's a list of links and resources to help you find more details in it:

- Annual State of Database DevOps report – `www.red-gate.com/ solutions/overview`

- Evolutionary Database Design – `www.martinfowler.com/articles/ evodb.html`

- Agile Database Techniques – www.amazon.com/Agile-Database-Techniques-Effective-Strategies/dp/0471202835

- Introduction to DevOps: DevOps and the Database – www.red-gate.com/simple-talk/sql/database-devops-sql/introduction-to-devops-devops-and-the-database/

- Azure SQL Database Deployment task – https://docs.microsoft.com/azure/devops/pipelines/tasks/deploy/sql-azure-dacpac-deployment

- GitHub Action for deploying updates to Azure SQL database – https://github.com/marketplace/actions/azure-sql-deploy

- Django: Migrations – https://docs.djangoproject.com/en/3.0/topics/migrations/

- Django: Writing Migrations – https://docs.djangoproject.com/en/3.0/howto/writing-migrations/

- Entity Framework Core – https://docs.microsoft.com/ef/core/

- Code First Migrations – https://docs.microsoft.com/ef/ef6/modeling/code-first/migrations/

- Synchronization via SQLPackage.exe and PowerShell – www.mssqltips.com/sqlservertip/4759/sql-server-database-schema-synchronization-via-sqlpackageexe-and-powershell/

- Unit testing in .NET Core and .NET Standard – https://docs.microsoft.com/dotnet/core/testing/

Index

A

AddRange() method, 65

Advanced data security (ADS), 30

Advanced Threat Protection, 129

Apache Spark, 12

Application Insights Agent, 293–299

Application Map, 296

Application Performance Management
(APM) service, 293

AVX and SIMD instructions, 4

Azure Blob, 7

Azure Cognitive Search index service, 226

Azure Cosmos DB, 197

Azure Data Studio (ADS), 22, 287

Azure Kubernetes Service, 56

Azure Monitor

    logs and metrics, 267

    long-term analytical options, 268

Azure portal, 287

Azure Portal experience, 287

Azure SQL, 1, 2, 4, 5, 10, 12, 193, 197

    abstraction and access level, 15

    adding data, 84, 85

    ADS, 30

    advantages, 197, 232

    aggregations

        grouping data, 94, 95

        multiple grouping, 95–97

        Windowing Functions, 97–101

    Bulk Copy API, 101, 102

cloud-native entity, 17

collation awareness, 204, 205

collations, 30

compute to data pushing, 70, 71

connection methods, 29

create database, 18–22

Cypher expressions, 211

data assets protection

    Always Encrypted feature, 130, 131

    dynamic data masking, 128–130

    features, 123

    permissions management,
        123–125

    RLS, 126–128

data monitoring

    change data capture, 123

    change tracking, 121–123

    example, 120

declarative vs. imperative, 71, 72

DTU or vCores, 24, 25

Elastic Pools, 18

Flightlines CSV file, 210

functions, 110–113

geometry *vs.* geography, 217, 218

graph capabilities, 198

graph processing support, 211, 212

graph structures, 208–210

hardware generation, 27, 28

identity and sequences, 91, 92

instance-level features, 17

319

Printed in the United States
By Bookmasters